D0712154

From Bonsai to Levi's

From Bonsai to Levi's

When West Meets East:
An Insider's Surprising Account
of How the Japanese Live

GEORGE FIELDS

MACMILLAN PUBLISHING COMPANY
New York

Macmillan Publishing Company
866 Third Avenue, New York, N.Y. 10022
Collier Macmillan Canada, Inc.

Material from *Yukagen Ikaga*, © 1982 by Kazue Morizaki, published
by Tokyo Shoseki Kabushiki Kaisha, reprinted by permission.

Levi's® is the registered trade name of Levi Strauss and Co., U.S.A.

Library of Congress Cataloging in Publication Data

Fields, George.
    From bonsai to Levi's.

    1. Japan—Civilization—1945–   . 2. National
characteristics, Japanese.   3. Consumers—Japan—
Attitudes.   4. Marketing—Japan.   I. Title.
DS822.5.F53   1983   952.04   83-22196
ISBN 0-02-537750-7

10   9   8   7   6   5   4   3   2   1

Printed in the United States of America

Acknowledgments

First, I want to thank Pierre Marquis and my colleagues in ASI Market Research, Japan and U.S., and our many clients, for making my intercultural explorations possible.

I also want to thank Mr. Hiroo Takase, the president of Yamate Shobo, for encouraging me to embark on a writing career; Jim Conte, for first suggesting that there might be a book in English; Mr. Hiroshi Yamaga, for his help in bringing my Japanese manuscripts into shape; and Ruth Stevens, for bringing the book to the attention of John Brockman Associates.

But above all, for this book, I am grateful to Patrick Filley and Melinda Corey of Macmillan, New York, for their invaluable advice in making the book suitable for a Western audience, and to John Brockman for bringing to their attention my Japanese effort.

Contents

From Bonsai to Levi's

Foreword

It has been almost twenty years since I left Japan, in my early youth, and ceased using Japanese, let alone writing it. I am, therefore, not a student of Japan but one who was, through the accident of birth, raised and educated in both the Japanese and Western systems, so I cannot take credit for my competency or otherwise in either the English or the Japanese language. When I returned to Japan, I increasingly realized a duality in my personality: when speaking Japanese, I was in fact in a Japanese conceptual framework; when speaking English, I reverted to my Western persona. As it was the latter under which I operated in business, it was not surprising that all my writings in my professional capacity were in English. Yet it always troubled me that when my English was translated into Japanese, it never seemed to be what I had actually written.

It was not until late 1981 that I ventured into writing in Japanese for publication. It all came about because of an article that had appeared in the September 1981 issue of *Fortune* magazine dealing with the activities of our company in Japan and my part in establishing it. This article attracted the attention of the Japanese monthly magazine, *Bungei Shun-jyu*. The magazine asked me to contribute an article on the subject of East-West cultural differences that led to difficulties in marketing Western products. As the magazine is held in high esteem in Japan, I was not reluctant to do so. While they naturally expected me to write the article in English, which they would translate, I was still troubled about the previous translations from English into Japanese. It then occurred to me that I gave many lectures in Japanese and that I tended to structure these somewhat differently than those I gave in English. To the editor's great surprise I volunteered to write the article in Japanese and obtained his reluctant acceptance by assuring him that he would have considerable editorial freedom.

I was resolved to write as if I were speaking in Japanese, which put me into a Japanese frame of reference. And this turned out to be eminently suited to my audience—the article seemed to be well accepted. The advice I received from Kanakura-san (the sub-editor) of *Bungei Shunjyu* at this early stage was invaluable and gave me considerable confidence. It was hard going at the beginning, but as I proceeded I found that my written Japanese started to flow more easily. After all, up until my high school years, I did study in Japan under the old Japanese system—which meant that my knowledge of written characters was greater than that of most of today's young Japanese. This was a source of continual amusement to my staff; to me, it was almost a personal revelation, a rediscovery that gave me a great deal of pleasure.

But writing a magazine article and writing a book are two separate matters. When one of the up-and-coming publishers in Tokyo first approached me to write a book on my experiences in Japan, I balked. First, there are hundreds of books on Japan and the Japanese, written by both foreigners and Japanese. How could there be a gap in the market? Second, could I really sustain my Japanese for that long a work? I am very grateful for the persistence of Hiroo Takase, the president of the Yamate Shobo Publishing Company. He had heard me commenting on Japanese business customs on one of the national T.V. network programs. The Japanese love to have themselves discussed from what they consider a new angle, and Takase-san felt that many of the things I said about the Japanese would be full of surprises to the Japanese reader! He finally convinced me.

As it turned out, I did manage to produce a manuscript over the course of the summer of 1982, entirely on the weekends, with constant nudging and encouragement from the editorial staff of Yamate Shobo. When it was finished—and I still would have liked a few more weekends to add and polish—they had the audacity to be astonished that I was able to turn out so much in Japanese in such a short time. In hindsight, I was probably able to do it because I simply wrote down everything I had come across in my twenty years as a Western-oriented market researcher in Japan, the events and anecdotes that had accumulated in my head; it really took little effort to parade them out.

Many, many books on intercultural aspects have been written by professors of history, sociology, psychology, and linguistics. I am making no attempt here to produce a cohesive theory of marketing in

Japan—except for two chapters on advertising/communication for which I do have my own theory. No marketer can use this book as a primer for marketing in Japan; it is not intended as such. Many Japanese readers were fascinated to learn what puzzled and confounded the Western marketer in Japan, which was this book's *raison d'être*. Many have been kind enough to say that I discussed aspects of which they themselves were not aware, and this has given the book a somewhat broader appeal than possibly first intended.

At the galley proof stage, one problem still remained. The book did not have a title. As I said, there are many books on the market entitled the Japanese this or that, with at least three by different authors called simply *The Japanese*. (One is by the eminent Edwin Reischauer of Harvard and a former ambassador to Japan.) My own inclination was for *The Inscrutable Japanese Consumer*, and we vacillated right up until the last minute. Yamate Shobo felt my title was too limited in appeal, so finally the word *consumer* was dropped and the title *Fukashigi na Nihonjin* was accepted. It translates roughly as *The Inscrutable Japanese*.

I have received many phone calls and letters from Japanese readers telling me that I should translate the book into English. The fact that the reverse process—from Japanese into English—would be adopted by a person with the name of Fields who is identified as a "foreign" business-man, seems to tickle my Japanese colleagues. However, just as I felt that the original was better written in Japanese for a Japanese audience, I felt equally strongly that it should be rewritten in English, not just trans-lated. Accordingly, I had a clause written into my contract with Yamate Shobo whereby I retained all English language rights. Since this is not a work of literature, the English-reading audiences' interest is not likely to coincide with that of the Japanese. Nevertheless, what I recount will be based on the same experiences and so, in essence, the book is the same. The student of Japanese is, however, advised not to compare the Japa-nese and English versions line by line.

Introduction
Even Old Japan-Hands
Find It Hard to Get to
the Japanese

The Gun Was Not Mightier Than the Sword

As all traders know, the exchange of goods brings differing cultures into contact. Since ancient times, people learned of the existence of other cultures through their products. Historians learned a great deal from the trading records kept by the Cretans, and from Marco Polo, a Venetian merchant, the West learned of the East. Today, the average American's view of Japan is not the same as it was twenty years ago—due almost entirely to exposure to Japanese goods.

Goods manufactured by hand not only represent the skills and creativity of the maker, but also conceal the "wisdom" of the culture from which they emanate. While the Japanese culture may appear to have been isolated until the arrival of Commodore Perry on the coasts of Shimoda, it was continuously stimulated long before that through the arrival of goods, artisans, and traders from China, the Korean peninsula, and Mongolia. The Silk Road continues to inspire the Japanese imagination: there is even a Ginza bar, with the name of one of its obscure capitals. Japanese curiosity about the outside did not awake just through the advent of the nineteenth-century West.

The guns brought to the small island of Tanegashima by the Portuguese in the sixteenth century changed the course of Japanese history. Nobunaga, a relatively small clan chief in the Nagoya area of the main island, achieved crucial victories in the field with their clever

[4]

use, at a period in Japanese history somewhat akin to the War of the Roses. Hideyoshi, who followed the short-lived Nobunaga, was probably inspired by the gun when he sent his warriors to the Korean peninsula—not the first, but one of the few instances of large-scale aggression onto foreign soil until Japan achieved its notoriety in more recent times. Typically, the Japanese react very quickly to new products and the ideas behind them. When Perry's blackships arrived on Shimoda, some of the sailors had their buttons ripped off by the curious populace. Up until then a sash—*obi*—kept Japanese clothing in place, and there was no need for buttons. More than a hundred years later, zippers manufactured by Y.K.K. of Japan dominate the worldwide market, thereby removing buttons from the trousers of Western males.

There is a time and place for a new product's acceptance and often it speaks for the culture. The Western gun, called the *Tanegashima* after the island to which it was originally introduced, abruptly entered the Japanese market and just as abruptly disappeared, at least for all intents and purposes as a weapon, for several hundred years. Japan was effectively closed to most foreign influences—and particularly that from the West—for over three hundred years. Yet it should be remembered that sixteenth-century Japan had the ability, based on imported technology, to manufacture guns. And the guns they made at that time were thought to be the equivalent of the Portuguese originals.

It is often said that we cannot turn back time, but the Japanese abandoned the powerful modern technology represented by the gun and returned to the more primitive sword. Though they had quickly perfected the manufacture of guns, they just as quickly abandoned it—and the opportunity for national military strength. There was simply no need for such a product once the internal strifes were solved and a period of peace ushered in. Indeed, this was an intriguing and unique phenomenon in history that Noel Perrin turned into a fascinating book, *Giving Up the Gun*. The existence of such a culture in Japan over three hundred years ago is of particular interest to the modern man confronted with the possibility of nuclear catastrophe: it shows that it is possible to prefer a less-advanced state of technology if the more advanced does not fulfill real needs.

I read Perrin's book with great interest because I saw in it an analogy to some of the events I was observing in the current Japanese marketplace. The reason that the gun was so short-lived in Japan—like some more recent Western products—is because its concept did not fit the basic cultural values prevailing in Japanese society at the time. Some products profoundly influence social modes and patterns and resistance is swept aside; others fail to make even a small dent. That the product concept is the key to success or failure remains the same throughout time.

The closing of Japan to foreigners left the West unaware of Japan's rejection of the gun, but if it had happened today it would have made news. Perhaps it would have been given as another example of Japan's unwillingness to accept Western products. Interestingly, like many things that happen in Japan, the people were unaware of the one instance in history in which cultural values were placed ahead of advancing technology—it took a foreigner to notice and write a book about it. It is symbolic that the last major incident in which the gun was used in Japan was to suppress the Christian uprising in Shimabara in 1637—in the southern end of Japan—an incident that was perceived as being Western inspired and even instigated.

One would assume that the Japanese would be ready and willing to accept all things emanating from the West. That this is not so was demonstrated by the gun. (This was also true in spiritual matters. Christianity has been a dismal marketing failure, with a very low conversion rate despite the fact that missionaries were not faced with a strongly militant incumbent religion. The problem was, and is, that the population, by and large, is nonreligious.) Nevertheless, bedazzled by the superficial ease in which the Japanese adopt Western ways, many a Western marketer has entered the Japanese market only to find his brand or product going the way of the *Tanegashima* gun.

It has been argued that by importing Western technology and by basing economic development on it, Japan has become Westernized. An illogical leap is made from this point: if certain Western products do not sell in Japan, it is because of a deliberate plot on the part of the Japanese. This viewpoint is now very fashionable.

When I returned to Japan in 1965, the expression "nontariff barrier" was not as much in vogue as it is today. Most American marketers were confident that all that needed to be done was to lower the tariff for their products and they would sell. My job was simply to introduce a certain Western technology. However, as it progressed, my work turned to the study of Japanese attitudes and the advancing of relevant hypotheses to explain perceived differences.

While there may be some disagreement among historians, market research as an industry was born in the United States in or about the thirties. A product of free enterprise capitalism, it cannot exist in the true sense in the totalitarian states; since Japan operated under such a system before the war, and since the so-called Taisho democracy of the twenties was short-lived, the concept that marketing activities should be based on consumer needs—the *raison d'être* of market research—is a very recent import to Japan. In 1965 I found that Japan's market research industry was still at a relatively formative stage. Japan had very rapidly entered a period of material prosperity from one of scarcity; manufacturers were busy fulfilling consumer demands; and there seemed little need for market research. This, of course, was not the case with the foreign entries for whom market research was almost a necessity for survival.

Over the years, thanks to my clients, I have been able to study why some products from the West have succeeded in Japan and why some failed. Life would be easy and my fortune would be made if a golden rule existed and I had discovered it. Alas, it is a bit like the guru who claims to have discovered the secrets of successful advertising. Such claims do not stand the test of the marketplace because they ignore the dynamic nature of society. What makes my work fascinating is that each case leads to new discoveries, but it's also frustrating because of the difficulties in systematizing knowledge. However, if systematic accumulation of experience didn't tell us something, there would be no need for historians. The rejection of the gun by the Japanese more than three hundred years ago tells us a great deal about that culture. So, even if I cannot formulate a general rule for success in the Japanese market, I have begun to realize that by studying the introduction of various Western products into Japan, I can learn something about Japanese culture that may have been overlooked by the more orthodox interculturalists. Anyway, it seemed worth trying.

Foreigners Who Are Fluent in Japanese Have a Handicap

I returned to Japan to practice market research, but in the early stages I often found my fluency in Japanese to be a handicap. My language ability was valued by my American head office and my Western clients, and it was undeniably a personal asset, but there were many unseen traps.

In the first place, language is only a skill, one that is relatively easy to acquire at conversation schools. True understanding, though, comes only from knowing the history and literature of the country. Perhaps because of the difficulty of the language—a very different structure from English—a lot of Japanese linguists acquire the skills but not the knowledge. For the average businessman, it is bad enough spending those interminable hours with language tapes; to go further is well-nigh an impossibility. The Japanese who are often ridiculed for their incompetency in conversational English actually have a considerable advantage over the Western businessman in that they have been steeped in Western literature, music, and movies even if only in translations.

The acquisition of superficial language skills can be a handicap if it leads the student to think he understands the culture. And the Japanese don't help matters: with their deep conviction that no foreigner can really understand their culture, they usually deal with the floundering efforts of the foreigner with benign neglect. In fact, a few words of Japanese are enough to elicit a profusion of flattering expressions of amazement at the foreigner's language proficiency—thoughts that really stem from a feeling of condescension.

For me, the trap was even greater. Not only had I been born in Japan, but I went to Japanese schools until high school, so I simply basked in my proficiency in the language. I completely overlooked the fact that my entire business experience was Western and based on fundamentally different values. (Articles and books on the Japanese management system, now in vogue, were at the time virtually nonexistent. In the late sixties, articles began to appear in such publications as the *Harvard Business Review*, including one from Peter Drucker in March 1971 entitled "What We Can Learn from Japanese Management," but it still took ten years before any such treatise was taken seriously. Unfortunately, the art of Japanese management as explored by Western management scientists is read more by the Japanese than the Westerner.) My confidence was not unusual if one were to consider the environment at the time. I was brought up on the power of the dollar. During my days as a student of economics, the Japanese themselves were sending teams to the United States to study their superior business management technology—the renowned quality circle concept, which the Japanese appear to have preempted, had its genesis in the United States. The underdog is in a better position—he is prepared to learn from and emulate the top dog. The Japanese, when faced with an external challenge, have historically had the facility to consider themselves the underdog and thus always tried harder.

As readers of recent management theory well know, the quality circle concept is that workers themselves are the best judge of what improvements can be implemented in the production process. To determine this, "circles" of those engaged in the actual process are formed, debating among themselves, how improvements can best be effected. This involves the participants in the problems and, more importantly, their solutions. The concept originated in the U.S. but was never implemented there because of the adversary situation between labor and management. This situation did not exist among the group-oriented Japanese, who readily took to the concept.

Now, I wasn't so stupid as to think that I could employ my Western management methods in Japan without adaptation. Nevertheless, I, like most of my Western colleagues, considered Japanese management techniques to be anachronistic, inefficient, and requiring enlightened Western guidance. None of my Japanese colleagues denied this viewpoint, although they knew otherwise. My relative youth—mid-thirties—fed fuel to the flames as I had absolute confidence and faith in what I had hitherto learned. I surely would have been more cautious if I had not been able to speak Japanese. My Japanese colleagues would also have been more resigned to my acts. On the other hand, as I said before, the Japanese do not help. Essentially, their treatment of those who can speak their language does not differ one iota from that toward those who have no competency. If there was cultural arrogance on the part of the Westerner in those days, the Japanese had a similar arrogance in the feeling that they were unfathomable to any foreigner. There is a streak of narcissism and self-indulgence in the Japanese. Most cultures believe that they are superior, but this is most certainly evident in the Japanese. They continually say that they are bad at explaining themselves to others. The truth is that they are convinced the effort is futile. (This lack of effort to explain extended to me, nominally a *gaijin* [foreigner], and my last seventeen years here have

seen my own attempt at a reorientation to the country of my birth.)
There is an inherent sense of isolation from the world among the
Japanese that can take dangerous turns. I can vouch for it; I lived in
Japan during World War II. The kamikaze tendency is still there,
under the surface.

I was in Japan during World War II for the simple reason that my
parents were there. My parents were there because of my father, a
Hiroshima-born Japanese who was exceptional in that he crossed to
Australia, of all places, to help establish the faculty of Oriental studies
at the University of Sydney. My mother—another exception—was
smitten with a Japanese silent movie star, Sessue Hayakawa, and decided she wanted to go to Japan. Her eyes fell on my father, who was
teaching at the University—the only one in the State at the time—and
his fate was sealed. Come to think of it, so was mine. In an act of
selfishness, he took his bride to Japan. Still hindsight wisdom is not
fair. He probably didn't think through the implication that a pure
society like Japan does not accept mixed bloods as part of its culture.
So, I was in Japan during World War II.

It is not surprising that Japan has been best introduced to the world
by foreigners; although there are some notable exceptions, such as
Professor Chie Nakane, Japanese intellectuals tend to speak amongst
themselves. Professor Chie Nakane is another one of those exceptions
that enrich a society. She is the first Japanese woman to graduate from
the hallowed halls of Todai—Tokyo University—comparable to Oxford or Harvard Business School. She later taught at London University and studied the Anglo-Saxon and Indian cultures to form her own
view of Japanese society. Thus, with Professor Nakane an exception,
international problems are of interest only if there is a direct link with
Japan—an air crash involving ten Japanese will be headlined, but one
with two hundred other nationalities will be relegated to a few col-
umns. In all fairness, this is simply a manifestation of provincialism
that is certainly not restricted to the Japanese. In any event, among
foreigners in Japan, this is known as the "*ware ware nihonjin*" (We the
Japanese) syndrome.

In the early days, I was frequently told by some of my Japanese
executives that "you just don't understand" whenever I tried to impose
my Western ways onto the company. The sentence ended with a shake
of the head that simply left me hostile. I have observed paranoia

developing among many expatriate businessmen, even those less well placed than I because of the language, as a result of being subjected to this treatment. It is only natural that through sheer defense of his dignity, the Western executive will try to impose his ideas on his Japanese associates, whose attitudes he rightly considers unconstructive. On an interpersonal level, things are never the same again once this happens. Patience is not the most notable characteristic of the successful Western businessman, but it is necessary in Japan.

The problem is compounded by the evangelical enthusiasm of the Westerner who tends to believe in absolutes and considers it his duty to impose the "correct" values on his associates who hold differing ones. The Japanese consider Western culture as that of "push," with little heed to the other's values. While this viewpoint is formed by observations of the late-nineteenth- to mid-twentieth-century West, this belief will not be dispelled over a single generation. In contrast, the Japanese, being largely nonreligious, are basically relativists. To put it another way, against the absolutist challenge, the natural reaction is to "draw back" and deflect the "shoving." There is a common Japanese expression, *"noren ni udeoshi,"* that my Japanese-English dictionary valiantly translates as "useless like beating the air." Beating the air is an active phrase and does not convey the spirit of this saying. A *noren* is a short curtain that hangs outside an establishment such as a sushi restaurant. *Udeoshi* means pushing with the arm. Naturally, there is no resistance from the *noren*, which simply gives way, but when the arm is removed it returns to its original position. Much Western evangelizing in Japan reminds me of *"noren ni udeoshi"*—it in no way disturbs the originally held values. The·same is true for the Western businessman's attempt at changing Japanese business methods.

There Are Two Types of Foreigners—Those Who Consider the Japanese as "Different" and Those Who Don't

It was Robert Benchley who chided the Westeners' tendency for simple categorizations. Along this line there are, broadly speaking, two types of foreigners in business in Japan: those who are convinced that the "Japanese are fundamentally different," and those who maintain that the "Japanese are fundamentally no different." There is always the problem of what criteria are measured, but let us say that generally their implied criteria are those that belong to the executive's more recent business environment. These two groups are, of course, natural enemies and futile arguments are advanced by both sides to prove their points. Many times I have been caught in the cross fire, and my instinct is not just to duck for cover but to escape from the scene as quickly as possible.

Since we are all members of the human race, there are bound to be many similarities. But cultures will differ, and to be obsessed by either simply clouds the fundamental issues. Most Japanese belong to the "Japan is different" syndrome. Since to wholeheartedly accept this proposition is to deny the Westerner's role in Japan, many Western businessmen succumb to the "Japan is similar" syndrome as an antidote. A common symptom of the disease is to be affronted by perceived differences; to ignore or deny their existence; or, worse still, to attempt to make the differences disappear. In international affairs, the latter attitude can lead to war. The positive aspect of this stance is that each side tries to bring the other to his way of thinking. However, such efforts are notably lacking on the Japanese side.

A common trap with perceived similarities is assuming that the reasons behind them are the same as elsewhere and, therefore, can be handled in a similar manner. The problem with this way of thinking is that the similarity could have arisen through a different process. Japanese youths love to wear jeans, but that doesn't mean that their motivations for first use are the same as those of their American counterparts. Similarities could be simply coincidental. The Japanese supermarkets are full of frozen foods, but the market has developed completely differently. Even words that were originally English, assume different connotations when used in Japan.

The Japanese—most of whom subscribe to the "different" point of view—are generally unfazed when any similarities between cultures are pointed out to them. With a deep conviction of their uniqueness, they simply consider that whatever it is that originally came from the West has since become Japanized. The dialogue between the Western "similar" syndrome and the Japanese "different" syndrome can be hilarious, with each side left bemused. While seeing through the emotional fog is difficult, it is essential for both sides.

The typical Japanese negative response to his Western business associate's suggestion, "since this is Japan, it can't be done," has been disproved time and time again. In fact, the Japanese are well known for their ability to easily absorb or adapt things from outside their culture. The negativism toward foreign suggestions appears to be caused by a latent resentment on the part of the Japanese to the idea that foreigners can change Japanese ways—only the Japanese are capable of initiating fundamental changes in their society or are permitted to do so. I know quite a few Western businessmen who found their suggestions to Japanese colleagues rejected on the grounds that "the Japanese are different," but much to their chagrin, seeing a Japanese competitor introduce the same idea, having brought it back from a trip overseas.

I can vouch for this. Before introducing a certain research technique to Japan, I asked a number of Japanese businessmen their views. Everyone I asked felt that the Japanese people would not respond to the technique; rejection was based on cultural, not methodological, grounds. Well, I ignored these views and was able to pioneer the market; our competitors are now using similar techniques. I would not be surprised if early opinions had been that Coca-Cola would not suit the Japanese palate. I know of a few who expressed the view that since there was a traditional form of take-home fried chicken—called *ka-raage*—Kentucky Fried would not be viable in Japan. This is like saying that since the Japanese do not have the custom of eating on the sidewalks, there would be no potential for McDonald's. Needless to say, all three are spectacular successes in Japan.

Love of New Things; Dislike of Revolution

I wonder how many market research firms subject their market to the same degree of scrutiny that they provide for their clients' markets? I was hired in Australia for the Japanese branch of a U.S. company (ASI Market Research) because of my Japanese background. I will expand on this later. The decision to open up in Japan was based on no more than two facts. First, the company's first overseas venture—in the U.K.—was making money pretesting commercials. Therefore, it seemed a good idea to expand the operation elsewhere. Australia had a developed commercial television market and an active market research industry, and seemed a logical choice for an extension of the company's services. Second, by far the largest commercial television market outside the U.S. was Japan. The size of the Japanese market is still the most commonly cited reason for attempt at entry.

I have already touched upon my depressing first encounter with Japanese business opinion, but by that time it was too late for me to report that fact to my head office unless I wanted to look for another job. Anyway, I had the optimism of relative youth and was not overly troubled by Japanese negativism. Through luck rather than good planning I survived the years since 1965 and am still here with the same crew, although the company's ownership has changed. The testing activity is now conducted by one of our divisions and is no longer the entire hub of our activity, but it is still going strong with about five thousand commercials tested to date, mostly for Japanese companies. So the original advice that the method was not applicable to Japan because Japan was different could be ignored.

I have recently had to go through the same experience again in introducing, in association with others, market simulation modeling techniques in Japan. Our current Japanese clients said that it wouldn't work, but through our Western clients, the technique was introduced. Now, with about fifty cases behind us, we are beginning to get reactions from our Japanese clients. Things haven't changed.

For the nonspecialist, simulation modeling technique is a computer-based technique that artificially produces a situation that can be assumed to apply to real life—it doesn't actually take place but the whole thing is simulated. The technique we use was developed by Professor Glen Urban at the Sloan School of Management at M.I.T.

Certainly, it is difficult to change basic customs and habits, but in recent years Japan has become one of the most innovative societies in the world. Transformation of the Japanese society over the last 150 years is the most dramatic the world has known. The Japanese may even surpass the Americans for their love of new things. The one major proviso is that the changes wrought in manners and consumption patterns may be misleading if projected to basic values. The task is to discern which existing values can be affected and which new values can be accepted.

In 1968 there was a new T.V. commercial by Coke that encountered some Japanese—and old Japan hand—resistance. At that time, a clean-cut young Japanese star was asked to drink Coke from the bottle, American style. This is called *rappa nomi*, which translates as drinking bugle style; i.e., the posture reminded the Japanese of the blowing of the bugle. It was seriously suggested that this went against conventional manners and was therefore not acceptable. Although the question was debated quite intensely, the producers of the commercial had their way and the commercial was aired, creating a new fashion. (The Japanese vending machine market, I am told, is one of the biggest in the world.) The gesture of drinking from the bottle may have appealed to the highly regimented Japanese youth as a small but harmless defiance of convention. The star, Yuzo Kayama, now playing young executive roles on T.V., was an establishment type and his gesture hardly represented revolution or a challenge to fundamental values. In fact, the Japanese were beginning to tolerate the release from rigid social codes, at least in the young, so the commercial was perfectly attuned to the times.

We should not, however, lose sight of the fact that the Japanese are essentially conservative and dislike revolutions. For example, the change in social organization that occurred in the Meiji period (1868–1912) was called "restoration," not "revolution."

While there are exceptions, few products are powerful enough in concept to revolutionize consumer values. The probability of success is much greater if the new product is part of the evolutionary process of society and comes from within that society. One would have to be foolhardy to expect that change can be easily imposed from outside. Many of the marketing mistakes and continued failures nevertheless are based on reckless disregard for the consumer's social environment.

This much is obvious. There are many Western products that have become integrated and part of the life of the Japanese consumer. And there are quite a few that have not equaled their Western success. In many ways it is more useful to explain why a product was not accepted. This is not to dwell on the negative but rather to contribute toward greater mutual understanding. By putting down on paper the specific examples that I have witnessed over almost twenty years, I hope to be doing the latter.

I did not follow Japanese consumers on their daily rounds of shopping because I wanted to use my observations to formulate serious sociological theories; it was simply my job. But acquisition of goods is one of the most basic types of social behavior and when it deviates from other known norms—in this instance, those of the Western consumer—I have had to try to explain the "aberration." At that point, it became obvious that to talk about norms in an intercultural context was simply nonsense. The Japanese consumer is not deviating from anything when he rejects a foreign product or service or positions it differently. Though, in the past, Westerners often accused the Japanese consumer of being illogical, the Japanese were, in fact, devastatingly consistent with their cultural values. Exploring these consistencies has turned out to be an unexpected side benefit of my work for almost two decades, and it forms the basis of this book.

1

Living in "Rabbit Hutches" Contributed to High Economic Growth

Influence of Village-Style Living Environment on Products

The Japanese Launder Several Times More Often Than the Westerner

Since the Second World War the Japanese living environment has been a product of steady industrialization and accelerated urbanization. From a historical context this environment is still a recent event and the influence that it has had on fundamental values must still be superficial; the average Japanese is far less concerned than the Westerner would expect. Japanese living conditions became a major issue when, in a European Economic Community report, the phrase "Japanese lived in rabbit hutches" appeared. It caused quite a stir here, but instead of resentment, the Japanese, who prefer to see themselves as underprivileged self-achievers, seemed to take almost perverse delight in it. As these living conditions have been only recently imposed on a national scale—notwithstanding urban ghettoes in such places as Edo, the old Tokyo, a phenomena that would have also existed in London from the seventeenth century on, as well as in ancient Rome—we can expect conditions to continue to change.

Urbanization is created by migration from nonindustrialized to industrialized areas of the country, and in this sense Tokyo and New York are alike. The fact that they are fundamentally different is not just because one is a homogeneous society and the other a heterogeneous one. The differences are more attributable to the historical evolution of each society and the values that bind them. Originally

called Edo, the city of Tokyo existed with the castle—now the Imperial Palace—at the center; the samurai were the aristocratic core of the
community surrounded by merchants and artisans living in the commercial districts. The town was in turn surrounded by farmers and
fishermen who brought produce in for the sustenance of the administrative town. In other words, the social organization was that of a
village.

Frank Gibney, a noted Japan hand and the author of several books
on Japan, points out in one of them that Tokyo is not a city but a
collection of twenty-three villages, referring to the same number of
wards in Tokyo. It could be argued that this would apply to any large
city, such as New York, Los Angeles, and London, in the sense that
ethnic or, more prevalently, economic strata will create distinct groupings into areas, but that is not what is meant. Even with my long
affiliation with Japan, I have only recently come to understand. For
example, I belong very much to Onarimon village. Now, Onarimon is
the name of the intersection that was originally one of the numerous
gates that sprinkled Edo. (It was through the gates that merchants
entered the samurai district.) It is a part, and only a very small part, of
the district of Shimbashi, which in turn belongs to the Minato ward,
one of the aforementioned twenty-three. In fact, Tokyo is fragmented
into further villages within each of the twenty-three wards, with their
characteristics not easily defined by social or economic criteria. (Ethnic groupings are very rare although they do exist as oddities of the
"foreign" residents, and tiny Chinatowns, etc.) Onarimon, not on the
map except as a name of a subway station, exists because it is a distinct
living community.

Practically all of our own business is generated outside the
Onarimon community since we are not a local retailer or a printing
shop and our clients are large corporations. However, the fabric of
community living is such that when we put new carpeting in the office
or get new fixtures, our general affairs department tends to contact the
local supplier. Lunch is brought in for our staff from the local sushi or
noodle store. We contribute to the community association—not a
chamber of commerce—that runs a festival each year centered around
a tiny Shinto shrine. The festival itself has an origin in the harvesting
rites of a farm village but very few who participate are conscious of
this fact. It is not just a question of forming business relationships; if

general affairs shopped around more, we might be able to get a cheaper carpet, but we would not be served with the same trust and reliability. In the village, a carpenter is always on hand; you get superb consideration and service and the best his skills can offer because he is a neighbor. Japan is an enormous market for consumer durables, a fact that would not surprise anybody in the world. However, a great deal of sales are still accounted for through tiny local appliance stores that cannot hope to compete with the large discount stores in price. But he is there to fix your T.V. set even on a Sunday night—and that may be worth paying a little extra.

Contrary to the belief held by many that Japan is a closed society, the fact that we are a foreign-capital firm has no effect on our relationship with the rest of the village community. This is because, as in any village, once you are accepted as a member, credentials other than origin become more relevant. For a newcomer to be accepted in the village community, he has to demonstrate that he does not plan to disrupt existing values; it also helps if he can bring distinct skills that will contribute to the welfare of the community. Obviously then to become an accepted member of the village requires effort; the origin of the company is not as important as whether one is acceptable, through ones' behavior, to the community. Foreign firms, which simply bring products over and do not make such an attempt, cannot hope to be successful. After all, the Japanese are not asking any more of that firm than they ask of their own.

While sociologists may object to the oversimplification, I believe the Tokyo-ite retains much more of his original roots than, say, the New Yorker, because of his transfer of village values to urban living. The Japanese often cite the cultural differences between Kanto—the eastern region dominated by Tokyo—and Kansai—the western region dominated by Osaka and other Japanese areas. At certain levels this is true. But the differences, to me, do not seem as great as those between a Midwesterner and an East Coaster in the United States; the geographic distance that separates Americans is not the cause. The best way to visualize it is to imagine the unlikely phenomenon of the transfer of Midwestern community values to the city of New York. This is the sort of thing you find in Tokyo.

The example of Tokyo can be extended to any reasonably sized city in Japan. Tokyo and Osaka represent the extreme forms. Since Japan is highly urbanized, with purely agricultural communities accounting for only a small proportion of the total, the primary demand for modern-day products is created in this unique urban-village environment. The Japanese, of course, take this for granted and don't even notice the effect it has on the development of markets for products. For example, on the one hand; Japan is a gigantic market for laundry detergents. On the other, on a per capita basis, it is a small market for furniture polish. Both facts can be easily explained by the "rabbit hutch" living conditions brought about by urbanization and the scarcity of land. Since there is little room to place furniture, there is less opportunity for the use of furniture polish.

The transference of village values to urban living could account for the Japanese fastidiousness and the extremely high frequency of laundering—on the average, about once every two days. The fact of the matter is that in the confined living space—a universal condition and not just for the urban underprivileged—there is nowhere to put the soiled clothes. As a result, the wash loads are small, and dirty clothes are not allowed to accumulate for very long. Hence, on international comparisons, a large market for detergents.

The Japanese Do Not Use a Lot of Baby (Talcum) Powder

The explanation for the relative sizes of the market for furniture polishes and detergents are obvious. But in my early professional days in Japan, I came across an unexplainable phenomenon. The Japanese change their baby's diapers more often than other cultures. (It doesn't follow from this that it is a giant market for disposable diapers, but that is another story.) Japanese mothers are always in close proximity to their infants; they even sleep with them, so the slightest whiff or a baby's cry leads to a diaper change. (The diaper is, of course, washed immediately, but disposable diapers of Western origin have added a new dimension.) This should mean that the consumption of baby powder would be extremely high.

In fact, a certain well-known Western brand's international market was lower than expected, and it was not a question of market share. Talcum powder has been used in Japan for a long time, and so the difficulties of expanding the market appeared not to be based on cultural objections. There was, however, a deviation from the Western norm in that most baby powder in Japan was sold in round cardboard containers or cans rather than the sprinkle-on canisters common in the West. This was assumed to be based on unknown cultural values and required further investigation. Observing the Japanese mother applying baby powder from the Japanese container is illuminating. She removes the lid and a powder puff emerges. The powder is gently applied to the baby's bottom with the puff; very little powder is wasted. The foreigner's first tendency was to surmise that this was because of the frugality of the Japanese mother, and more importantly, that it was consistent with the Japanese mother's valuing "skinship" (she even used to carry the baby on her back). A focus group soon revealed that the Japanese mother had a far more practical bent. It had to do with the confined quarters in which the people live. The diaper could be changed in the living room, the dining room, or the kitchen; even the bathroom is in close proximity to the other rooms. It is certainly not pleasant to have powder flying around the place and getting into things, so the sprinkle-on method was highly suspect. The round can with a puff provided the most appropriate method of application, and it did reduce product usage. We must also note that frequent diaper changes, in themselves, lessen diaper rash, further reducing the need for talcum powder.

But the poor baby powder faced further problems. Although generically the product is talcum powder, the major brands heavily identify the product with its major use, i.e., for babies. The name of the major Japanese brand, Siccarol, is almost a translation of talcum powder, but it showed a picture of a baby on the can. The Johnson & Johnson packaging is the same as it is worldwide, no picture of a baby but the word *baby* instead—with the same effect. The Japanese tend to categorize and classify not only items but modes of behavior from which only acknowledged eccentrics deviate. The word *nonconformist*, or even *conformist*, is not a common word in the Japanese vocabulary. (My Japanese-English dictionary cannot give a single word for "conformist," described as a "person who obeys customs and the law," which would seem to be practically everybody in the Japanese society!) This tendency to classify is extended to literal interpretations of a title, caption, product description, or whatever. Once you are placed in a category, you're stuck there.

Since the Japanese bathe often—I hesitate to say more often than anybody, but they are well up there—if talcum powder usage could be extended to adults and not limited just to babies the market could grow enormously. Even taking the space problem into account, theoretically it would be a quantum leap in product usage.

A fairly recent American marketing success story that is fast becoming a classic is Johnson & Johnson's ability to extend its Baby Shampoo usage to adults with its "mildness" concept. It is an extremely impressive strategy and saved the product from languishing in a static baby product market. I feel such an attempt would be difficult, if not doomed, in Japan although nothing can be impossible for the marketing geniuses of Johnson & Johnson. In any event, baby powder is truly stuck in the baby products category—a pity, since talcum powder was known to have been used by some Japanese women a few generations ago. There are other factors to inhibit the growth of the baby powder market that need not be gone into here. The point of this story is that it is very difficult for a mere product, no matter how well marketed, to buck culturally induced attitudes. This is an often ignored truism that we shall encounter again. I hasten to add that Johnson & Johnson does not face the problem; they have recently become highly successful in the market, obviously adept at picking up the appropriate cultural cues.

The purpose of this chapter is to discuss the effects of confined space on the acceptance of modern consumer products; the baby powder example has caused me to digress. So, to return to the central theme, let us take as an example a Western product that was successful in Japan: Tupperware. The *raison d'être* of this product in the West is its excellent ability to preserve things, especially food, and its contribution to home storage. We could surmise that in the small Japanese home, rather than "preservation" *per se*, "storage" is the key word. While the product's efficiency is measured in terms of time in the West, the Japanese housewife who shops often—another issue that is discussed later—has no need to keep food in her home for an extended period; rather, her primary concern is how efficiently she can utilize space when she *has* to keep something, even if for only a short period. The philosophy of "letting the other guy stock it" is not just limited to Toyota. The refrigerator is really an extension of storage space and must be used carefully in this sense. Not surprisingly then, the design of Tupperware containers and their ability to stack well in the refrigerator could be their primary value. On the scale of time versus space, the latter is weighted more heavily in Japan. Therefore, the intrinsic value of the same plastic container is not the same in the East as it is in the West.

The Rabbit Hutch Is Inundated With Consumer Durables

Rabbit hutch living has a more profound impact on the development of the Japanese economy and extends well beyond the single products—detergents, talcum powder, furniture polish, diapers, and plastic containers—discussed so far. Not only have current environmental conditions changed Japanese attitudes, but they have contributed to the economic prosperity of modern Japan. This proposition evolved through a slide presentation I give on the Japanese consumer. I cannot claim to be the originator of the presentation itself; it was brilliantly conceived and created by an American colleague, Fred Perry, a Japan hand with whom I worked in developing our operation in Japan.

I met Fred in 1966 while he was still working for Gillette in Japan. As he had previously worked for the advertising agency Hakuhodo— second in size to the giant Dentsu, the world's largest—he had a superb grasp of the Japanese consumer market, a quality still rare these days but almost nonexistent then in a Westerner. Fred was working on a book, *The Japanese Consumer*, coauthored by Boyd Dementhe. A by-product of the book was numerous photographs of Japanese people in their daily surroundings, which became the genesis of the slide presentation we gave to businessmen visiting Japan. Gradually I evolved my own style of presentation, but I have to admit that Fred's dynamic ways and enthusiasm made his presentations hard to match. In the early days Fred was the presenter, and I enjoyed listening to the ways he changed the narrative according to the audience. My own presentations were also unscripted and a new angle would intrude as we tried to explain a picture for our foreign visitors. Interestingly, for some reason, the presentations never had the same impact when presented outside of Japan—in the United States, Europe, or Australia. At least as far as I'm concerned, insights never occurred during those presentations.

Still, without a doubt, the greatest value of the presentation was not in the accompanying narrative—"feeding false pearls to real swine," as a professor of mine used to say—but in the actual scenes presented. The average Japanese home remains an impenetrable fortress to most foreigners. The Japanese say *"hyakubun wa ikkenni shikazu,"* which translates as "a hundred listenings do not amount to one viewing," or more simply "seeing is believing." So we enjoyed taking our visitors through a photographic tour of the Japanese home—the porch, the living room, the kitchen, the bathroom, the bedroom. However, the presentation was originally developed around 1966, and Japan was growing very rapidly and continued to grow at a real rate of 10 percent or more. Therefore, between 1966 and 1973, real income had more than doubled. Even if fundamental values do not change that rapidly, such income growth must very visibly affect consumer life-styles. Our Japanese friends began to note that some of the scenes were looking rather outdated and, interestingly, some scenes more than others. My original inclination was to update and replace the slides, but then suddenly I realized the importance of comparing the old slides with the new, a juxtaposing technique that I used to use by running U.S. and Japanese commercials back to back. The viewer sensed the differences far more easily than possible with just words. In this instance, the technique of showing more or less the same scene from two time periods is used for two purposes; first, to show how much Japan has changed visibly, and second, to show how little it has changed in its fundamentals. This was not always obvious, and required some cultural commentary.

At last, in line with most modern cities, Japanese residential styles have moved dramatically from private homes to apartments—an inevitable consequence of limited space and high land prices, although it was surprisingly slow to happen. Things have changed so much that there are small children who have never lived on a tatami floor, which would have been almost unimaginable to the majority of Japanese only twenty years ago. With labor costs rising, the craftsman-produced tatami—the compressed straw mat—flooring is a lot more expensive than the Western floor with carpet. Even a Westerner who has never been to Japan is probably familiar with the tatami from visits to Japanese restaurants—the kind where you have to remove your shoes. It is difficult to explain how fundamentally important the tatami floor was to the way the Japanese lived. It affected what one wore, the furniture, the garden—seen at a lower eye level than its Western counterpart. Social manners and styles were affected because there was a great difference in the way people socialized, sitting on the floor as opposed to sitting on a chair—the latter having greater mobility. The Japanese are more sedentary and certainly quieter in their movements in the home.

In turning to the photographs of the middle-class living rooms called the *chanoma*—literally, space for tea—we are separated by ten years. In that decade, the occupant's real income has more than doubled. But he has been unable to increase his living space because real estate values have increased at a faster rate than his income. In the Western sense, his living style may not seem to have changed much, but careful examination of the photos will reveal a profound difference.

In 1966 the *kotatsu* occupied the center of the room. This is a table that has an electronic heating element under its top. In winter the top is lifted and a floor-length coverlet is placed underneath that warms the knees of the whole family while they sit around the table. This is still a popular heating device that is safe and also space saving; if necessary the table can be removed and a mattress rolled out as a bed for the night.

In the later photo the *kotatsu* is gone, and an air conditioner that cools the house in summer also provides heating. Gone also is the small black-and-white T.V. set; it has been replaced by a color set. (Color T.V. penetration passed that of the United States quite quickly and is currently at saturation with a majority of homes having two sets.) Although from a functional point of view a rug is totally unnecessary over the soft tatami flooring, nevertheless it is what the family now sits on. Thus the same space has now been upgraded by an avalanche of consumer durables. The confined environment turned consumer energy toward household items with a vengeance. It was a boon to the manufacturers of consumer durables and, especially electronics.

The expanding domestic demand enabled the manufacturer not only to work at full capacity, but also to retool in the newest equipment. Domestic competition was severe, but buoyed by the demand, products continued to improve enabling them to be successfully exported. The rest is history. I believe the Japanese have a much greater attachment to consumer durables than Westerners and, of course, they should, since they live in such close proximity to them. The refrigerator could be in the Western-style living room, and the washing machine in the bathroom.

Of course, there is a certain attachment to expensive consumer durables in every culture, particularly for such items as automobiles and stereo equipment. But utilitarian items, such as washing machines and refrigerators, have a higher psychological positioning in Japan simply because they occupy relatively more space in the total living environment. They occupy a position in the Japanese home akin to furniture in the Western.

The Japanese perception of cars also differs fundamentally from that of the Westerner and particularly in those wide open cultures as the American and the Australian, major cities such as New York and Chicago perhaps excepted. The car, in Japan, is an extension of space. This is reflected in advertisements that show unrealistic stretches of open road, obviously in a foreign land. In essence, the car represents an extension of one's spatial horizon. Excluding the sports car segment, which is aimed at the young in Japan, juxtaposing U.S. and Japanese family-car advertising immediately brings home this point. The heavy emphasis of functionality gives way to social and life-style positioning in Japanese advertising overlaid with the concept of spatial freedom. In Japan, like "my home," "my car" is a place of family communion.

In any event, the consumer durables explosion provided a valuable safety valve to a growing Japanese economy and consumer society. No problems of excess capacity for the manufacturer, and, therefore, the theory that the confined living space contributed to Japan's outstanding economic growth.

The Japanese National Railways Contribute to Vitamin Sales

The scarcity of land and population density have also affected some markets in unexpected ways. But it must be emphasized that these living conditions are a relatively recent phenomena in Japanese history—perhaps just as Mexico City is to Mexico—and the attitudes affected are not based on long-term cultural values. The way the Japanese coped with the situation, without a doubt, followed established cultural patterns. Japan, like the United Kingdom, another small island nation, developed an intricate network of transportation quite early. Before the intrusion of the West via the blackships of Commodore Perry, Japan had a centralized government with a bureaucratic infrastructure that required a communication network. Traveling by foot or horse may be primitive, but it is still a mode of transport and, as in seventeenth- and eighteenth-century England, there were numerous travelers in Japan carrying information from one center to another. The railway, which originated in England and spread through Europe in no time, was one of the first foci of the new Japanese government, in a country opened forcefully to the West. Rightly they identified the railway as one of the best means to catch up with the West. The development of the railroads was one of the major reasons Japan industrialized ahead of its neighboring giant, China, which continued her feudalistic slumber.

The Japanese are second only to the Swiss in their use of the railroad. It was the Japanese National Railways that developed the bullet train and made the world aware of the high technological standards of the Japanese. But the very same National Railways has one of the most disastrous performance records of any enterprise in the world; accounts for the bulk of Japan's national debt; continues to lose market share to others; charges more than the competition; and its labor and management are continuously feuding. Yet, for good or bad, it is still central to the Japanese conscious.

Rush-hour travel conditions are symbolic of the status of Japan's railway. Of course, rush-hour transportation problems exist in most major cities, but only a few foreign businessmen are willing to brave the Tokyo conditions. As mentioned, Japan was originally an agrarian society. As industrialization progressed, so did urbanization; land prices skyrocketed in cities such as Tokyo, forcing the average worker further and further away from his workplace. While this situation may seem the same as in New York or any other major Western metropolis, one product category was affected by this induced condition in a uniquely Japanese way.

Slightly over ten years ago, a multinational Western corporation looked at Japan's market potential for its vitamin product. Although the market has since rapidly matured, vitamins were then still regarded as a major growth category. And unlike now, there were few restrictions by the Japanese FDA. It seemed an attractive market to enter but it had been entirely developed by Japanese brands. Actually, the Westerners' decision to investigate the market came when the market growth had peaked, so the timing was not the best—but that is hindsight.

In any event, let us assume that the concept was somewhat akin to the one-a-day pill. It is well known that with vitamin use there is considerable waste, the body flushes out rather than stores most excess vitamins. But, if the vitamin were in granule form, the concept was that the ingredients would be released into the body at varying speeds, providing required vitamins throughout the day. A cold remedy using the same principle had been successfully introduced into Japan.

The Japanese consumer wasn't interested in nutritional supplements, believing that if one maintains a reasonable diet, nutrition is generally not a problem. In fact, Japanese cuisine is exceptionally well balanced nutritionally, which contributes to Japan having one of the highest life expectancy rates in the world—far exceeding that of the United States and recently surpassing the Scandinavians, the previous record holders.

That being the case, why did the Japanese consume so many proprietary brand vitamins? The answer is that their expected benefits were very specific and quick. Abstract benefits of nutritional balance were not what the consumer needed. From multiple vitamins, the Japanese consumer expected "fatigue prevention/cure"; from vitamin C, "removal of freckles and skin blemishes, bleaching of the skin tanned by the summer sun (!)"; and from the various tonic drinks, "sexual energizing." Since the Westerners planned to introduce a multiple vitamin, the concept of "nutritional balance" proved to be no threat to the incumbents, and the fatigue-related benefits had been preempted by strong existing brands, precluding entry of a new one.

Why should the most successful vitamin concept be fatigue related? It may seem as if I am stretching the point, but it is the result of the postwar commuting conditions. Immediately after the war the Japanese worker suffered from nutritional deficiencies and at the same time had to cope with a brutal commuting system. If one's nutritional intake is inadequate, one is fatigued. While the claim is no longer allowed, there was a tenuous link between improving one's vitamin intake and preventing tiredness.

There was a Japanese Ministry of Health study that showed that the Japanese white-collar worker expended more calories getting to and from work than at work. A major Japanese vitamin, with garlic (believed to contribute to the male's sexual potency), was popped into the mouth of about half the male white-collar workers, no doubt providing psychological solace to the dedicated, fatigued workaholics. So the brutal commuting conditions, by courtesy of the National Railways, contributed to the growth of the Japanese vitamin market.

While the reader may prefer to take this idea with a grain of salt, I believe it. Another idea my Japanese colleagues hold in good faith is that commuting conditions revolutionized Japanese breakfast habits—culturally, a most difficult task. If one has to rise at dawn and be pummeled and squashed in a train bursting at the seams, the traditional Japanese breakfast of bean-paste soup, dried fish, pickles, and rice is not appropriate. A quick cup of coffee or toast at home or a bowl of noodles at the station kiosk or the "morning set"—an economical combination of boiled egg, toast, and coffee—at the coffee shop near the office is far better. And it has benefitted Western products—coffee and bread, as well as other breakfast foods.

2

"No, No" to Making a Cake in a Rice Cooker

Modernization Is Not Synonymous With Westernization

Drinking Coca-Cola, But at Heart a Japanese

Whether imported or locally manufactured, a foreign product's failure is often due to the marketer being bedazzled by the so-called Westernization of the Japanese life-style. Certainly, cultures are influenced by the taking in of foreign elements. Some of these elements will be absorbed, some rejected, and on the rare occasion some will become a catalyst for cultural change. In any event, the new cultural entry, like a bacterium entering the host's body, would be expected to create some reactions, although most bacteria that enter our body have little effect on it.

The Japanese refer to the opening of the Meiji era as *bunmei kaika*, meaning "the coming of civilization and enlightenment," and there was, superficially at least, complete acceptance of things Western in a country that had been closed off from the rest of the world for over three centuries. A similar phenomenon occurred at the end of World War II. The very same nation that had mounted kamikaze suicide attacks turned around and welcomed American influence with open arms. Both were results of the traumatic acknowledgment that there was a force more powerful than their own, but national pride was preserved because the superiority was seen as being material rather than spiritual. There is an underlying faith that the Japanese race will always adapt to adversity yet eventually prevail. The moment of adver-

[30]

sity is accepted with stoicism, but like a swinging pendulum, the sense of national feeling returns. I fear that we are now entering such a phase.

Western influences are visibly evident in Japan. Regretfully, businessmen will make judgments by observing their immediate environment. The post–World War II businessman, be he Western or Japanese, saw the marketplace changing as a result of the industrial revolution that emanated from the West. Since all economically advanced nations were Western and all technologically advanced products came from the West, Westernization was equated with modernization. When a Westerner comes to the East and sees Western products being used, he feels more secure in the environment, somehow feeling that the local inhabitants are Westernized. This is a form of cultural arrogance, but one that can be forgiven as it is not a conscious form of condescension. Nevertheless, I often like to say that a New Yorker who eats sushi is no more Easternized than a Tokyo-ite who eats hamburgers is Westernized.

Coming into contact with a different culture often generates a sense of anxiety, so when the Western observer sees the Japanese consuming Cokes and Big Macs with relish, it does seem as if the Japanese are not fundamentally different from Westerners. The observer then thinks that his own methods—marketing, financial, personnel management, or whatever—are easily transferable. He holds the illusion that the Cokes and hamburgers impart the producers' value system to the consumers. The foreigner who consumes sushi is also more approachable to the Japanese, so the leap in logic exists on both sides.

In the historical context, Japan suffered from a shortage of foreign exchange. The Japanese government artificially undervalued the yen for longer than was necessary; this, along with other policies, helped create a mighty export machine that was sprung on the unprepared West. Until recently, the average Japanese consumer found imported foreign products scarce curiosities. These were times when "from the United States" was considered an effective advertising-copy phrase. This tendency was at its peak in 1965 when I returned to Japan. We have a habit of not knowing that we are on the peak until later. We seldom realize that the crest of the wave is only a temporary phenomenon.

Faith in permanency or a continuation of a trend by many ensures that there will always be those who lose money on the stock market. Establishing a new company in a different culture is no joke; if I knew then what I know now I certainly would not have tried. The Western cliché, ignorance is bliss, certainly applied to me, but fortunately I had the confidence of relative youth, the security of a prosperous economic environment, and the crest of Western cultural confidence to help me along.

The Japanese have a saying, "Even a dog will bump into something if he walks enough"—in other words, the good salesman wears out his shoe leather. I was told that you had to have introductions before you went and saw anybody in Japan, but since the few I had were not enough on which to base a business, I had the brazenness to make calls cold. Admittedly I did have an advantage over my Japanese colleagues in that the Japanese are curious about what a foreigner has to offer. Now that I am older and better known, this has become more difficult. In any event my job was to call on clients and develop business for a new firm. It was in these early activities that I ran into a significant Western marketing failure.

Since our only reason for entering the Japanese market was that it was the second largest T.V. market in the world—surely the most naive of reasons—I certainly cannot take a holier-than-thou attitude in recounting another's market entry failure. Although this might sound strange coming from a market researcher, we all know that luck is a large part of any product's success. None of us, in those days, perceived the trap of confusing modernization with Westernization. Observing this product's failure at such close range made me realize this truth fairly early in my professional career in Japan. I have told my clients the story of this case so often that some of them will cry, "No, not again!" (Even *Fortune* referred to it as "Fields' classic.")

The "cake mix" case, since it occurred so early in my Japanese experience, has had considerable impact on my approach to marketing in Japan. It all started when my head office notified me that their client, General Mills, had formed a joint venture with the major Japanese confectionery firm Morinaga and that I should follow up.

In the days of calling cold, such tips are precious. I was able to get in touch with the American management and got to know a first-class young marketing pro. We were both young, and we both shared a common professional view of marketing. I was entirely on his side and his approach was entirely consistent with my systematic approach. Our company's emphasis on advertising research meant that I only heard about the process in which the decision to launch a cake mix in Japan was made. Since I knew all about the success of the Betty Crocker cake mix in the United States and elsewhere, I was not surprised that General Mills had selected it as the product with which to enter the Japanese market, a market in which any sort of cake mix was yet to be introduced. Hindsight is easy, and I cannot confidently claim that if I had been engaged in the pre-launch research I would have avoided the trap. I probably would have fallen into the same hole as my friends at General Mills.

The Oven as Womb, and the Cake as the Baby; and the Rice Cooker?

Even now, I have to explain to my Japanese audience what a cake mix is (I relate the case as an example of the difference between a technical concept and a marketing concept), so obviously the strenuous efforts by General Mills and Morinaga fifteen or so years ago made but a ripple on the Japanese waters. I explain that in the West cakes are traditionally baked at home, that shop-bought cakes account for only a small proportion of cakes consumed—a reversal of the Japanese situation.

The initial introduction of the cake mix in the U.S. is, in fact, a good example of how skillful marketing overcame cultural resistance. This product, that took the drudgery out of baking a cake and even more importantly promised to be failure proof, was strangely unsuccessful when first launched. This was a surprise as the concept seemed to be made to order for the American housewife who was putting increasing value on her own time and moving toward convenience products.

I rather suspect that the psychological ramifications of baking a cake have become somewhat exaggerated over time, but the analogy that the oven was the womb and the cake was the baby coming out into the world was certainly neat. The act had an important position in American culture and reflects the perceived role of the female at a certain point in history. Some postulated that the female could not overcome her feeling of guilt in resorting to convenience foods and it made them resist the product.

It was then suggested that to assuage the housewife's sense of guilt, she should have a hand in the product's preparation, and not just put the product into the oven. Today, such a concern would be inconceivable. But, at that time values were different and the role of the female was largely seen as being that of a maternal provider to her family in the home. A cake mix was then introduced that required the addition of an egg or two. It was said that by adding her personal touch in this way the housewife felt that she was not betraying her perceived role. This cake mix outsold the one that was completely self-contained.

The lesson here seems applicable when we enter another culture: a step-by-step process is more likely to succeed and one should not attempt to leap from one plateau to a higher one in a single jump. I saw something similar happen in Australia in the fifties when I was a novice researcher. The concept of a fully automatic washing machine was rejected by the Australian housewife who still thought that the power wringer was the greatest invention since the refrigerator. She rejected the fully automatic out of hand as being a totally unnecessary and unthinkable extravagance. As a result, the twin-tub was the major seller in those days. Of course, even in Australia, with an imagined rugged pioneering tradition and a very conservative view of the feminine role in society, the fully automatic machine became the mode not so long afterward. Interestingly, the twin-tub is still the mode in Japan, the lord of highly developed electric appliances.

To return to the cake mix: General Mills added to their marketing genius by turning a warm, "real" personality, Betty Crocker, into a brand name for their cake mix. Before the days of T.V., Crocker had a radio program in which she gave personalized hints on cooking—obviously an authority. Her face, neither middle-aged nor young, adorned the package. Betty Crocker was a person who baked cakes; she was not a manufacturing process. It is on such marketing touches that corporate fortunes are made. (Betty Crocker spawned imitators, and the advertising agency I worked for in Australia came up with Betty King, an antipodean twin of Crocker.)

"Why Not the Rice Cooker?" Says an American Manufacturer

Still, like human beings, all products mature and cease to grow eventually. The teenager seldom imagines that he will someday be old, and at the time of growth it is hard for a manufacturer to imagine that his product's sales will slow down. The railways in the U.S. in the twenties and now the automobile industry are such examples. Almost thirty years ago, A.D.H. Kaplan of the Brookings Institute discovered that of the top hundred-largest industrial corporations in 1909 ranked by size of assets, sixty-four had lost their position to newcomers by 1948.

The cake mix market had matured in the U.S. and poor Betty Crocker was becoming old. It is a truism that an industry then seeks to expand internationally, to hitherto unconquered areas. Initially, cake mixes entered other Western cultures that shared the same cultural roots and, not surprisingly, succeeded in quite a few—but not in all. That pool was now exhausted. Japan was becoming a logical target; her standard of living was rising rapidly, and, even more importantly, she was clearly displaying a penchant for Western products.

A closer examination of the Japanese market revealed extremely promising features. The Japanese had always bought rather than made cakes—this being regarded as a specialized skill. What seemed significant was that they were now buying more and more Western cakes, and in fact, the number of Japanese-type cake shops were decreasing while the Western-type pastry outlets were increasing. Though per capita consumption of Western-type cakes was very small, Japan's population, roughly half that of the U.S., still made it a respectable market. Considered together with the perceived Westernization of Japanese eating habits, there appeared to be a major opportunity for a cake product.

There is, however, always a catch, and in this case it seemed, on the surface, formidable: virtually none of the Japanese homes at the time had an oven! The poor Japanese housewife was being denied the opportunity of making her own cakes; she was forced into buying expensive shop cakes and hence restricting her level of consumption because she lacked an oven in her own kitchen—or so it seemed. If she could be given the means, she would not only buy fewer shop cakes, but she would also increase her family's consumption by making inexpensive cakes at home. The emotional satisfaction would enhance the economic benefits.

Many Japanese now have ovens in their homes, but in the mid-sixties ovens were almost nonexistent in Japan. To a good marketing man problems exist only to be solved. This indeed was the case with the original cake mix launch in the United States with the brilliant one-or-two egg concept. The proposed solution to the Japanese problem was nothing short of brilliant. While the Japanese home lacked an oven, it had a piece of equipment that no Western home has: the automatic rice cooker. Although volume consumption of rice has been declining in Japan because of the availability of other foods, rice still remains the core of the Japanese food culture. Menu census after menu census, including the latest, show that about 90 percent of the main evening meal is centered around rice. I do not know whether the initial introduction of the automatic rice cooker encountered rationalized objections in Japan, but by the mid-sixties, it had become standard equipment in every Japanese kitchen.

I can only imagine the delight of the research and development people back in Minneapolis when this fact was presented to them. It turned out to be perfectly within their technical expertise to create a cake mix that could be used in an automatic rice cooker. In fact, the resulting cake was of very high standards, at least according to the Japanese housewives who tested it; I am not a cake eater and am therefore not competent to judge. So the decision to enter the market by this means was a *fait accompli* when I met the General Mills executives in 1966; everything seemed to fall into place and I thought the project exciting and intriguing. The Japanese housewife would not identify with the foreign personality of Betty Crocker, so the product was given a new name, Cakeron. In Japan, the word "cake" denotes non-Japanese *kashi* (cake); what's more, it had just the right sound to Japanese ears. (Many foreign-sounding Japanese brand names do not need a specific meaning and in fact, the lack of meaning can later turn it into a semigeneric that indefinitely preempts the market for that brand.)

I became involved in the project after some advertising concepts had already been developed and tested. Tests suggested interest in the product, but on hindsight this was probably just curiosity, and the test design could not predict possible repeat purchase after trial. Of course, nobody expects that standard advertising pre-testing will prognosticate the product's performance in the marketplace.

Interestingly, when Cakeron was launched, it caused a minor stampede by other Japanese brands to enter the market. For a short time there was quite a profusion of me-toos on the supermarket shelves. However, in both product quality and volume of advertising Cakeron was clearly the leader. As is characteristic of the market the others merely wished to pick up some overflow from the brand leader without putting in too much effort. It is a marketing truism that the number of imitators of a new product is a poor guide to the eventual level to which the product will settle. Nevertheless, we all see clearest what is dangling before our nose. So, at first, influenced by effective advertising, the stores were well stocked with Cakeron and all seemed to be going as hoped. However, the repeat orders came much slower than expected, and it was soon realized that this market was no pushover.

Morinaga-General Mills was marvelously professional and I enjoyed visiting them and discussing the various ramifications of the Japanese market. However, when we decided to conduct a series of what the trade calls, focus group discussions, I was quite unaware of the seriousness of the situation. For the uninitiated, a focus group is a deceptively simple technique whereby a few people gather around a table and hold a discussion session on a predetermined topic. Since anybody can conduct these sessions, their quality ranges from extremely useful to downright misleading. Based on the principle of group dynamics, its aim is to peel away at the rationalizations till we come to the core attitude or motivation—those aspects that a person may not be aware of himself. In other words, it is a technique of psychological probing.

The technique was used surprisingly little when I came to Japan; advertisers seemed to rely heavily on statistical data alone. It has since, however, quickly become part of the standard repertory of the Japanese marketer. I was literally forced into using the technique when we started to realize that the advertising approaches that had tested well in the West were not performing in Japan. It was not enough to tell the client that something is so; it was also necessary to at least hypothesize why it should be so. It was essentially the same in this case—why was the Japanese housewife resisting the Cakeron concept?

"I Won't Use the Rice Cooker," Said the Japanese Housewife, "and Don't Ask Me Why"

Research is occasionally able to give a flash of insight into a situation. Unfortunately, it seems mostly to simply confirm or deny assumptions. Worse, the most significant aspect may lie buried because we become obsessed with the peripherals. What is so obvious, once it is pointed out, was missed at the outset. The moderator of the series of housewives group discussion sessions initially treated the matter as a possible product problem. Did they have trouble following the instructions? Was the cake too dry or too moist? Was it too sweet or not sweet enough? Was it the wrong sort of cake that was being pushed? And the color? The odor? Or taking another angle, did the advertising fail to communicate the product's benefits? Did they dislike the way the advertising was made? By failing to see the benefits, did they feel the product was not worth the price? And so on and so on. Market researchers would be familiar with the routine structuring of these probes.

Observing the Japanese group sessions was, in itself, a revelation of certain aspects of the culture. I was told, when I had first returned to Japan, that the focus group technique would not work there, since the Japanese were shy about expressing themselves in front of others. Actually, it turned out that they were better respondents in a group session than in a one-to-one interview. For the latter, no matter how skillful the interviewer, he is still a stranger, and the Japanese are not usually prone to open their hearts to a stranger. On the other hand, in a group situation they are with others like themselves. We are very careful to gather those with similar life-styles and backgrounds and age to generate rapport among the participants. The Japanese do not like to be faced with conflict in a group situation. Since they live in essential harmony, there is a great degree of interpersonal trust and very candid views are exchanged without any animosity.

A skillful moderator remains unobtrusive. There is plenty of time— the sessions usually run a course of two hours—to warm up the participants so the swapping of anecdotes start. The Japanese are marvelous in groups because they are attentive and interested in what others have to say. An American focus group and a Japanese one immediately start off differently. For example, when a new idea is introduced to the

American group, an opinion—for or against—is expressed very quickly. Somebody is just as quickly going to disagree with that opinion, sometimes just for the sake of scoring a point. This can lead to active debate, which can be enlightening but can produce the bane of group discussions, the group dominator.

A dominator is not common in a Japanese group, although they do occasionally occur. Since opinions are not immediately expressed, to the first-time listener the opening part of a session can be agonizingly slow. When an idea is introduced, a more typical pattern would be for Mrs. Suzuki to express a very tentative reaction. However, Mrs. Saitoh may pick up on some nuances of her comments and add a few of her own. And so it goes. Gradually the idea will be positioned and a consensus formed. This is how decisions are made in Japan, so it is not surprising that this research procedure is suitable.

So, after talking about cakes in general for warm-up, the moderator began to focus on various aspects of Cakeron. We seemed to be getting nowhere. Yes, there was the customary vagueness, but nobody was giving us a coherent reason why they would not buy again. There was nothing wrong with the Cakeron cake.

Then it came and it went something like this.

Mrs. Suzuki: "But doesn't it have vanilla in it?"
Mrs. Kobayashi: "Yes, chocolate, too."
Mrs. Saitoh: "Don't you think it will remain?"
Mrs. Fujiwara: "I suppose you can wash it off but . . ."

The scales fell off my eyes and I sat up.

The moderator: "What do you mean?"
Mrs. Kobayashi: "Well those things have a scent."
Mrs. Saitoh: "Wouldn't it come on to the rice?"
Mrs. Tanaka: "If you really scrubbed the cooker, it would be okay."
Mrs. Saitoh: "Well, I don't know about you, but I cook more than I need for dinner and leave some rice for breakfast, and perhaps my lunch. Then I have to go out for the shopping in the afternoon. Then it's time to cook the rice for dinner."
Hearty agreement by the assembled. Stop! They need go no further.

This simple product had come up against two formidable, interrelated cultural factors. First take the less important of the two. The rice cooker is in almost constant use. The Health Ministry surveys show that rice-centered meals are served in the majority of Japanese homes for most evening meals. That is why every home had an automatic rice cooker. Although quantitatively, rice's position was deteriorating, it was still preeminent on the Japanese dinner table. Put this together with the Japanese housewives penchant for shopping almost every day and spending a lot of time on shopping, you have an instrument that is seldom without rice. Between coming home from shopping and preparing for the next meal, the housewife is not likely to have enough time to make a cake in the rice cooker. A reminder: she also cooked more rice than she needed for the evening so she could have some for breakfast or for her own lunch. She was hardly likely to invest in another rice cooker just to make a cake, especially since cake making was not part of her routine.

But even if she only occasionally used the rice cooker for the cake, there would still be an adequate market, for even 5 percent of the Japanese market is equivalent to a substantial portion of some of the smaller European markets. No, it wasn't the frequency of use that was the problem, it was her reluctance to use the instrument at all! But why? We have to digress a little before revealing the horrible truth that, no doubt, some readers have already guessed.

Rice Is Still at the Core of the Japanese Culture

To understand the problem that Cakeron faced, we must understand the position of rice in the Japanese culture. I heard one foreign correspondent say that in Japan, rice is symbolic of the culture. It is highly polished and refined. All traces of the husk is removed to such an extent that the remainder is somewhat glutenous and soft compared with rice cooked in other parts of the world. Like their rice, the Japanese like to think of their culture as being extremely pure; things brought in from outside are placed on the surface and do not disturb the essential core. Fried rice is a Chinese dish; the traditional way the Japanese consume their rice is to have it in a separate bowl with all other items on different plates.

There are some foreign influences—such as curry to top the rice—but not essentially disturbing the base. Perhaps foreign enterprises in Japan can only be tolerated if, like the curry, they do not disturb the

Japanese core. When a foreigner eats sushi, he first responds to the fish or the other items that top the rice. A Japanese connoisseur of sushi will say that you can judge a truly first-class sushi restaurant and the *itamae* (cook) by the quality of the rice. It is certainly not a supporting player to the fish but plays an equal role.

Recently I saw a revival of a Japanese postwar film classic by the venerated Japanese director, Keisuke Kinoshita. Unlike Kurosawa, who is renowned in the West and even Mizoguchi or Ozu who have their Western following, Kinoshita is virtually unknown. He is still alive and well and the Japanese have rightly bestowed the title of *kyosho* (great master) on him. However, his films have been not well received at Western film festivals, mainly because he disappoints the Western expectation of exoticism, which Mizoguchi and others provide, or technical flamboyance, which Kurosawa provides, or Oriental introspection, which Ozu provides. His works are a peculiar blend of nineteenth-century Western romanticism and Japanese sentimentality. In *Narayama Bushiko*, which is probably his greatest film, the importance of rice is pervasive.

The story centers on a small farm in a bleak village in northeastern Japan during the Edo period (1615–1867). Growing and harvesting rice is the central activity of village life. Living conditions of this region were extremely harsh and, like some parts of India today, famine and starvation were not unknown. The villagers paid their dues to the landlord and the government officials in terms of rice, essentially protection money for the lord to maintain his army and bureaucracy. Throughout the Edo period, rank was designated in terms of rice. A clan chief like Date, the character in the film, had theoretically a large domain because his rank was 20,000 *koku* (*koku* is a measuring unit for rice; one *koku* is 4.9629 bushels). So 20,000 *koku* was enough to feed a large number of officials and soldiers. Each of these officials and soldiers also had their ranks designated by a number of *koku*, going as low as 5 or 10 for a foot soldier, which meant he had only enough to feed his family and could not afford to feed any servants. The *hatamoto*, who were the elite "head office" staff that surrounded the shogun, may only have a few hundred *koku*, as compared to the few thousand designated to a minor clan chief—equivalent of a branch manager with line responsibilities. However, the *hatamoto*'s few hundred *koku* was worth more than the few thousand of the clan chief because he did not have the responsibility of feeding a large dependent group of employees. Rice, then, was a standard of value and designated one's place in society.

For the village peasants in the film, rice was not a standard of value but a quintessential item of life, and lack of it meant starvation and death. Over the years the village had preserved a sad custom called *ubasute*: when a person became aged and feeble and was no longer able to contribute to the production of rice and became a burden to the community, he was taken up a mountain behind the village and abandoned to starve or, more mercifully if in winter, to freeze to death. Even today, there is a railway station in the quiet countryside by the name of *Ubasute*, and Kinoshita's film opens and closes with a shot of the station, the final scene showing young people getting off the train with their ski packs, presumably going up the very slopes that may have been the paths that led to the sad final spots for the aged.

The old lady of the story, played by the very great Japanese actress Kinuyo Tanaka, is quietly preparing for that day when her son will have to take her up the slopes. Each day is becoming a burden, as both are devoted to each other, and there is a strong parallel with the situation a family faces when one of the loved ones is terminally ill. Not only does she not question or fight her ultimate outcome, she welcomes it; not all the aged in the film are quite so acquiescent to such a fate but the ultimate end is inescapable. In a scene that surely must go down in film history as being one of the most poignant, the son sets off for the hills on a cold winter's day with his mother on his back. The mother had set the date and she is not as disturbed as her son; she knows that the son must set a brave example to the community and observe tribal laws for the preservation of the community.

Before departing she prepares for herself three *onigiris*, balls of pure, white rice, the best the village can produce. She carries this pathetic parcel very carefully to the place of her ultimate doom. In one of the final scenes the forlorn little figure sits with great dignity amidst some skeletons in a bleak open area atop the mountain. Her son, having set her down, runs down the slope sobbing and stumbling, but the rules are that he must not look back. Snow starts to fall just as the little old lady had calculated, which is why she picked that time. What I remember most about the film is the way she quietly placed the three balls of rice in front of her. She was going to partake in the last ritual of her life. Corny? Perhaps. Morbid, no—certainly not the way Kino-shita presented it. At least it brought tears to the eyes of one cynical middle-aged man who failed to be overwhelmed by E.T.

Perhaps I have gone too far in emphasizing the importance of rice in modern Japan. But it was not long ago that a young bride was judged on the way she cooked the rice; just like the young Western bride may have been judged on the cake she baked! The irony of this last example has surely not escaped the reader. Rice cooking is undeniably still a daily ritual in the Japanese home. But the chore is no longer onerous, thanks to the automatic rice cooker. It has become an important per-former in a ritual.

So we now return to the purity of the rice, a quality the cake does not possess. It must have many things added to the flour, not least of which is flavoring such as vanilla, chocolate, etc.

Flashback:

> *Mrs. Suzuki*: "But doesn't it have vanilla in it?"
> *Mrs. Kobayashi*: "Yes, chocolate, too."
> *Mrs. Saitoh*: "Don't you think it will remain?"
> *Mrs. Fujiwara*: "I suppose you can wash it off but . . ."

Yes, the essential problem was that psychologically, the cake mix ran the danger of contaminating the rice. Whether this fear is rational or not does not matter. When I first discussed this with my friend, the marketing manager for the client, neither of us felt that we faced an insurmountable cultural barrier. All good marketing men consider discovering the problem as the first step to success. The overcoming of the cultural resistance to the cake mix in the U.S. is, after all, a classic example of how such a problem was brilliantly handled.

The closest analogy I can think of for a Japanese housewife making a cake in a rice cooker is for an English housewife to brew coffee in her teapot. She cannot tamper with an age-old ritual. In an admirable example of cutting one's losses and getting out, the General Mills and Morinaga joint venture on cake mixes was dissolved.

A Product, of Course, Does Not Create Its Own Needs

The term, "marketing concept" is quite difficult to translate into Japanese, although the equivalent Japanese words do exist. The word *concept*, which the Westerner freely uses in debates at even the lowest intellectual level, is seldom used in Japanese conversation since it springs from Western philosophical terminology. Therefore, I used to have considerable difficulty in explaining marketing or advertising concepts in my lectures in Japan. I used this cake mix example to illustrate that it was really a technical concept and *not* a marketing concept. In other words, a product that was technically excellent was sprung on the consumer who perceived no need for it. If it was a marketing concept, it must be based on perceived consumer needs, or, if the category was entirely new, it must be capable of creating such a need. Deep-rooted cultural resistance to the concept relegated it to a technical rather than a marketing concept.

Actually, the term "marketing concept" was coined by Theodore Levitt during the 1950s, in the *Harvard Business Review*, and it has had considerable impact on subsequent marketing thought. An example he gave in his article is particularly meaningful to me in the light of other Japanese observations. The Penn Central, when Levitt wrote the article, was already in trouble but not yet bankrupt. However, since the turn of the century railway companies, even those that occupied the top positions, were struggling for survival or had given up the fight against the onslaught of the automobile and, later, the airplane. Levitt pointed out that this was because the companies saw themselves as railways rather than as being in the business of transportation. A true market moves with consumer needs. The Japanese National Railway is today, like most nationally owned railways, in dire straits because it too has operated as a railway rather than as a link between and a means to develop communities. None of the private Japanese railway companies are railway companies in the pure sense. Long before the marketing concept was talked about—in fact, well before World War II—private Japanese railway companies began to build department stores at their terminals. When the passengers left the train, they could go straight into a department store to do their shopping. Then the stores started to run major exhibitions, usually on the upper floors, which increased customer traffic through the stores and in turn increased passenger traffic on the railways. They bought the land around their tracks and developed community centers. Railway companies bought professional baseball teams and built stadiums along their tracks. A marketing concept put to effective practice.

So the cake mix was not a marketing concept, but there is a postscript to this story. Teflon, the Dupont product that prevents food from sticking to pots and pans, was successfully introduced into Japan. But, it is not used in rice cookers! It imparts a slight color to the inner surface!

If there were to be a post-postscript, it is that now even though a respectable proportion of Japanese homes have ovens, there has not been a major launch of any cake mix. Since there would be no cultural hang-up in using the oven for baking a cake, is it simply that no one is game to try because of the previous disaster, or is there another reason why the Japanese woman is not interested in baking a cake? I can only guess that since the Japanese have no tradition of cooking extensively with an oven, they have not yet decided how they want to use it. Only the Japanese love of appliances introduced the Western oven into the kitchen in the first place. Now, the Japanese use the oven only for reheating and simmering foods—which is how they've always cooked before the advent of the oven. It may take another generation before it is used for baking cakes—but by that time perhaps cake baking may be out of vogue in the West too!

3

"In Japan, the Woman Is the Boss?"

Differing Roles of the Housewife in Society as Revealed in Her Shopping Behavior

The Housewife as Sovereign

To market researchers, who are the tools of marketing management in getting the consumer to buy more, no one is more important than the housewife. There is no difference between East and West in this sense. In the degree of control she exercises on the purse strings, she is nearly a god in Japan. Our own consumer research business in Japan focuses on the housewife for about 70 percent of our activities.

A great deal of research is, not surprisingly, concerned with the success or failure of individual products, and we tend to miss the forest for the trees. It is this book's theme that reactions to individual products are often based on culturally conditioned attitudes; therefore, if comparisons can be made between cultures, synthesizing them may reveal important cultural peculiarities.

It was from the originally fragmentary observations collected in this book that I pieced together what I have come to postulate as the fundamentally different roles played by the Japanese housewife and her Western counterpart. Granted that all Western societies cannot be lumped together, my observations would at least apply to the three Western societies in which I have in one way or another worked—the United States, Australia, and the United Kingdom.

Statistically, Japan has the highest relative savings rate in the world. It is reported that the Swiss are higher in the absolute amount they keep in their banks, but in relation to income the Japanese far exceed everybody else. The Germans follow but are far behind, and it would not surprise my American readers that the U.S. is even further behind despite its large total wealth. Saving is supposed to be a Puritan virtue, but they do not have a monopoly on it. The prewar Japanese children were taught the life of Kinjiro Ninomiya, who, as an impoverished farm boy, studied even while carrying firewood on his back, saved his money, repaid his parents, etc. Somewhere in Tokyo is a statue of him as a little boy, walking and reading at the same time, with firewood on his back. Of course, he put whatever he earned to good use, especially education, and went on to a successful career. The modern day embodiment of these virtues is the Japanese housewife who accomplishes her savings feat as well as spends her considerable energy on the education of her children. For the latter, the Japanese even have a word: *kyoiku mama*, which simply means "education mother." Kinjiro Ninomiya, incidentally, later changed his name to Sontoku, which literally translates to "venerate virtue," when his place in society was secured. Although he acquired a fortune later, he did not flaunt it. As a boss, I rather suspect he may have been seen as a stingy old man and quite hard to work for. I had a similar experience working for the founder of a company who had strong Scottish virtues that seemed similar to those held by Sontoku. Frugality and modesty are Confucian teachings, and Confucianism is still the strongest force in Japanese social values.

The bald statement that the housewife is entirely responsible for the family savings *and* planning—unlike Fagin, she doesn't hoard the money, but has specific plans for future spending—seems to surprise some Westerners who are not familiar with Japan. I have found this a dangerous statement to make unless explained carefully. About ten years or so ago, during a brief return home from Japan, I was interviewed by a reporter from the *Sunday Telegraph* in Sydney. My associate in Australia had planted the idea with some of the media that my "unusual" experience as an Australian running a business in Japan might be of interest to their readers. Being a mass circulation Sunday paper, the reporter was of course not really interested in my business experiences *per se*. She was interested in the role of the Japanese woman, and it would not have been surprising that she, along with many others, subscribed to the prevalent image of the demure Japanese female succumbing to the tyranny of the Japanese male, trembling and quaking at the whims of her lord and master.

Post–World War II Australian society was extremely straitlaced—my copy of *Portnoy's Complaint* was confiscated at the airport on that visit—and as male-dominated as Victorian England. It was not difficult for nonstereotypical female behavior to stimulate the imagination of the Victorian male to unrealistic limits, and the Japanese professional woman was extremely adept at that art, practiced superbly in the boudoir of the eighteenth- and nineteenth-century playground of Yoshiwara and continued to this day, in the bars all over Japan. If he understood the language, the Western customer would have been thoroughly disillusioned with the matter-of-fact discussions his butterflies were having amongst themselves. The Japanese female is, by and large, very pragmatic, and on the whole, less romantic than her Western counterpart.

It was to correct the West's skewed perception of the Japanese female that I responded to the very charming reporter's questions; it was before the day of militant feminism and, besides, she did not give the impression of a battling feminist so I was less cautious than I would be now. It is absolutely true that within a large Japanese corporation, the inferior treatment of the female in terms of promotion verges on disgrace and is an appalling waste of an extremely well-educated and intelligent segment of the work force. The situation is being corrected, though perhaps not at a pace that is desirable to many of us.

Granting this, it must be pointed out that the Westerner often has the fault of following absolute value scales and tends to jump to conclusions when the other's behavior doesn't fit. For example, a typical question posed by a Westerner is "How can any woman tolerate a husband who returns late practically every night? Isn't that simply treating a woman as a domestic servant?" On Western value scales, yes. However, many Japanese women resent the Western interpretation of their role as a wife as that of an oppressed species. In any event, public statements on male-female roles are fraught with danger, as the Sydney interview proved.

I find I am culturally ambivalent on this matter. When I am speaking with my Japanese clients or colleagues I tend to put forward the Western viewpoint. Since my readers here are Western, I will do my best to put forward the Japanese side and simply make the philosophical point that, on value judgments, we should agree to disagree. This was the situation with my Australian interviewer when I stated that, in some ways, the Japanese housewife was given more responsibility in the home than her Australian counterpart and that she displayed remarkable managerial competence.

"Oh?"—a raised eyebrow. Rather hastily I explained that the Japanese housewife was virtually the minister of finance and had very wide discretionary power over her husband's pay envelope that was, in the great majority of cases, handed over to her in its entirety. This happens to be fact, not conjecture, and has been verified by repeated surveys by banks. The wife allocates the funds, which includes handing her husband his daily pocket money. While there may be protestations and pleadings in some cases, on all accounts she tends to hold firm, like any good secretary to the treasury or minister of finance.

Our own studies show that the Japanese housewife keeps a sophisticated and quite meticulous record of daily accounts. All expenditures are carefully entered into books given to her by banks, insurance companies, and as premiums for magazine subscriptions, much as businessmen receive pocket or desk diaries from their suppliers. (Incidentally, Japanese banks make door to door calls on housewives to solicit their savings.) Examination of these record books is a revelation to the market researcher. Apart from her daily expenditures, accounts are kept for educational and leisure expenses, as well as provisions made for a rainy day. Many even budget for a deficit to be repayable twice a year—the Japanese have a biannual bonus system that provides lump-sum payments for nonroutine expenditures, such as consumer durables.

Well, I was still in bed on that Sunday morning when the interview appeared in the *Telegraph*. I was featured on the back page, in a large photograph, with the headline, "In Japan the Woman's the Boss!" As usual, I got to the breakfast table after everybody else and was confronted with an Australian chorus of "Did you say this?!" My family was not a bit impressed that I had made the Sunday papers; obviously they felt I had made an ass of myself. Now, I did not say "in Japan, the woman is the boss." All I said was that she had almost total control of family finances; but in the West, the person who controls the purse strings is supposed to occupy the seat of power, and that's how they saw it.

The Japanese Husband Is a Feminist?!

A little later I attended a Foreign Correspondents' Club luncheon in Tokyo at which three Japanese leaders of the feminist movement were invited to speak. Their after-lunch speeches tended to be of fairly standard stuff, being read from a script and lacking the fire of American feminists. As a result, I don't really remember what was said on the formal part of the occasion except that they seemed to be concerned with women's participation in broadly social issues and consumer movements, rather than militantly seeking legal and other remedies. I do, however, remember vividly a segment of the question and answer session.

One of the speakers had built a career as a professional photographer, was articulate not just in her own language but also in English, and seemed to be in her early thirties. She certainly was not a stereotypical, demure, subservient Japanese woman, but her manners and behavior were still that of a Japanese female. She had been married to an American, and had published a book of photographs featuring American black communities; she then returned to Japan.

The question from an American woman reporter was of the expected kind, why do the Japanese women continue to put up with their subservient roles as a housebound wife. The reply that came back, however, was totally unexpected and shook the audience that was 90 percent Western. Her immediate response to the question was that the Japanese housewife was not as subservient to her husband as many Westerners thought, to which the audience reacted with more than a murmur. Clearly expecting another kind of reply, they found the one given to be ludicrous. Some laughed openly. The speaker was put into the position of having to defend her controversial statement, which she did, eloquently. Knowing that attack is the best form of defense she described how Americans did not treat their women well and listed specific situations in which they were treated better in Japan.

"We Japanese women don't particularly feel that men are doing us a favor when wives are invited to accompany their husbands to a business function," she stated. "Japanese wives would tend to feel that that is the man's business and why should she be forced into partaking in his area of responsibility? It is an imposition rather than a favor." Any

Western manager who, with all goodwill, has asked his Japanese employees to bring their wives to a party would attest to the sheer misery some of them obviously go through at such a function. This career woman knew what she was talking about. "I've been to American business cocktail parties and all the men do is talk about business. If the wives are not in some business, they are totally ignored in the conversation. After all, wives have their own interests and hobbies and would not expect or compel their husbands to join them in their own female groups." Now, here was a leader of the Japanese feminist movement, invited to speak on the female role in Japan, defending the abominable behavior of the Japanese husband in business! The place went into an uproar.

Whether the wife's sharing of her husband's business experience is a right or an obligation depends entirely on where you stand. Japanese wives who take an active interest in their husbands' business are considered bad wives, interest being construed as interference. This is a hen or the egg situation that cannot be resolved overnight. Whether the Western value that spouses should share all or the Japanese value that there are distinct roles to play impinges on the equal rights of males or females seems a moot point.

The brave little photographer was visibly annoyed with the audience's reaction and continued. "One of the things I found objectionable in the U.S. was that I couldn't go out alone. If I'm sitting alone in a hotel coffee shop I'm invariably approached by a man and some can be quite persistent." (On this I knew she was not alone. I remember one Western female business associate telling me she envied the fact that men could go down to a bar alone to unwind while she was often forced to call for room service just to avoid unwanted attention.) Women are much less likely to be pestered in Japanese cities than in most Western cities. The speaker cited the fact that violent acts toward women are much more prevalent in the U.S. than in Japan. But there are much fewer violent acts against anybody in Japan, so it probably has little to do with equal rights for sexes although women are, of course, much easier prey, especially in matters of sex.

Though she probably thought she was delivering a *coup de grace* with her concluding remarks, I felt she spoiled her case by becoming personal. "Japanese men are shy in public and have been brought up to feel that it is not manly to fawn over women. Still, in private, they are gentle. Western men are cold at home. I was surprised to find how gentle a Japanese man can be. When I'm tired after work, I have been offered a gentle massage." This of course had nothing to do with race or culture but simply the particular men involved and the particular stage of the relationship. Our photographer so overstated her case that by the time she sat down her central point was entirely lost—even in something as basic as the male-female relationship, cultural differences profoundly influence what is considered right and wrong. It is a matter of personal values, and it is not the right of one culture to consider that another is doing wrong.

Holding the Purse Strings Without Authority

The Japanese Consumer presentation, the concept of which was originally developed by my colleague, Fred Perry, is devoid of statistics and concentrates on showing slice-of-life photographic slides of the consumer in action. There are spots in it where I pause to make a point and one of them shows the housewife doing her bookkeeping in the evening. To be more precise, there are two slides, one that's about fifteen years old and one taken only a few years ago: in the earlier photo she is using an abacus, in the latter, an electronic calculator.

We use this technique throughout the presentation mostly to point out some of the dramatic changes that have occurred in the past ten years or so but here it is the opposite. Nothing has fundamentally changed, even when twice as many married women—almost 50 percent—have a separate source of income from their husbands'.

This does not surprise the Japanese viewer; he knows it is true. As daughters acquire a sense of the female role by watching their mothers, this scene of nightly bookkeeping is likely to continue at least into the current generation. I have already mentioned how meticulously these books are kept and how the housewife budgets such items as education, leisure time activities, and future major investment expenditures, most notably the house. (Incidentally, while the average American moves at least once, the house in which a Japanese couple invests their life savings is, in most cases, the only house they will own in their lifetime.) This slide follows the Japanese adage, "*byakubun wa ikkenni shikazu*," one hundred hearings are not the equivalent of one seeing; in other words, "seeing is believing."

This slide starts the story of the Japanese housewife as we follow her on her daily rounds. The differences that are visually evident still have to be explained. Luckily data figuratively fell into my lap. We were looking into the Japanese housewife's attitudes and behavior toward fresh foods both in shopping habits and food preparation. It occurred to me that it would be interesting to see how much time she allocated to these respective chores.

How did she allocate her time over the whole day? A study had been conducted by NHK, the National Broadcasting Network, which is equivalent to the BBC in England, on the very matter. Although not strictly comparable, somewhat similar data for Australia became available. In the context of this argument, we must assume that the American or British patterns are closer to that of Australia than that of Japan, which seems fairly safe as they are based on values rooted in Western civilization. At least, even if the comparison is not, strictly speaking, scientific, it helped to make sense of the observations I have developed over the years.

When we limit our observations to the full-time housewife, though they be few in either culture, some of the differences are not surprising. The Japanese housewife spends far less time cleaning the house and polishing the furniture—her house is much smaller and as a consequence she has relatively little furniture. To counterbalance this, she spends a lot more time laundering.

The next observation came as a surprise even to my Japanese colleagues—at least, it had not previously occurred to them. An old-time Westerner in Japan, married to a Japanese, challenged me on it, but I stand by my findings: namely, that the Japanese housewife spends far less time in the kitchen than her Western counterpart. Of course, in the old farm village, pickling the vegetables and drying the fish would have consumed considerably more of her time, but that applies to the rural West too, with different kinds of pickling, the canning of fruit, and the making of jam. It is also true that processed foods have greatly lessened the time a Western woman spends in the kitchen—in many American homes, it may be that dinner comes straight out of the refrigerator. Even conceding this last point, there are just so many waking hours in a week available, and there is one indisputable statistic—the Japanese woman spends a great deal of time shopping. In the last count about 75 percent of the women questioned said they shopped on the previous day. I believe the relative emphasis of shopping time over kitchen time in Japan still stands and is the opposite of that in the West, if only psychologically.

There is, in fact, less need to spend a lot of time preparing a Japanese meal, which is largely ingredient- rather than course-oriented. Cooks rarely use ovens for a routine meal, and frying and boiling on gas burners or electrical rings suffices in most cases. No homemade cakes, pies, casseroles, or Western soups occupy the time of the average Japanese housewife. The Japanese soup is almost always the instant variety using prepared seasonings, though sometimes it is freshly prepared using recently purchased ingredients. One should not be misled, by some of the elaborate courses served at high-class Japanese restaurants, into thinking that the procedure is the same in the home, although meals in both the restaurant and home are rooted in the same concept.

Like nouvelle cuisine (but preceding it), the actual ingredients selected for the table are of crucial importance to the Japanese meal. Freshness is, of course, a key criterion. The Japanese like to see what is served and appreciate the color and other indications of quality; a lot of the meals in the popular Japanese restaurants are prepared in front of the diner, and you don't select the course, you select the items. The Japanese consumer retains the values of a farming community, where the source of the produce is very close to the table. Japanese society is, surprisingly, closer to the Southeast Asian, e.g., Vietnam and Thailand, than it is to the Chinese. These social values fundamentally affect the attitudes toward food and, as we shall see, the basic systems of marketing—the way the product ultimately reaches the consumer.

Planned Impulsive Shopping Japanese Style

Change of scene; we now follow our housewife on her shopping rounds. Already there is one thing that is missing that many of her Western sisters carry on such an occasion. No, I don't mean a credit card. The Japanese consumer does not have a shopping list. We inserted a question in one of our surveys to check on this and the response did indeed verify that few carried a list. Perhaps this is because she shops almost every day, she doesn't need to be concerned with forgetting something—truly a nuisance for the Western housewife who shops in bulk and only a few times a week.

But that is only part of the story. In many cases, the Japanese housewife does not have a shopping list because she really doesn't know what she is going to buy before she leaves home. While I may be exaggerating slightly, we see it revealed as a rule by her general pattern of store visits. She may go to the fish shop first or to the butcher, but that is the extent of the variation. (Some go to the fresh food section of the supermarket first, but they are in the minority.)

No survey data can give the true picture of what really goes on. She scrutinizes the fresh foods available for quality and price. She looks for the best buy of the day, often assisted in this by the information given out that day on T.V. Her preference for the small, specialty fresh food stores over the supermarket is reasonable since, known to the storekeeper, she can seek reliable advice, an aspect in which the impersonal supermarket cannot compete. Whether the first purchase be relatively inexpensive imported beef that is miraculously available because she is a good customer or the more usual pork or fish of the season, this first purchase takes the most time, and once it is made the rest of the shopping falls into place. It is at this point that what is to be served that night at dinner starts to become clear and not, as is usually the case for a Western housewife, before she leaves home. After the vegetables to go with the meat or fish are purchased, the Japanese housewife heads for the supermarket.

Our data show that the majority of housewives visit more than one store on their average shopping trip. She visits the supermarket because there she can get a good buy on such items as detergents, coffee, and toilet tissue. In product categories, where brand discrimination and loyalty is low, small changes in price dramatically affect the brand's share. The Japanese housewife is now acting out her role as minister of finance helped by the Japanese cuisine, although I'm not sure which comes first.

The continuing recession in the West has played havoc with the household budget, and I would not be surprised if the Western housewife—the middle-class American housewife—spends more time scrutinizing her finances when shopping. However, she still tends to buy from one source and most likely has more or less decided on the dinner menu before leaving home—even if the decision is to buy frozen foods. After comparing the behavior patterns, I contend that the Western housewife emphasizes her creative role as housekeeper while the Japanese housewife, as demonstrated, emphasizes her role at the treasury.

This daily shopping pattern has serious consequences for foreign manufacturers though the causal link is not immediately obvious. Given the housewife's habit of buying often and in small quantities, a very intricate network of service has developed on every suburban block that means, in every city, an ever continuing string of retail outlets. Japan, with half the population of the United States, has the same number of retail outlets. Two-thirds of the stores are, even now, family owned with less than four employees. The statistics work out as one retail outlet for every fourteen dwellings if we include the numerous small eating establishments.

While Japan is about the same as California in area, the population is more concentrated because of the uninhabitability of the mountainous regions, which comprise one-third of the country. In other words, if you visualize every retail store in the United States shoved into less than half of California, that is Japan. Needless to say, there is a store within walking distance of every urban dwelling. Since the Japanese housewife carries only small quantities after her shopping, there is no need for a car.

Japan is one of the few advanced societies where family-size Coca-Cola is sold through the liquor store, not in the supermarket. Family-size bottles, really any size bottle of soft drink or beer, is too heavy for a housewife to carry. All she has to do is phone the local liquor store-owner, who will deliver the necessary number of bottles to her door, within minutes, on his scooter. Rice is also delivered by the local rice merchant. This community of servicing pulsates from early morning to night. The village conducts active trading with neighboring villages but is little concerned with the outsider beyond them.

So far, these small stores serve a real need, but economic pressure from the larger stores is great and in the future their numbers will probably decline. In the sixties many felt this event was imminent, but it ignored the deeply rooted cultural base of this system, which economic forces alone will not change. Two and a half million retail outlets constitute a powerful political force at the local level, and the government has responded by protecting them from the larger outlets by placing many restrictions on the activities of the big competitors.

It is not only the Japanese farmer who is protected from the more efficient large-scale producers. Small Japanese businesses are also being protected from larger operations—presumably at the expense of the consumer in that the inefficiency and high cost of distribution keep the price of consumer goods higher than need be. But this may be the price the housewife is prepared to pay for the intimate service she receives, at least for the time being.

Which Comes First, the Freezer or Frozen Foods?

The initial attraction of frozen foods in the West was convenience in quality and storage. Also, in some parts of the United States, some fresh items were simply not available. However, our studies show that most Japanese consume the frozen food the day it is purchased! With little space to store things, but, even more importantly with little desire to store, frozen foods didn't take-off in Japan. The need to stock makes frozen food buying a rational, planned decision in the U.S., but without this need, as in Japan, frozen foods are much more likely to be bought on impulse. After making her primary purchases, the housewife looks in at the supermarket. She may see an out-of-season vegetable or a hamburger that is just the thing for a late-night snack for her son who is studying for exams. Since it is for that day's evening meal or for supper, she buys just enough for immediate consumption.

In the United States the market for freezer compartments and freezers developed as the demand for frozen foods grew. In Japan nothing very much happened until the very astute electrical appliance manufacturers began looking for ways to prop up the maturing refrigerator market. We have seen the important positioning of consumer durables in the confined Japanese home. You are never too far from any appliance, and as they represent the rise in the quality of life, there is a much greater emotional involvement with them. However, refrigerators have a very long life cycle; unlike cars, there are few parts to wear out quickly. Since the Japanese have a love affair with durables, it was not as farfetched as it sounds that the latest thing—the large freezer compartment—could be promoted as an innovation even if there was no immediate need for it. Attraction to the new feature would speed up the replacement cycle.

This newfangled piece of equipment had a compartment in which to place frozen food, so this in turn generated interest in a still-limited range of frozen foods. The manufacturers of frozen foods have to thank those in the electrical appliance field for promoting their market for them and not *vice versa*, as was the case in the United States.

The Advent of the Working Housewife

So far the social effects of working women are not as profound as expected. It is my contention—but not really an original one, as many Japanese scholars hold this view—that a large part of urban Japanese society is based on values held over from an agrarian village society. Therefore the lack of impact of the working wife on social mores is not surprising. After all, farmers' wives work just as hard as their husbands to support the family. And the division of the male-female roles has not changed; even if she is working in the office, finances are still the housewife's responsibility. She still shops almost every day, though now it's on the way home from work. Since husbands work longer hours, these chores still, by and large, fall on the wife's shoulders. So many food manufacturers who expected revolutions in food habits were disappointed. Food life is changing and quite rapidly, but it is taking quite a steady, consistent path and has more to do with modernization than with the fact that more women are out working.

Is the Japanese woman becoming Westernized? They are cooking more Western-style meals. Also the divorce rate is rising and more women are divorcing their husbands than the other way around. Some argue that these signify that the women are becoming Westernized. As for the divorce rate, I prefer to argue that it is the result of more and more women acquiring economic independence. Unhappy marriages existed in Victorian England too, but there were fewer divorces; the dire economic consequence to a woman of leaving her husband was probably a greater inhibitor than any social stigma.

An independent Japanese woman will effect significant social change, but this does not mean that she is necessarily acquiring Western values in the process. As we have seen in the career photographer, she need not necessarily see her newly acquired independence as putting her closer to her Western sisters.

The Japanese woman seems to be evolving a new role for herself in society but in a distinctly Japanese way, something that could be said for the Japanese society as a whole, which continues to modernize. As far as we who do business here, it is best not to impute prematurely Western attitudes and values because of superficially observed behavior or appearance.

Will the Japanese Female Remain Conservative?

A recent international survey that was conducted in many Western countries by Gallup and included Japan showed Japanese women to be the most conservative on the traditional role of their domestic responsibilities and childbearing. In general, then, the survey supports my observations in this chapter as applied to the current status. However, one cannot be so complacent. Although I still maintain that the women's role in Japanese society will evolve somewhat differently to that in the West, the following letter to *Asahi*, a Japanese newspaper, by Naoko Atobe, a seventeen-year-old high school girl, clearly shows that traditional values will not remain unchallenged.

> "HOME IS THE PLACE FOR WOMEN" IS NOT FOR ME.
>
> Your paper the other day carried the results of a poll on the female issue. According to it, an overwhelming majority of Japanese women agree with the idea that "the husband goes out to work and the wife protects the home." It seems that in our society, the commonly held idea that it is best for a woman to have a happy marriage and enter the home, is deeply rooted. Parents who think "a girl should go to finishing school and then go off as a bride" are also in the majority.
>
> However, why is it that there is an increase in part-time workers who are mature women who have completed bringing up their children? Isn't it that not a few find a purpose in living through work? I think the time has come to throw away the viewpoint that "women are for the home only."
>
> My parents are of the opinion that "women should also be educated" so they have helped me prepare for the university examinations, but they seem to hold with the common view when it comes to my post graduation. However, I would like to have a job and continue it for life. My life does not belong to anybody else. It exists for me. I would like to do the things I want to do and extend my abilities to the limit.
>
> Certainly, it is tremendously difficult to continue with work. In the first place, I may not be able to find work in which I can involve myself wholeheartedly. However, I am not going to abandon hope. After all, even for me, a female, there may be unforeseen possibilities.

Things are going to change, and not necessarily because social values will change from within. Like many things that have happened in Japan, they will be externally imposed. This is inevitable if we consider the following startling demographic facts:

- The Japanese woman now has the longest life expectancy in the world but had a very low expectancy until the end of World War II. She now has an average of 1.65 children, versus 5 for prewar.
- Before the war, the time taken to raise children was nineteen years, but today it's nine years, so a woman spends ten years less of her life in bringing up her children.
- If graduation from college or marriage of the youngest is the point at which women are completely released from the responsibilities of looking after their children, then before the war, statistically, the average woman was already dead for eight to nine years when this point was reached; today she lives for another twenty-four years.
- If entry of the youngest child to primary school is the end of the intensive period for child rearing, the prewar woman, on the average, had only eight years or so left till death, but today she lives another forty-three years or so—more than the life expectancy of the prewar male.

The revolution has already occurred without most males realizing it. Economic independence of women will be a key to how far and how quickly social values will be changed. With a rapidly aging population, women are likely to win a greater position in economic life simply by being very rapidly drawn into the work force.

4

Brand Preferences in a Vertical Society

Pre- and Post-Marriage Purchases

*Why Are Some Japanese Brands Invincible? Marriage Causes
Transformation in the Female Consumer*

In the previous chapter I discussed the Japanese housewife as a consumer. A noted Japanese female sociologist, Chie Nakane, applied the
expression Vertical Society to Japan in her book *The Logic of a Vertical
Society*. Nakane was among the first batch of women who graduated
from the prestigious Todai (Tokyo University) after the Second World
War, the doors having been opened through the liberalizing decrees of
the U.S. occupying forces. Still, at that time, neither Oxford nor
Dartmouth College nor the Harvard Business School admitted
women, and Japan boasts a number of excellent women's universities
from prewar days, so females were not actually excluded from higher
education.

To go back in time a bit, the first novel in the world, *The Tales of
Genji*—a towering classic in literature—was written by a Japanese
woman, Shikibu (Lady) Murasaki (circa 978–1031). Seishonagon, another woman writing in the same period (circa 965–1020) and the
author of a book of essays, *Pillow Talk*—which, contrary to that suggested by the English title, has nothing to do with bedroom manners—is also a monument to the intellectual maturity of the early
Japanese woman. Women, as in Western societies, had to put up with
discrimination and lack of social opportunities but the stereotype image of the Japanese woman is based on the samurai culture, starting a

little before the Edo period. Even then, in relation to Western societies, Japan was not a cultural backwoods, having produced remarkable women artists, writers, and even politicians throughout history.

Thus, because of her bilingual orientation, Nakane may seem to be
unique; she is among an elite corps and the Japanese are not a bit
surprised that she is a woman. After her graduation she studied in the
West, lectured at London University, researched in India, and returned to Japan to illuminate her compatriots as to the Japanese society
in relation to others. Her book in English, *Japanese Society*, is required
reading for a novice on Japan. The Vertical Society as described by
Nakane is not as simple as it sounds, and the vertical structure is more
fluid and, in historical terms, the established positions more transitory
than most would suspect. However, this aspect is best left to her book.

All societies work on social rankings; apparently the instincts of the
herd are impossible to shake, as goings on in the monkey cage illustrate. In the case of Japan the rules of the Vertical Society affect our
marketing and lay traps for the unwary Westerner. However, in some
ways, the Japanese woman is less constricted by these rules than the
male, which makes her a more interesting consumer. But even so she
cannot be independent of society and she shares the same basic values
as the male. Even though society continues to evolve rapidly, there are
still stronger social constraints on her, as a wife and mother, than are
on the male.

The Japanese word *shakaijin*, which the dictionary gives as "a public
person" or a "member of society," is a word freely used in daily
conversation when referring to children who have graduated or started
working. One is not a *shakaijin* while dependent on parents or still a
student. When equivalent words do not exist between English and
Japanese, I have developed a habit of making a mental note as they
invariably signify important differences between the cultures—either
in scale of values, perceptions, or attitudes. (For example, the Japanese
do not have a strict equivalent for the word *privacy*, and since Japanese
words just do not convey the right feeling, the preferred translation is
praibashii; in other words, "privacy" pronounced in a Japanese
manner.)

The concept of *shakaijin* has a great deal to do with the Vertical
Society, in which everyone's position is fairly clearly defined. When
boys and girls reach twenty, they are invited to a ceremony called

seijinshiki—a ceremony for becoming an adult—held by the ward office. Although many tribes have initiation ceremonies and some religions have their own rituals in this respect, I am not aware of any modern Western society that has such a nondenominational rite organized at the public level. What is important in our context is that even behavioral patterns seem to change virtually overnight at the arrival of this and other designated stages.

When one becomes a *shakaijin*, one stops wearing jeans and going to rock concerts. Men even stop going to movies. There are few social constraints for the male until he becomes a *shakaijin*. Women are somewhat more restricted, though they have a slightly longer period of freedom because relatively few consider a job as a career and working in an office doesn't really make them a *shakaijin*; it is just a preparatory period for marriage that, for the great majority, occurs around the age of twenty-five. Like most things in Japan, even marriage is timed for a specific moment. The female becomes a true *shakaijin* when she gets married because, by definition, this means that one acquires social responsibilities and obligations. While she is working as an office girl she spends her money on herself or saves for the marriage dowry, but most live or are at least supported by their parents to a great extent. Once married, they find they have little time for themselves.

For this reason a market for overseas group traveling—most notably for Europe—has developed among unmarried Japanese women. The short period of freedom is taken much more seriously by women, who want to make the best of it before drudgery sets in. If we say that once she marries, apart from the honeymoon, the opportunity for such travel evaporates for all but the lucky few, to the Westerner the picture would seem exceedingly grim. However, in the Japanese Vertical Society, this is a natural event, like growing up and going to work, so it is accepted.

When the Japanese man enters a corporation, initially at least, he expects that he will stay with it for the rest of his working life. In a Vertical Society a steady progression up the corporate ladder is expected—although, like anywhere, not necessarily realized. The Japanese woman marries such a man and immediately starts establishing a horizontal relationship in the community—through the various suppliers of merchandise and services, including the bank; neighbors; and when the child starts going to school, fellow parents. Vertical social progress depends entirely on the husband; so she displays great concern for his health and well-being. The work horse must be fed, clothed, and exercised. Social advancement can also be attained through the scholastic achievement of the child in a meritocratic environment, so the *kyoiku mama* (another uniquely Japanese word, the "education mama") is an extremely visible entity. Since the sphere of activity becomes narrowed to the community to which she belongs, the housewife is extremely sensitive to horizontal relationships. The vertical and horizontal cross threads make her a much more complex consumer than the male.

The horizontal thread makes the Japanese female conscious of and concerned about what her peers buy. The vertical thread creates a respect for authority and provides stability for brands manufactured by major corporations. The Japanese like to think that theirs is a relatively classless society. However, class is determined by the university you attend and where you work. Officials of such ministries as finance and MITI (Ministry of International Trade and Industries) are at the top of the pecking order. Not far behind the top ministry officials are senior executives of major corporations. In any case, top ministry officials join these corporations as directors, so business and government constitute a chummy establishment. Another splendid Japanese word is *amakudari*, which literally translates as "descent from heaven," but its specific meaning is the act of a government official joining a private corporation on his retirement.

Actually, the major corporations only account for a minority of employees, which is contrary to popular thinking. Even the renowned lifetime employment system only applies to establishment employees. So the numerous medium- and small-size corporations constitute the lower strata of the Vertical Society. Let it be said that most foreign corporations belong to the lower end of the employment ladder, compensated for by a certain smart image that appeals to the new social mavericks.

The fact that major corporations impart employment security and social status is well understood by the housewife, who tends to ascribe similar qualities to major brand names. The Procter & Gambles in the United States and the Unilevers in Europe are conglomerates that market a diversity of products. On the principle that "soups" can't be associated with "soap," both companies push the merit of an individual brand rather than the corporate umbrella. Recently, there was a rather ludicrous incident of some Americans accusing the Procter & Gamble corporation executives of practicing Satanism all because of its trademark symbol. The company was concerned enough to take legal action for slander and libel while conducting a survey to see if there were any repercussions on their brands. They need not have worried. Even for such market leaders as Crest toothpaste and Head & Shoulders shampoo, most Americans could not name the manufacturer. This would never happen in Japan where there is an acute awareness of the company that produces the goods, at least *after* marriage. If a brand wishes to be a trendsetter without the backing of a corporate image, it is better to concentrate on the unmarried female.

Outsiders Are Excluded From the Distribution System

Before dealing with the less interesting males, at least as consumers, let us examine the "shopping village" that is an important part of the females' horizontal society, and the retail outlets that constitute it. When I returned to Japan in the mid-sixties, two very large U.S.-headquartered, multinational food companies had set up operations in Japan and were examining the distribution situation. They no doubt discovered that a small number of their retail customers accounted for a large proportion of their business, perhaps 70 percent of sales through 20 percent of outlets; known as Pareto's Law, this is not an unusual phenomenon in business. With the sort of numbers involved, servicing the 80 percent of smaller outlets directly with one's own sales force was not only too costly but well-nigh impossible. Even the major Japanese manufacturers use numerous wholesalers to distribute their goods.

When wholesale figures are quoted, in Western terms, the Japanese distribution system generates the feeling of an Alice in Wonderland. There are 2.4 million retailers in Japan and to service them there are 400,000 wholesalers—one wholesaler to every six retailers; and these figures have not changed greatly in the past twenty years. Only one wholesaler in six deals directly with the source of supply. In other words, you start off with wholesaler *A* with a large warehouse. Your neatly boxed products are split out and parceled to a medium-size wholesaler *B*—and, of course, there are more *B*-type wholesalers than there are the *A*-type. For many of the products, *B* is not the final destination and, in an even smaller quantity, products go to wholesaler *C*—and maybe even *D*—who makes deliveries, sometimes daily, to customers in his neighboring "village."

It is not surprising that major Western corporations expressed impatience with this system. The long chain of handling points before the product gets to the retailer means that one cannot control the marketing of the product. Incidentally, a better way of looking at these wholesalers may be as warehousing points, at each point the warehouse gets smaller and more dispersed. Here again we have the influence of the confined land and the Japanese mastery at inventory control, which ultimately shows up in the cost efficiency of a Toyota over Detroit.

However, if these numerous wholesalers are mostly serving even more numerous retailers, 80 percent of whom only account for 30 percent of business, why not bypass the system and go to the few who account for the bulk of the business? In other words, what the two major Western corporations thought of and probably successfully applied elsewhere was not to bother with the 80 percent—they could be left to the wholesalers—but to cut out the wholesalers in the case of the 20 percent who accounted for 70 percent of the sales. If the sales force approached the major retailers directly, marketing strategies could be put into use far more effectively than through a, in most cases, disinterested third party. By cutting out the middleman, the cost of distribution can be substantially reduced. The two organizations who set up a Western-style direct sales force failed in this very logical approach.

Logic is fine if the set of premises one selects are correct. When their logical approach failed, disconsolate Western marketing executives accused the Japanese of being totally illogical. The logic was applied within Western parameters; failure to understand that cultural factors were at the base of the illogical or archaic Japanese distribution system was costly for the two corporations. Within Japanese parameters, the system has its internal logic. Both of these Western organizations have gone through fundamental restructuring in Japan since then.

To explain the anomaly of the Japanese distribution system, I use a truncated version of Nakane's models of society. Of course, Nakane did not apply her model to marketing, but it explains very well the system of wholesalers and retailers.

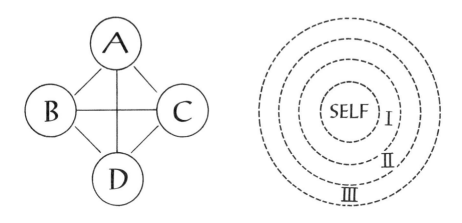

The diagram on the left is more or less the Western social arrangement. Direct relationships are formed between blocks and equilibrium is reached when the blocks are of roughly similar strength. The Austro-Hungarian Empire was run on this principle and it also seems the basis of Dr. Kissinger's view of world diplomacy. Retailer *A* can be approached by newcomer *E*, or a new product can enter and disturb the equilibrium if it has a specific power (quality) to offer that is new and attractive. Some marketing models are also constructed on this principle.

The diagram on the right, on the other hand, represents a totally different organization. Instead of a direct line relationship there are a series of concentric circles, like the ripples on a pond when a pebble is dropped. Nakane calls the center circle the primary circle, surrounded by the secondary circle, with the tertiary circle being the outermost circle. There are no others beyond the tertiary, which is the outer limits of the universe, so to speak. The best way to understand the primary circle is to see it as a village, an analogy I have used throughout this book. The village has close relationships with neighboring villages; not only do they trade, but marriages occur between members of the villages.

This concept of society is not unique to Japan and is similar to those throughout Southeast Asia. They are essentially those of rice paddy societies in which inhabitants tend to be less mobile than those in societies that depend on cattle—you can move your cattle around but you can't pick up your rice paddy and take it with you. This tends to lead the members of the society to view most human relationships as long lasting. I was struck by the similarity of the Japanese society with that of the Vietnamese as Frances FitzGerald described it in *Fire in the Lake*. However, very few Japanese, who consider themselves members of an advanced industrial society, will identify with the Vietnamese. It seemed to me that the American military strategists in Vietnam were making the same sort of mistake that was made, in a smaller way, by the Western marketer in Japan. Instead of treating the village—the primary circle—as an immovable entity that would only respond through the secondary circle, the Americans were dealing with the village directly from the tertiary circle and even, at times, moved them under protective custody. The Vietcong were burrowing into the primary circle and had the advantage of being identified as members of the community.

As applied to the distribution of products in Japan, let us say that the shops on a commercial street belong to the primary circle. Their secondary circle contains the wholesalers who service them. This relationship has been going on for years and is expected to continue into the foreseeable future. Now enters a manufacturer from the outer world, the tertiary circle, i.e., the two foreign manufacturers with their direct sales force. The stranger thinks he has a very tangible offer to make, eminently to the benefit of the retailer. He has all the facts to show that establishing a relationship with him will lead to increased profits but nothing happens. The retailer procrastinates and is unable to respond. The newcomer shakes his head in disbelief. How is it that this perfectly logical offer is not accepted? His credentials are immaculate.

In the cultural context the offer is not so logical. The relationship between those in the primary and secondary circles is of a longstanding, almost permanent nature. Certainly, at times, there may be more profitable options available. However, like villagers who trust each other, the known relationship has proven to be beneficial over the years; besides, it is not a one-way relationship that can be terminated at any time. No contracts are needed to sustain it because the relationship is a natural outcome and not artificially created. The risk of terminating this arrangement and accepting a new but perhaps more transitory arrangement is substantial. After all, although the offer may be attractive now, there is no guarantee that it will be repeated. Unlike the wholesaler in the secondary circle, you can't even be sure that the stranger from the tertiary circle will still be there tomorrow. The new multinationals who established a direct sales force to approach the major retailers simply ignored this basic and very logical structure. They did not have the patience of trying, over time, to get themselves into the secondary circle and become an identifiable member of the community. Only now are national wholesalers being formed by the linking up of provincial wholesalers. A few years ago, I was lecturing in the city of Nagoya—the third largest in Japan—and was surprised when told that all the wholesalers were Nagoya-based. So again, the circle principle of society was demonstrated with respect to marketing.

Evidence of this societal system abounds when one lives and works in Japan for any length of time. The primary circle is first the family, then the school, and finally the company. In fact, Japanese workers often use the same word, *uchi*, to refer to their homes and company—the two are synonymous by being the primary circle. An active and successful businessman in Japan is one who has expanded his secondary circle. A *gaijin* (a foreign resident) I know was sitting at a yakitori restaurant one night and heard a group of Japanese workers continuously refer to *uchi* this and *uchi* that. He remarked to his English-speaking Japanese colleague on how home-oriented Japanese workers seemed to be; the latter then realized the foreigner's misinterpretation—the Japanese workers were not talking about their homes; they were talking shop! The word *uchi* does mean "my home," but it also means "my company."

Some foreigners are upset that Japanese seldom invite them to their homes, a common custom in the West. Apart from the confined space that makes the home as an area of entertainment impractical, it is not because he is a foreigner but because he is still in the tertiary circle. The Japanese will only go drinking or eating with someone who has established himself as one who is likely to qualify for a long-term relationship, but they don't even invite other Japanese who belong to the tertiary circle.

I belong to the American Club in Tokyo and also to some Japanese clubs. In the former I could be sitting at the bar and strike up an acquaintanceship with another fellow member who's not in the same line of business but has some mutual interests—it could be the baseball game we are both watching. This seldom if ever happens in a Japanese club; most members are only interested in their circle, which means that if you are a businessman, only with those with whom you have some business relationship. Therefore, the term, Vertical Society, used so often to describe the Japanese society, is not only a misnomer, it is somewhat misleading in that within the vertical structure there are intercrossing circles.

You Can Sell Johnnie Walker Black But Not Red— Because It's Too Cheap

For Japanese men, social strata considerations also weigh heavily. A case that illustrates this well has its genesis in the days when Japan was said to have a shortage of foreign currency and was permitted to operate behind the barrier of an artificially weak yen and direct import controls. One such protected industry was whiskey. Not only was overseas travel beyond the reach of the average Japanese some twenty or so years ago, but Scotch whiskey seemed the ultimate luxury. How I remember the joy I elicited when I arrived with my one bottle of Johnnie Walker in the early sixties—now you are allowed three and nobody gets excited, thousands of other Japanese travelers are bringing in their own. In those days, not only was there a high tariff, but there was a quota that restricted imports to four or so brands, which was very nice for those companies that had exclusive agencies for them.

Needless to say a bottle of Scotch was a great status symbol, especially in a Ginza bar; it was much more favorable than being seen with the local Suntory whiskey. Of course, most of those who were seen drinking Scotch in the bars were drinking Suntory at home—as is still the case. One would expect that once Scotch became competitive in price with the local brands—actually only two, but dominated by Suntory—they would make great inroads to the market. Well, the price dropped but the inroads didn't appear.

Johnnie Walker is probably the best-known Scotch brand in the world, and in most markets its lower-priced Red outsells the Black. In Japan, under the quota system, it was better to concentrate on Black with its higher margin for profit. If you were bringing one in duty-free, you brought the Black. So *Johnnie-kuro* (Johnnie-Black) became the representative premium-grade Scotch in Japan and had great prestige attached to it. When the market was liberalized, efforts were made to sell Red since it was competitive in price with the local premium-grade whiskeys. However, the availability of the lower-priced Johnnie Walker did not particularly excite the Japanese consumer. It is not hard to understand why: to be seen drinking Red was a clear reminder that one was *not* at the status of Black. Although Logan is a higher-priced grade of White Horse whiskey, this fact is little known, which probably helped the brand to beat out Johnnie Walker Red in this price category in the Japanese market. If Red was initially the major brand and the consumer was given the opportunity to step-up to Black the story may have been different. Stepping-down is not an option.

In a vertical society one is expected to rise, not fall. You are generally not demoted from a vice presidency to a section head even in the U.S., though in the American system the worker has the option of leaving, or being fired, before it happens. In the Japanese system of lifetime employment, once the high growth-rate slowed down, automatic progression up the corporate ladder was no longer possible. (It never was assured, but in the past *more* could go up to the next rung.) A group of workers has evolved in major Japanese corporations that is called *madogiwa-zoku* (the tribe that sits at the window). These are the salaried workers who have been passed over for promotion; they sit at their desks all day with very little to do. Most of them hang on rather than quit because even the window seat is a specified position and better than going out into a world in which one's position may not be well defined.

Johnnie Walker and the other Scotch whiskeys were successful before liberalization because they could be identified with the elite. Now that Scotch is more readily available their luster as a status symbol has diminished considerably, but worse still their positioning in society has become hazy. If the motivation to purchase is only on visible symbols and not on inherent product quality, then the brand is in trouble.

Suntory Reserve When You Become Section Head

In contrast to Johnnie Walker, Suntory's progression in the market followed the logic of a vertical society. The various Suntory brands have clearly defined ranks and therefore different positions in society. Many have been added in recent years commensurate with the Japanese economy. When I first returned to Japan, in 1960, the best selling Suntory was a light whiskey called Red. A few years later I noticed that the popular brand was Kaku—in a square bottle and priced higher than Red. A premium-grade Suntory brand was already available in a bottle shaped similar to the Scotch whiskey brand Old Parr, and this was called Old. Its affectionate nickname now is *daruma*, coming from the Buddhist saint Dharma, a fat and jolly character who is also a patron of electoral victories for politicians.

In 1965, on my third return visit to Japan, Suntory Old was for senior executives, who have since moved on to Suntory Reserve, the latter being priced higher than Old, the previous prestige drink that is now consumed by everyone, including women. The progression of the Suntory brands reflects the progression of the Japanese economy. When a Japanese salaried worker selects a Suntory brand, he does so according to his position in the company. As the middle level is overwhelmingly the majority—not just in the company but according to the self-perceived Japanese image of social class—Suntory Old dominates the Japanese market. The largest increase is registered by Reserve, which is the one you are to reach for when you attain the section-head level in a large company or the division-head level in a medium-sized company. The Suntory strategy has been consistent with social values and astutely timed.

In contrast, since Scotch is a generic and not a brand name, with liberalization and the availability of a variety of brands, instead of expanding the market the various brands simply fell into disarray with more splitting the same pie; only a few well-marketed brands being the exception in holding their volume. Scotch brands that were previously only available in department stores and liquor stores became available at supermarkets, many priced lower than the leading Suntory brand. Without a clear knowledge of the specific brand the consumer simply became confused. It was safer to reach for the clearly defined Suntory brand—you knew what you were getting.

What happened to the leader, Johnnie Walker Black, is particularly illuminating. One rather suspects that as a brand leader in a small but tightly controlled market, liberalization was not necessarily welcomed. Apart from the so-called challenge of the miscellaneous brands entering the market, there was the real threat of parallel imports undercutting the price; in other words, theoretically, anybody could make arrangements to import the brand from, say, Hong Kong, and offer it to the consumer at a lower price than that offered by the exclusive agent. (Actually, it wasn't quite as simple as that.) Presumably to meet this price challenge, Johnnie Walker—or rather, the accredited importer—reduced its shelf price, which promptly reduced its sale!

To understand this anomaly we must go back to the fact that, at the sort of price being charged for the brand in the store, it was hardly a daily consumption item. It sold in the department stores at roughly 10,000 yen, which, even at the stronger rate prevailing now, is between $40 to $50 a bottle. Thus the bulk of Johnnie Walker sales were as gifts. (Japanese give and are given things to an extraordinary extent, acting as a social as well as an economic move.) So, when Johnnie Walker reduced its price 10 to 20 percent, it effectively reduced its value as a gift. If you are accustomed to giving a person a gift of a certain designated value, you can hardly reduce that value—at least not in an obvious way. Hence, the phenomenon of a price reduction leading to a sales reduction—a perfectly logical consequence of the consumer's positioning of the brand.

Returning to the neat social progression that the Suntory brand was able to effect, we can see a parallel in cars. In the mid-seventies, Yuzo Kayama progressed from playing the clean-cut collegiate in movies to portraying clean-cut junior managers in establishment corporations. He was then appearing in the Datsun Blue Bird commercials. At that time the Blue Bird was positioned as the first car for the junior executive. No longer. Now, it is Kenji Sawada for the same car, also known as Julie, an ex–semi-rock star who plays distinctly nonestablishment types because with improvement in ownership standards Blue Bird is now positioned to a different target. Sociostereotyping is prevalent for actors and although this may be considered the kiss of death to the professional actor in the United States, it is more of an indication of success in Japan. The actor Kiyoshi Atsumi has been playing the role of Tora-san for more than ten years in a popular movie series, and his other roles seem to be extensions of the Tora-san persona.

Tora-san has, in fact, achieved a *Guinness Book* status, having appeared in thirty-one major release films, all box-office successes. He is the bumbling Mr. Everyman, and in a brilliant move, IBM has used him—or the stereotype that he portrays—for their personal computer commercials in Japan. The reader will most probably recall that it was Charlie Chaplin in his tramp personality that IBM used for their personal computer T.V. campaign in the U.S. They had to resort to a historical portrayal for their U.S. campaign but in Tora-san were able to find a contemporary Japanese equivalent. While not quite as extreme as Tora-san, many T.V. and film stars appear to have achieved popularity by being closely identified with a particular social type. In turn this helps the advertisers clearly position their products by their use.

While the changing of cars to suit one's changing status is not unusual in the U.S., the switches are certainly not as orderly or as predictable as in Japan. During a recent visit to a U.S. corporate headquarters I was impressed with the diversity of cars in the senior parking lot—there was even a DeLorean. However, go down to a corporate parking lot in Japan and you will see rows of black Toyota Crowns and Nissan Cedrics—the acknowledged company cars. Imported cars only have about 2 percent of the Japanese market and most of the Mercedes, BMWs, Cadillacs, etc., are not owned by senior executives of corporations but by those in what the Japanese call the free occupations—doctors, authors, and the professions, i.e., the few who are outside the defined social structure—or owners of small businesses. If it's a large American car, it probably belongs to a local crime boss.

This changing of cars also has something to do with the village, to which I refer with monotonous regularity. If you have to do business in the Japanese community and you are the president of a Japanese company it is only proper that you drive a Japanese car. For the younger employee this should not be an issue. Still, to drive a 5 million yen ($25,000) BMW may be difficult when your boss drives a Nissan Skyline—consumer life for the male is indeed constricted.

The Secret of the Battle of the Titans; Shiseido Cosmetics Versus Lion Dentifrice

But it is not only the foreign marketer that walks away with miso soup on his face. A Japanese manufacturer with the help of Western technology managed to transform the market for male toiletries; this was the giant Lion Dentifrice company, which has about 70 percent of the Japanese toothpaste market. In a joint venture with Bristol-Myers of the U.S.A., Vitalis Hair Liquid was introduced to the Japanese male consumer who mostly used pomade, a solid and sticky hair dressing, on his hair. Lion's powerful distribution and marketing completely transformed the male hairdressing market that is now predominantly liquid. Vitalis was a pioneer and monopolized the genre for a short time, but of course other entries soon followed. What was unexpected was that the real challenge came not from the existing male hair products manufacturers who were completely left at the starting line—one even had to change its corporate name to a more modern one and hired Charles Bronson to promote its image—but from a female cosmetic company.

Even if it is inevitable that a new category will eventually see the entry of the second, third, or more brands, the brand that is first is usually able to hold onto the lead, unless there is gross mismanagement. Not only was it surprising that the serious challenge came from Shiseido, the female cosmetic giant, but that the commanding share of Vitalis rapidly eroded and, in fact, has now almost evaporated. Those were the days when I had just set up shop in Japan and, based on my Western marketing experience, I confidently predicted that Shiseido would probably do only moderately well in the male toiletries category. After all, the Revlons and Max Factors were not particularly successful in launching male lines, presumably because of their strong feminine image.

Again I was ignoring the different cultural factors; I now know better not to blindly extrapolate Western marketing situations to Japan. There is no difference in Japanese between the words *cosmetics* and *toiletries*—the one word *keshohin* covers both. Anything that is used to adorn and transform oneself is *keshohin* and thus it is unisex in concept—females may do more of it, but it isn't limited to them. In fact, the Japanese have been forced to attach male and female prefixes to *keshohin* to differentiate between cosmetics and male toiletries. So there was no image problem for a *keshohin* maker, Shiseido, to come out with female *and* male *keshohins*.

Just how, virtually overnight, Shiseido overhauled Vitalis' position in the male liquid hair dressing market would require a detailed analysis of its advertising—very Japanese as against the more rational Vitalis approach—and other marketing factors. However, it is interesting to note that Shiseido's MG5 hair dressing—tonic and liquid—was followed by a range of male toiletries, all under the umbrella of Shiseido while Vitalis was left to fight its battle alone. After a while the single Vitalis bottle started to look rather desolate amidst the MG5 product line and later the Bravas line (more were to follow from Shiseido, such as the eccentric Tactics line of products). In other words, since the MG5 segment was established, Shiseido's tactics were the same as those adopted by Suntory, i.e., a product for each social status. Again the consumer was not locked into one position and, like the whiskey drinker that moved up the ladder from Suntory Old to Reserve and the car owner who moved from the Nissan Blue Bird to Skyline, he could now move from MG5 to Bravas. Like the Johnnie Walker drinker, the Vitalis user had nowhere to go when he had outgrown his brand.

5

The Taste of First Love Is Calpis

Japlish and Form Have Their Intrinsic Values

Mutations of the English Language

Modern conversational and written Japanese is riddled with imported words. It all started with the traumatic opening to Western civilization some 150 years ago. A literate and advanced society in its own ways, Japan had no time to cope with the influx of ideas and products that just did not have their equivalents in its culture. Certain words that were introduced more than a century ago—and in the case of the Portuguese, several centuries ago—are not even recognized to have a foreign origin because Chinese characters are used rather than the phonetic *katakana* writing that generally signifies that the word is of Western origin. Just to name a few, the well-known dish tempura is really an import from Portugal. *Kappa* (mackintosh), *juban* (under-shirt), and *shabon* (soap) are all of European origin, and the reader can test his knowledge of language by guessing where they come from. Other so-called Japanese words—but this time in the phonetic *katakana*—are *manto* (a cape) from the French, *noruma* (the norm) from the Russian, *arerugii* (allergy) supposedly from the German, and so on. The point is that each is pronounced in a typically Japanese way and is unrecognizable to those who come from the countries from which the words originated.

A friend who was learning Japanese lamented that it was easier to learn straight Japanese than Japlish. Who would have guessed that *saytar* was "sweater," and *tone-neru* was "tunnel." Even in my case it took a few years before realizing the source of some Japlish. I was accustomed to driving behind large trailers with the words "National Railway *Kontena*" before catching on to the fact that the word *kontena* came from "container." I was also accustomed to hearing the disc jockey on my car radio announcing that the music was from a *santora* version and assumed that *santora* was the name of a record label. It wasn't; it meant sound track version, from the sound track of a movie.

This illustrates a special Japanese genius for adaptation. Some imported words are superior to the originals in their speed of communication. For example, *pasokon* is "personal computer," *afureko* is "after recording" (dubbing after the scene is shot), *stamen* is "starting member of baseball team," *patocar* is the "police patrol car," *autome* is "automation"—and I'm only scratching the surface of the words that continue to enter the Japanese vocabulary. The Japanese—from the northern island of Hokkaido to the southern tip of Kyushu plus Okinawa—continue to add words to their everyday speech and take it in stride. In my own company the slide presentation "The Japanese Consumer" has been abbreviated very naturally to *japakon*. The transparencies used for other presentations are *tranpas*.

I do not subscribe to the French abhorrence of Franglais. Perhaps because of my own background, I do not believe that purity of the language *per se* is meaningful. English is a hodgepodge of Latin, German, French, etc., and is none the worse for it. In fact, Shakespeare's England was the most dynamic period for language innovation. The two most innovative societies in the post–World War II period are the American and the Japanese, and to me it is no coincidence that both are nightmares for the language purists. You cannot freeze a language that is a living organism of a changing society. When a language becomes static, that culture is atrophying.

So, learning Japanese is a horrendous challenge because no sooner have you mastered the existing vocabulary than you have to cope with a new set. I was away from the Japanese language for twenty years and I can speak from firsthand experience. Some of the new creations based on Western words are just brilliant. One that I found particularly ingenious was a peculiarly Japanese term for a low-priced cabaret—low cost because the hostesses are said to be amateurs who engaged in this profession in their spare time. The Japanese word for part-time worker is *arubaito*, which comes from the German *Arbeit* (work). The word for this low-cost cabaret is, therefore, *arusaro*, short for *Arbeit* saloon.

I hope any British reader would not be offended or consider it ludicrous if I say that I find Elizabethan vigor in the way the modern Japanese use words. There are some Japanese scholars who would disagree strongly with this viewpoint as they, like the French, are concerned with the mongrelization of the language. I ascribe to another school of thought—that the entry of new words is an index of the vitality of the language. In any case the Japanese language can no longer be purged of foreign-derived words and is richer for them, though some have changed from the original and are there to snare the foreigner as well as the Japanese translator. When a Japanese says "she is *sumato* [smart]," he is referring to the way the woman dresses and not her intelligence quotient. *Yuniku* (unique) does not have the strength of the English word and implies something that is just a little different. To be called *naive* in Japan could be a compliment and not an insult.

In advertising, Japlish allows the creator to break out of the constricted Japanese mould. *Stoppu rukku* (stop-look) was coined for a swimsuit that stopped men in their tracks. The following year it was the *jumpu rukku* (jump-look) swimsuit that made men leap out of their seats. Reading through the fashion section of the women's magazines provides special pleasures. There is "A *mannishu* [mannish] *taipu* [type] that leaves a lingering taste that is *hardo* [hard, e.i., tough]." "Cotton for the *wairudo* [wild] *kantori* [country] tribe"; or the reader can indulge in a "*richii* [rich] *hai-sensu* [high sense]" but what does "high sense" mean? In any case, never mind where the word comes from! If it fits the culture it will stay and if it doesn't it will be discarded. It brings me back to the theme of this book: some Western products will go to great heights in Japan and some will fail.

Rapidity of Word Creation Leads to Some Gaffes—But Only in Western Eyes

Patience is seen as a key word for a Westerner to succeed in Japan, but the Japanese self-image is not of a patient race but rather that of a race of *sekkachis*—a nation of impatient, running Sammys. The haste to adapt foreign words before they are fully understood sometimes leads to hilarious results to Westerners. A famous Japanese soft drink is Calpis. This is a milky, sweet concentrate, technically speaking made by lactic acid fermentation of milk. *Nyusan inryo* [lactic bacterium drink] is a commonly understood product category but not in the West.

The Calpis brand, a pioneer in its category, is credited with one of the most famous early advertising hit phrases: "The taste of first love is Calpis." When they tried to export this brand to the West the name was greeted first with incredulity and then with a giggle. The foreign-resident's joke is "Where does Calpis come from? From Cals, of course!" A well-known line of fruit juice is called My Juice. The leading coffee creamer is Creap. There is a snack called Krap; another, called Snatch, was withdrawn just in time, but the package that was test marketed is a foreigner's collector's item. Such a withdrawal has a prewar precedent that had diplomatic repercussions—and the sexual pun was quite appropriate. As the brother of the Emperor, Prince Chichibu was the senior member of the imperial family. A new ship, the pride of the Japanese passenger liners, was to be named *Chichibu Maru*. About that time, for various scholastic reasons that escape me, the education ministry standardized the Latin spellings of Japanese words, and one of them was to change the more prevalent "chi" to "ti." "She" was changed to "si," but to my ears the previous spelling came closer to the actual pronunciations. The ship was renamed *Titibu Maru*, which tended to raise a snicker among the vulgar foreigners. Rumor has it that before the launching ceremony—I nearly said the Christening—the British passed a discreet word to the Japanese foreign office that the prefix "tit" was sometimes used among cruder circles in a context that was somewhat inappropriate for a carrier of the Japanese flag. Rather abruptly the ship's name was changed to *Kamakura Maru*—a difficult but eminently safer name.

Still, it is all in the mind of the hearer, and focusing on what a word actually means seems a Western trait. If you are a resident of Japan you soon become used to strange sounding words. Since my Japanese was of prewar vintage, when I first returned I tended to hear verbal nuances in Western-derived words, but as I have now merged into the scene as a local I have lost this sensitivity, as I am continuously reminded by the remarks of foreign associates who are new on the scene.

For example, today in Japan, Facom is a respected name in the computer business, but in the mid-sixties when we switched to computerization with the use of an IBM machine the name was unknown. Back then I had had a visit from a Facom salesman—he was quick off the mark to visit a small company like ours not just because of the nature of our business but, more likely, because their service bureau was less than a block from our office. Having established my caller's credentials, I asked him for the name of his service to which he replied Facom. Now, to understand the impact of his reply I must point out that the Japanese do not have the "a" sound, and in this context it was closer to a "u." Thus what he said came perilously close to a word not commonly uttered in polite company. Of course, I promptly relayed the incident to my Western colleagues. It makes a good story when I say that having explained the Western implications of the name, the salesman duly came back with a proposal that they pronounce the name as *Fakim*. While Facom survived and went on to great things, another service bureau, started at the time by Sanyo Electric did not survive; it was called Sacom. So the joke then was that you either Facom'd or Sacom'd. Senior executives or not, boys will be boys.

When Soup Is Not Soup, When Rice Is Not Rice

Foreign-derived words have their serious side for the marketer. One of the first things the foreign businessman has to learn when he comes to Japan is to be careful about straight translations. There are many reasons for this that can be easily surmised and would apply to any language, but one that is often missed and bedevils the marketer is that the Japanese use traditional Japanese words and foreign-derived words to subtly distinguish product categories and perceptions of a product. The most popular liquid food in Japan is *miso shiru* (miso being soy bean paste), which is consumed almost everyday with a rice meal. There is no other way to translate *miso shiru* than "miso soup." However, the Japanese also have the word *supu*—in other words "soup"—to them, *miso shiru* is *not* a soup. In fact, for their clear liquid recipe, with other items, they have the word *osumashi*." Both *miso shiru* and *osumashi* depend on soy flavoring but the former on paste and the latter on sauce. Of course, that is like saying potage and consommé, except that for these two there is the generic, soup. In the Japanese case the only common factor is that they are both a liquid rather than a solid form of food. To this then a new, Western-derived category has been added, *supu*.

This is not just a verbal categorization; it has enormous impact on the market. *Supu*—the Western-variety soup—will seldom be served with a rice-based traditional meal. This, in turn, means that its main serving occasion will not be the evening meal, for the majority of main meals are rice based. However, a respectable market developed for Western soup—mainly corn potage—at breakfast. Why breakfast? Because the Japanese have always served *miso shiru*—i.e., a liquid food— with their traditional breakfast; there is no resistance to this type of food in the morning. The "soup for breakfast" concept in the U.S. was not successful, so the situation is virtually reversed. More young people, and especially children, are having a bread-based breakfast and you can't have *miso shiru* (please, don't call it miso soup!) with bread. The traditional Japanese breakfast tends to have things with salty flavors, so it is a lot easier to get soup onto the table than cornflakes.

Unfortunately, a vice president in charge of international, covering Latin America and Asia—a very common combination that never made sense to me—reading about this in New York or Chicago would never know what this really meant, since everything is rendered into English. I met one vice president who was quite excited at the vast potential for Western soup because there was already a tradition of consuming soup. It turned out that he was referring to miso soup. If only a fraction of the miso soup consumption could be converted to Western soup, then this constituted a major marketing success. He thought *miso shiru* was a competitor. Western soups are not and are never likely to be in competition with *miso shiru*. In Japanese eyes they belong to a different genre, and in marketing terms that is all that matters.

In one focus group we asked the Japanese housewife about the type of utensils she used when serving Western soup and *miso shiru*. The reply: she served soup in a Western bowl or cup and the *miso shiru* in a lacquered Japanese bowl. When we suggested serving Western soup in a lacquer bowl, or vice versa, the housewives found the suggestion simply incredible and the whole idea preposterous. So, by calling the product *supu* and not *oshiru*, she had clearly categorized the two as being fundamentally and irreconcilably different. We are not looking here only at words, but at the importance of form. In the West there will be no other way to describe *miso shiru* than to call it miso soup. Just like *supu*, to the Japanese, Worcestershire and the other varieties are *sosu* and are not in the same genre as *shoyu* (soy sauce). In the same way that "soup" doesn't threaten *miso shiru*, "sauce" cannot threaten the position of *shoyu*. The Western category may change over time, but that remains to be seen.

An even more interesting differentiation by the use of words and the Japanese attention to form concerns rice. When rice is served Western style—not in a Japanese bowl or with Japanese dishes—it is called *raisu* (rice). When served in a Japanese context it is *gohan*. The two are not the same product in perception, even though physically and in substance they are exactly the same. Mixed rice has another terminology. For foreign-origin foods, it is *kare raisu* (curried rice), *chikin raisu* (chicken rice), etc. But if the chicken is cooked Japanese-style with egg, it is *oyako donburi*. There are still more ways to say rice; it depends on how it is served: *sekihan* is red rice with red beans, which is served on ceremonious occasions; *kama meshi* is rice cooked in a pot with mushrooms, *meshi* suggesting a less formal, country-style cuisine; and the various *gohans* are another way of denoting rice dishes. Since rice is of basic importance to the culture, its name changes with the various dishes.

The distinction of form and substance is really a philosophical issue, and the Japanese have a different approach to it. A good illustration is that to the Westerner, water is water. When you heat it, it either becomes warm water, hot water, or boiling water. It is still water, you have just added an adjective to describe its state. However, in Japan the word for cold water is *mizu*; for warm water, *yu* is used. The two are not the same; they are sensually different; i.e., as they are different in presentation, they cannot be the same thing.

This is a basic difference in the way of looking at things and leads to the Westerner's frequent misconception that "the Japanese value form over substance." It has ramifications in advertising: the Westerner insists on dividing concept from execution with the emphasis on the concept; the Japanese will often emphasize execution, which to Westerners, would place him as a marketing primitive. This difference is reflected in the Japanese emphasis on packaging ("how can the contents be any good if they have not taken the trouble to wrap it properly?"). The nonbranded, discount products have not had as much success here as they have in Western markets. Where else in the world does a bookstore attendant carefully put a cover on a $2.50 paperback.

The idea of wrapping gifts comes predominantly from department stores, and cynics have suggested that you are buying the wrapper from the department store and not the contents of the package. The Westerner sees what's under the wrapper; the Japanese see significance in the fact that it comes from a major department store (their wrapping paper) rather than from the local supermarket. Illogical? Not really, because in the act of giving gifts you are evaluating the giver's intent, not the gift. I think this logic also applies in the West if we place it in a different light. After all, everyone is pleased to receive something to which the giver has obviously given a lot of thought, and that has little to do with the monetary value of the gift.

Nowhere is this attention to form more important to the manufacturer than in advertising. The concept or the sales proposition is, of course, the key, but it is not everything, even in the West. David Ogilvy, the founder of Ogilvy, Benson and Mather, now one of the largest advertising agencies in the world, once said something to the effect that you should give the consumer a first-class ticket to your product. The customer should not be transported to the product by shoddy means. He will enjoy the benefits at the end even more if he has enjoyed the ride. A foreign advertiser has to be extra careful in presenting a product to the local audience and must recognize it to be a social act. A T.V. commercial that enters the Japanese living room must first remove its shoes so to speak. The Japanese expression "*do-soku de fumikomu*" means stepping into a room with shoes with soil on them and suggests brutish bad manners. Even if it is the custom in your country to walk into a room with your shoes on, it does not mean that it is acceptable to another. Advertising may have its own etiquette, but I have seen many Western advertising disasters because of the Westerner's refusal to accept this proposition. I do not believe that just because an advertising campaign has been successful in the rest of the world—I don't care even if it was twenty or more countries—it logically follows that it will be successful in any of the remaining countries.

One Way for Western Drugs, Another for Herbal Remedies

The Japanese habit of distinguishing foreign from their own is based on the historical development of the written Japanese language. At first there was only the Chinese ideographs. The Japanese language existed but an imported system of writing had to be fitted to it. Once they had mastered reading and writing skills it was typical of Japanese ingenuity that they developed a system of phonetic letters that they combined with the original Chinese ideographs to evolve a form of writing more suitable to their language. More importantly, it is more flexible than the original Chinese. The phonetic letters are called *kana* but later even this developed into *hiragana* and *katakana*, two similar systems but with different letters. The former is applied to traditional Japanese expressions, always in combination with the appropriate Chinese ideographs. The latter is almost always applied to foreign-derived words or, even more significantly, to pseudo-foreign words and is independent of the *kanji* (Chinese ideographs). (The ramifications of all this are discussed in detail in Chapter 7.)

In the context of the current discussion, the use of *katakana* or *kanji* instantly tells the Japanese consumer the nature of the product. Thus the drug may serve exactly the same symptoms—and at times even be constituted similarly—but if the name is in *katakana* it originated from Western-style laboratories. If its name is in *kanji* then it is a herbal remedy based on thousands of years of Oriental wisdom. The images generated for the two drugs are vastly different.

As usual, the Western manufacturer usually goes wrong in looking for some meaning or some inference from a name. Pampers, the disposable diaper, is a leading brand in Japan and is called exactly that. The name is very appropriate for the product in English but is meaningless to the vast majority of Japanese. It does, however, have the right sound. Since a comparable quality product did not exist in the disposable diaper category until the arrival of Pampers, the name quickly became generic; housewives started to go into the store asking for Pampers rather than disposable diapers. (Although Pampers does not command the per capita consumption of the United States, it certainly has provided a viable new option to the mothers.)

Much earlier the same thing happened with Band-Aids. Again the words mean something in English but absolutely nothing in Japanese;

it went on to become generic for all adhesive plasters. In many, many foreign products the names are incomprehensible to the Japanese consumer but this does not preclude their success. There is one important proviso: it should sound right to Japanese ears and be easily readable when written in *katakana*. Whether the name is used in other parts of the world is not important.

Nowadays the use of *katakana* no longer ensures that the brand is seen as of Western origin. Certain product categories, regardless of the brands or whether they are Japanese or foreign, use *katakana*, which simply implies that the technology is probably of Western origin. Thus, in detergents, there is Hi-Top, a Japanese brand, as well as Cheer, the Procter and Gamble brand. During the first oil shock (the dramatic jump in oil prices when OPEC was formed, bringing an awareness of the need for energy conservation), a Japanese manufacturer made an interesting attempt by using a brand name in *hiragana*, phonetic writing used in the context of traditional Japanese. The brand was called *Seseragi*, which means a "little stream." By divorcing itself from Western technology and by making a no-phosphates claim the brand was positioned to appeal to those with concern for environmental purity. The brand was not successful probably because, to most people, this was of minor concern; but at least the imagery it created was clear.

The mixing of the two forms of writing—*katakana* and *kanji*—in a brand name seldom works. This combination seems to cause schizophrenia in the consumer, who ends up turning away from the product because he or she has difficulty making a decision. Just how important this symbolic perception through writing is was unwittingly demonstrated by a European manufacturer. His brand had reached Asia as far as Hong Kong and was doing reasonably well, so he decided to bring it to Japan. The trouble was that he insisted on a multilingual label, one that could be used throughout Asia. It apparently did not concern the Singaporeans or the Hong Kongese that the instructions on the package were crowded with English, Chinese, and Arabic. With the addition of Japan to his Asian market, he dropped the Arabic and replaced it with, naturally, Japanese.

When tested in its original package the product had very poor acceptance; probes quickly indicated that the package generated a poor image. "Blind" tests of the product easily demonstrated that it was the poor perception of the package that lowered the product's acceptance. My client was distinctly annoyed—if the consumer didn't like a package that was acceptable in other parts of the world, then there was something wrong with the consumer. In design, the package was exactly the same as that of the rest of the world; the only difference was that it carried multilingual instructions on the back. Most Asian countries have experienced a colonial past and have learned to accept and assimilate multilingual inputs. Japan has been selective in this process: European languages presented no problems because historically they represented the advanced technologies. But by having non-European languages on the label—Chinese in this case—the product was immediately down-graded. It is a human tendency to adjust to the lowest common denominator and, while this condescension toward other Asian cultures in terms of their technological accomplishments may be objectionable on principle, it is a fact of the marketplace that we are forced to accept. The consumer is the sovereign in the matter of choice.

When Words Don't Exist

I have already mentioned that the word *privacy* did not exist in Japan in the strict sense and is best transmitted in the Japlish, *praibashii*. The fact that words are in common use in one language and not another can often be significant in revealing essential differences in cultural values. The area of marketing abounds in examples. The fact that the Japanese don't distinguish between female cosmetics and male toiletries—they are both *keshohin*—has already been discussed. Similar to this is the case when deodorants were first introduced—by the same people that brought over Vitalis. Unlike hair tonic and liquid, however, deodorants hardly took Japan by storm. The Japanese had great difficulty rendering the word into Japanese. The first attempt was in Chinese ideographs, but it came out sounding awful: "a drug that prevents odor and suppresses perspiration." So it was decided to create a generic in Japlish: *deodoranto*. But nobody understood the word and the manufacturer was back to where he started and had to explain it in the very same *kanji* ideographs.

Significantly, there are a lot more odor-related words in English than in Japanese, and they are all in common use: smell, scent, odor, fragrance, and aroma. In Japanese, only two words are needed: *kaori*, when the sensation is pleasant, and *nioi*, when it is neutral or unpleasant. The Japanese market for perfume is late in developing on a per capita basis and the lack of scent-related words indicate that it is lower in the value scale of society as compared with the West. Research in the perception of body odor revealed that if the odor was considered unnatural, then it was a form of sickness so one should go the doctor or at least go to the chemist. The item you bought was therapeutic rather than preventive, the opposite to the use of deodorants.

The adjective for a bad smell is *kusai*, and the Japanese still use the words *butter kusai* to refer to overly Westernized items or trends. The words sprung up when the hitherto isolated inhabitants of the Japanese islands came into contact with Europeans whom they found distinctly smelly. Since they saw the Westerner consuming a high smelling product, butter, the "butter" prefix stuck. The Japanese observation is not off the mark, as animal fats do have an effect on the body odor. To the Japanese, the Westerner on a diet of meat must have had a strong smell in the days when all the Japanese ate was vegetable proteins and fish. Body odor, then, in Japan was a form of physical aberration that had to be treated, and those who suffered from it were in a minority. Odors created from foods such as garlic were not considered a real problem, as they eventually went away.

The Japanese have great difficulty in distinguishing deodorants from colognes, though the two are very different in their functions for a Westerner. Deodorants have settled more as a perspiration suppressant in Japan but even here there are problems, as perspiration is a natural secretion and many feel it is harmful to suppress it. The market still languishes.

Just in case the reader has received the impression that the Japanese language has a smaller vocabulary than the English, as illustrated by the limited number of odor-related words, let me say that there are other words that do not have strict equivalents in the English language. By definition alone, I have difficulty in explaining these to English-speaking people and in reverse, such cases are greeted by my Japanese audience with great amusement. (Some bath words are dealt with in Chapter 8.)

The Japanese language is full of texture- and color-related words that either have no equivalent in English or, at least, are not part of daily conversation. In food, there are words in constant use that describe gourmet pleasures, such as "teeth feel," "mouth feel," "tongue feel," and "throat sensation." There are other words that defy translation that describe the sensation when one bites into something, such as *sakusaku, karikari, shikoshiko, paripari*, etc. To describe red, there are words such as *akane, kurenai, enji, usubeni, kokibeni, sabishu, sakurairo, tokiiro*, not to mention *koraru reddo* (coral red). Yes, red is an important color in Japan; for example, the gates that signify the entrance to a shrine, the *torii*, are painted red.

What are we to make of all this? Just that language is not simply a means to communicate with one another but that it also signifies a value system. Japlish is not just an object of fun for those who are familiar with the original words; it is an incredibly ingenious way of expanding the traditional vocabulary and it must be taken seriously when communicating to a Japanese consumer in advertising. Do not insist that the Japanese copy is translatable into a system that you understand. That is the tail wagging the dog. When you are marketing in Japan, all that matters is that it makes sense to the Japanese consumer.

6

The Art of Saying It Without Words

Fantasies of Being Different; "Don't you know Suzuki-san?! He's 5 feet 7 inches tall, has dark hair, and wears glasses."

Why Don't We Teach the Japanese How to Advertise?

Western marketers who arrived in Japan in the sixties were almost unanimously scornful of Japanese advertising. Entering their room in the Hotel Okura, they switch on the T.V. to examine Japanese commercials and what do they see? Nothing but "mood" commercials, with no message—or so it seemed. "To the end, I couldn't understand what they were advertising!" was the commonly raised cry. Even putting aside the language barrier, there seemed to be a great deal in what they said. The sixties were halcyon days of American marketing. The United States was said to have invented the "marketing concept." Europe was conquered. The Japanese were sending their best students to Harvard to find out what marketing was all about. The Japanese were advertising differently because they did not know better. That was the perception.

I am writing this book now because such an optimistic outlook swept me back to Japan. Despite my Japanese background, or perhaps because of it, I too had the missionary zeal of bringing enlightenment to the Japanese shores with research techniques for testing T.V. commercials. Just as I did not enter this occupation by any preconceived plan, it was pure accident that brought me back to Japan.

On hindsight, opening a research company in Japan and expecting to have Japanese clients was a crazy decision. I doubt if it would have been made in the current context, because the West no longer represents the authority it once did. But as I've said, there was an American marketing euphoria in the sixties and for me, it turned out to be fortunate. And since I can assure you that fortunes are not made in market research, it was all for love.

Other U.S. service organizations have entered Japan, and many have fared rather badly because they were offering a "name" that meant little to the Japanese. A representative who is used to being the kingpin in most other markets must often learn humility. It is daunting to have somebody ask, "What is American Express? A trucking company?" It is worse for advertising agencies, as the Japanese firmly believe that they have a unique system of communication that no foreigner can penetrate. Westerners simply should have something specific to offer. Our specific technique was not available in Japan, and our speed in installing it enabled us to establish a bridgehead and later expand.

Our technique began in the movie and program testing field, as the company that scouted me to start up its branch operation in Japan was a fully owned subsidiary of Columbia Pictures. There are far more commercials made than movies or T.V. programs so adaptation of the technique for T.V. advertising testing propelled the relatively unknown research company in those days to one of the top ten in size in the United States in just a few years. It moved the technique to the United Kingdom with almost equal success.

The success in the U.K. led to examining the rest of the world. The main question always was, how big was the commercial television market? With that in mind, the company thought it would make sense to move to another English-speaking country—Australia. Australia had a developed commercial broadcasting network somewhere between that of the U.K. and the United States. There were no cultural barriers and besides, advertising was increasingly dominated by U.S.- and U.K.-headquartered multinationals. But Japan was another story. The only reason to approach it was its sheer size.

As I said, just switching on the T.V. set in the hotel room showed the Western viewer the primitive state of Japanese advertising. Japanese marketers were crying out for Western know-how. If they were not adopting Western ways, it was only because they were not shown the light. The scene was supposedly set for the U.S. and the U.K. to repeat their success with marketing strategy in Australia and Europe.

Chance Leads to a Cultural Re-entry

So a guy turned up in Sydney in June 1965, from the United States. I was not long in a senior management position for one of the largest research companies in Australia and was certainly not looking for a job. I had returned to Japan, once privately and twice on business, in the last five years. My latest return was in 1964, as a member of a government-sponsored mission to examine the tourism market of Japan, and the obvious dynamism of the country, preparing for the Olympics, had a tremendous impact on me. Everybody seemed to be marching toward a target. The rather poor memories of immediate postwar Japan had tended to obliterate my earlier and better memories of the country, but I was again drawn to the culture which, after all, was partly mine by birth. Still, I did not expect to return.

One morning, I had a call in my office from a colleague who was also a member of the survey mission to Japan the previous year. "George, there is a guy called Pierre Marquis who is in town and who is looking into opening a branch in Australia for a company called Audience Studies (now ASI Market Research). He's quite an interesting bloke and when I told him about you, he said he would like to see you. Why don't you give it a go!"

I went.

June is early winter in Sydney but the skies are clear and the sun bright; Pierre was ensconced in the penthouse suite. There are two sights that I never tire of seeing: one is a snowcapped Mount Fuji from one of its five lakes and the other is Sydney harbor on a sunny day. Both are wonders of nature and both have a considerable impact on the life-style and culture of the inhabitants. So one could say that Pierre had managed the greatest stage setting possible for our first encounter.

The door of the penthouse opened and a friendly visage appeared: a man, not very tall for an American, stretched out a hand with a cheerful "Hi." That was the handshake that was to change the course of my life.

Market research as an occupation can hardly be described as encouraging flamboyance, although there are some notable exceptions and we are forever fighting a bad image. I cannot deny a certain academic trait in myself. So I was overwhelmed by the outward going Pierre Marquis.

Pierre was and still is an entrepreneur, a man who builds businesses, while I prided myself and still do, as a professional. So on the surface we were like oil and water, totally and fundamentally contrasting personalities, and one might think we would be quite incompatible. But still there is the view that opposites do better in marriage with each augmenting what the other does not have.

I was thirty-seven then and Pierre barely forty. The relationship between the head office chairman and the branch general manager was to last fourteen years.

One can say it is a small world, the greatest cliché of all times, but I know most of us are continuously amazed at life's coincidences. In any event, that day, circumstances seemed to converge for Pierre to make a quick offer. I was not used to American business methods but even for an American, the decision was delivered with devastating speed. It meant uprooting myself and moving my family to Japan with prospects that seemed uncertain. I balked. Still I was eager to get back after my exposure to the pre-Olympics excitement of Tokyo. The conditions were not good enough. But Pierre had to leave the next day, and as is characteristic of the man, he acted with great persistence and firm persuasiveness. So here I am still in Japan and glad of it.

But Why Don't the Japanese React the Way We Do?

Was I worried about working again in Japan? No, not at all. I am a confirmed optimist and Pierre was even worse. I was enamored of the technique, the vibrancy, and the excitement in the young organization I spent some time with in the U.S., and it never occurred to me that the Japanese would not be waiting for us with outstretched arms. When I started revisiting old contacts, it came as a small shock that the Japanese businessmen were singularly unimpressed with what we had to offer. "You see," they would say, "Japan is different." In my best Australian way, I said to myself, "Bullshit." Still it was not a bit what I expected. As a visitor, I was led to believe that the Japanese aspired to and welcomed everything Western. As a resident, I found otherwise.

Despite opposing Japanese views, after some experiments, it became quickly obvious that there were no operational problems and so we were rolling, creating a minor stir in the Japanese advertising community. We were pretesting commercials before they went on the air, that is, trying to assess their effectiveness before rather than after the event.

I will try to give a feeling of how things developed as we went along. The method involved gathering a group of people in the theater and measuring them in various ways—before, during, immediately after, and some time after exposure to a commercial.

We quickly accumulated results which produced "norms"—averages against which the performance of individual commercials could be compared. Our Western clients who used us elsewhere and particularly in the States tended to compare their commercial's Japanese data with what they were used to back home. In this respect, compared with my Japanese clients who had no such problems, I was encountering trouble from some of my Western clients. Quite often their favorite approaches were not testing well or at least not up to the standards they were used to.

I was in trouble. There is a tendency to blame the research technique if one continues to fail to get good results. If performance on Japanese commercial testing continuously ranks you in the lower quartiles, then there must be something wrong with the research, since the same approach scored well in the U.S., the reasoning went. To their Western eyes it was galling to see "inane" Japanese approaches outscoring their hard-hitting ones. Nevertheless, a major European marketer who now dominates a category, decided to go with our data.

Whether advertising research can accurately assess a commercial's effectiveness is a moot point. What really concerned me was why some scores should deviate so widely between two cultures.

Can Any Culture Claim Superiority in Advertising?

In the sixties, the Japanese advertising industry was not contemptuous of Western advertising approaches. Some Japanese had joined their Western colleagues in criticizing Japanese creative efforts. To them too, it was a letdown when a technique imported from the United States failed to prove their point. It was their insatiable curiosity about anything Western that prompted me to have U.S. commercials that tested well sent over to Japan. When a reel of these commercials was shown to my Japanese friends in advertising, it was fascinating to watch their bemusement and listen to the debate that ensued. The contrast with my Western friends was startling. A reel of Japanese commercials usually produced sniggers and condescending remarks. These early attitudes contributed just as much to the relative lack of Western success in the Japanese consumer market as the daunting distribution system did. The Westerners lost golden opportunities. And some of the major successes—Nescafe, Coca-Cola, Levi's, Colac (a number one laxative in Japan from Vicks)—all were supported by campaigns that were developed here in Japan.

Back in the sixties, a reporter from a U.S. business journal phoned me because he had heard of our research activities in the advertising field. I had had a few appearances in the Australian press, in a very minor way, but not the real big time—the U.S. media! Naturally, I was delighted and decided to take him to lunch so that I could enthusiastically expound on my experience. It turned out he wasn't much interested in what I had to say—perhaps it was because I had invited him to lunch. The session turned out to be mostly my listening to his complaints about Japanese advertising. One example stuck in my mind, for some reason, and the question he had posed in it. I'm only sorry I did not have an answer for the question then.

The case he cited was a press advertisement for a major brand of stereo equipment. "It showed," he said, "a young girl reclining on a carpeted floor. Very Westernized; no chairs, but very plush carpeting. Few apartments for Japanese are like that. Anyway, behind her is this stereo set, and what do you think is in front of her, on the carpet? Lemons! She had one of them in her hand, was practically nuzzling it. So I went to the advertising director and asked him what lemons had to do with hi-fi." The reporter looked at me triumphantly and said, "He couldn't answer, of course."

After all these years, I found the answer to the problem. In the U.S., which had reached a state of economic affluence still only to be dreamed of in the rest of the world, stereos were bought, to some extent, because of the sounds they produced. I have earlier dealt with the romance the Japanese householder had with consumer durables. In the days when that stereo ad had appeared, the kind of apartment it

depicted was certainly unattainable by the young man who yearned
for the stereo set. But the stereo set was creeping into the range of
attainable items. But why the lemons? It was an expensive fruit, but
above all, it symbolizes freshness, youth, wholesomeness, and many
other qualities that cannot be put into words. The ad presented a
setting for the young man's dreams, and the most attainable thing—
even more than the girl with the lemon—was the stereo set.

In startling contrast to Western contempt, evidenced in this epi-
sode, in a book published as recently as 1978 on the twenty-five-
year history of T.V. commercials in Japan, the following statement
appears:

The senior who guided Japanese T.V. advertising is the United States. . . .
Since its start, Japanese T.V. advertising has owed a great deal in production
and creative techniques, as well as in theory and in research to the United
States. . . . There are now two thoughts. The first holds that while this may
have been true at the beginning, Japanese T.V. advertising is now proceeding
along an independent path, technology has reached world standards, and so
we no longer have a great deal to learn from foreign sources. The second
holds that with respect to institutional and comparative advertising (meaning
the brand X approach) and in VTR (video tape recorder) technology, the
United States is still far ahead of others and we have a lot to learn. Both are
correct.

The writer goes on to examine, in great detail, U.S. advertising for
selected product categories over the years. Here were campaigns for
brands that were unheard of in Japan dissected and discussed seriously. There was the Marlboro man, the Gulf tire, Burlington socks,
Whirlpool, Union Carbide, and so on. I know of no American or
European advertising man who has visited Japan who has taken the
pain of studying Japanese campaigns to this extent. The Westerners
were too busy displaying their reel of "best U.S. commercials" so that
the Japanese could learn from them. Recently, as the Japanese have
gained more self-confidence, these gentlemen have completely disappeared from the scene.

Of course, no culture can claim to have the best methods of communicating to all people. Japanese advertising is certainly not transferable
to the West. Everybody will agree to that. Then why does the West
expect that theirs will translate well into a Japanese environment? The
battle is still constantly fought in my office.

How Can a Commercial Sell If It's Not Communicating Something

Despite the constant reassurance from my Japanese friends that they were fundamentally different from Westerners, even I couldn't accept the fact that "mood" could be a primary ingredient in most successful commercials. Actually, it is quite difficult to define a successful commercial, and a philosophical debate still rages in the industry. Like good philosophers, we can only agree to disagree and accept the fact that there are no absolutes in this business. Since Japanese are relativists, they seemed to be less upset than my Western clients that our research was not producing the "golden rule."

In my early research in Japan, I found some interesting differences. In a nutshell, the Japanese were scoring higher on the measurement that concerned their reactions to *how the commercial was made* (the "interest" score). But in Japan, the measurements that related to what the commercial was saying about the product—the "communication" scores—were abysmally low. However, those measurements that indicated a positive shift in attitude toward the advertised product and those that indicated subjective interest in the product came out the same in Japan and the U.S. (These are labeled as scores that relate to "persuasion.") If we postulate that the purpose of a commercial is to persuade the viewer to buy the product, these findings suggested that the creators of commercials in the United States and Japan achieved the objectives through different routes. In other words, the Japanese emphasized the way things were said, while the Westerners stressed what was being said.

When I first discussed these results with my Western colleagues in advertising, the invariable response was, "Of course! What do you expect? Japanese scores are bound to be lower for communication. Most of them are mood commercials." Still, if that was the case, all we had to do was to import Western approaches and render them into Japanese to improve the communication scores. But that didn't happen. There must have been something wrong in the technique for obtaining the measurements.

Actually, the answer lay in the data and the categories. Drop all those terminologies such as "interest," "communication," and "persuasion" and instead, sort the measurements into two categories—those reliant on words and verbal articulation and conversely those not reliant on them. Then suddenly there was consistency. The Americans produced considerably higher scores in word-reliant measurements than the Japanese, while for the non-word-reliant, the Japanese produced either higher scores or scores that were the same as those of the U.S. The data were telling us that the weights in the mix between verbal and nonverbal communications were different in the two cultures. I will examine why this should be so in the next chapter.

Not all Japanese commercials that had high interest were persuasive. When we looked at those that were, then suddenly we became aware that there were elements of the product benefits that were communicated visually and not necessarily verbally. That did not make that commercial a "mood" commercial, although it may have seemed that way to the Westerners.

A good example is a launch commercial for Toyota Cresta in Japan. Two versions were made on the same concept. One is called "Engine" and the other "Bird." The first, "Engine," is a fairly straight, to the point presentation of the mechanical excellence of the new car.

"Bird" has the same aural message but superimposes on it the scene of an open road and the symbol of a bird. Many of my Western friends pick the first as more modern and contemporary and therefore more effective. The "Bird," they feel, obscures the central message and is somewhat trite and old-fashioned.

However, tests showed that in all scores except comprehension of the advertising message—not surprising, since this is taken immediately after exposure and since the aural message was the same— "Bird" scored significantly better than "Engine." Not only was interest higher, but both message retention and favorable attitude shift were higher.

I have often maintained that the motivation toward purchasing a popular car model varies significantly between Americans and the Japanese. Mechanical qualities were often taken for granted by the Japanese, but the emotional aspects were very important. To the space-starved Japanese, owning a family car was like adding another room to one's house—an impossibility to the average Japanese home owner, who was already using all the space available. The mobility of the car afforded psychological escape and freedom, well symbolized by the "open road" and the "bird" in the more successful Toyota

Cresta commercial. The fact that one merely joined a weekend line of other cars is really irrelevant when one prefers to pursue a fantasy.

Foreigners Are the E.T.*s of Japanese Advertising*

Japan has almost always been under the shadow of the more "advanced" great powers—China, Russia, the United States. Like the "bird" in the previous example, foreigners too are used "symbolically" in Japanese advertising. Recently, CBS' "Evening News With Dan Rather" ran a short segment on the use of *gaijins* (foreigners) in Japanese advertising, and an article on the same subject appeared in the *New York Times*. But neither explained the phenomenon.

Until *E.T.* came along, I subscribed to a fairly simplistic theory that in the land where everybody was alike, the foreign stars provided glamour and fantasy with their blond or red hair and, of course, blue eyes. They also provided product differentiation of a kind that Japanese stars who tended to be identified with stereotype roles could not. While this element is still present, the advent of *E.T.* and the seemingly unrelated smash success of the other, less publicized movie, *Elephant Man*, has made me add another rationale to this phenomenon.

Both *E.T.* and *Elephant Man* confront us with a fear of the out-of-the-ordinary and yet tell us that the fear is misplaced and that the "ugly" unknowns are extremely loveable, like household pets.

In Japan's history, the foreigner has been regarded as a potential invader, and the exaggerated fear that foreigners will lead to the destruction of the "Japanese way of life" led to the closing of Japan to the rest of the world for three hundred years. Before that, there had been the attempted invasion by the Mongols and a minor challenge to the established value system by the Christians. Japan opened its doors to the world under the threat of the guns of the Western blackships. "*Krofune torai!*" ("The blackships have come!") is part of the Japanese modern vocabulary. The doors were again closed during World War II and again forcefully reopened by the victorious Allied forces.

Xenophobia has delayed trade liberalization and is plaguing international relationships now. Until *E.T.* came along, the Westerners felt the same about those from outer space, who were always seen as invaders about to destroy our civilization. So there is the link—loveable and "tame" foreigners who are kept by Japanese brands help greatly to alleviate the national inferiority complex and create gratitude toward the brands that were able to hire them.

Until recently, Japanese companies were simply not able to afford the huge salaries the Western stars demanded. The use of these stars coincides with the ascension of Japan as an economic colossus. The first major star to appear in Japanese T.V. advertising was Charles Bronson, who was used to prop up the flagging fortunes of a traditional Japanese male toiletries brand. The company had one of the leading brands but unfortunately, it had a prewar image, hardly appropriate in a country where young men associated the war with defeat and humiliation and the advent of the conquering American heroes. The brand name was changed to Mandom, after Yanagiya (its original name) got clobbered by brands with Western names such as Vitalis. The advent of Bronson was in 1970. He was followed in 1972 by the French star, Alain Delon, for a fashion house, Renoun, by David Niven for Mandom in 1973, by Sammy Davis, Jr., for Suntory, by Peter Fonda, again for Renoun, Orson Welles for Nikka Whiskey, Sophia Loren for Honda motor bike, and so on. Now even John McEnroe. All these companies who used foreign stars were *nonverbally* communicating the fact that they were of international status.

In other cases, when the brand had no Japanese tradition, it was simply not possible to use Japanese actors. This would apply to such products as jeans and coffee in their early stages of introduction. However, this explanation does not seem to hold anymore; so as far as I'm concerned, it is "Welcome, *E.T.*" The flood of foreigners, predictably, upset traditionalists. The following is an extract of a huffy editorial from the newspaper *Asahi* of July 2, 1976.

For some reason, even kids and babies are crazy about these blue eyes. I am startled to see a large close-up of imbecilic expressions on a foreign woman, in broad daylight, on my T.V. screen. Commercials which are offensive to the ear keep popping up, using English, French, and something like Japanese pronounced with a physically inadequate tongue. . . .

Surely, there are no other countries like this anywhere in the world? Can you imagine a Japanese appearing in a foreign commercial, spouting broken English? . . .

What I really can't understand is why foreign stars have to appear to advertise Japanese products. In the first place, what effects can the advertiser expect by using a foreign star? Does it mean that the fact a foreigner is using it provides a guarantee for product quality? . . .

The editorial goes on further. It must have seemed to the writer like the infamous Rokumeikan period, a time after the opening of Japan when the establishment went all agog about anything Western and even held a ball at which obviously uncomfortable Japanese women danced to the strains of the Viennese waltz. However, Japan appears to have matured considerably since the days of the acerbic editorial, and as has been characteristic in other aspects, the Japanese have accepted the change and absorbed its effects. Foreign stars flood the Japanese screen, but now only newly arrived foreigners are surprised and ask why. The use of foreigners is now just another way of saying it without words.

7

But Why Want to Say It Without Words?

You Don't Have to Be Able to Pronounce a Word to Know What It Means

Playing with Chinese Characters

Now that we know what kinds of advertising the Japanese prefer, we should look at why they like it. Having reduced a complex issue into incomprehensible simplicity, I shall now compound the error by leading you through some experiments that tell us that the average Japanese mechanism for receiving messages may be different from that of the average Westerner. The first was an experiment that I stumbled on through a friend.

A person who helped and influenced my early work in Japan was Fred Perry, an American who for a number of years was vice-president of ASI in Japan. Fred was already here when I had arrived in 1965 and displayed a remarkable command of the language and even more importantly a grasp of the culture. He introduced me to a psycholinguist, George Lambert, who was also an American, delving into the intricacies of the Japanese language, among many other things, for his Ph.D. at the Sorbonne. (George was also fluent in French.) Japanese linguists have increased in numbers since then but both Fred and George were well qualified for the Japanese epithet *henna gaijin* (an odd foreigner), in those days.

I consider both to have a touch of genius, probably mastering the Japanese language in double-quick time, compared to many others who toil for years without making headway. Fred and George went

very different ways, the former entering the world of business, marrying a Japanese woman, and building a career and family in Japan.
George was more eccentric, a lone wolf with absolutely no interest in
becoming a part of a business organization. My recollection is of an
intellectual hobo in the best of senses.

George was serious about the use of Chinese characters as a method
of clinical psychological testing. This he called the "*tsukuriji* test" (a
test using made-up characters). Even to this day, I have used his work
as part of my presentation on Japanese advertising. In any event, his
theory when presented continues to interest many of the Western
advertisers who operate here.

To understand the *tsukuriji* test, we should remember that since
Chinese characters are learned from early school days by the Japanese,
their meanings are instantly recognized and of course the origin of
these characters is not considered. However, the Westerner, such as
George Lambert, coming to his learning late in life, cannot help ana-
lyzing the components of these characters. The Westerner thus often
notices things that would escape the average Japanese. For example,
when the two characters 女 (female) and 子 (child) are combined, the
resultant character 好 signifies "love" or "like" and is indeed logical,
considering the relationship of mother and child. On the other hand,
if logic was the only consideration, it could also mean other things
such as "girl," "mother," "cute," or "birth." The fact is that such
interpretations would never occur to the Japanese and would seem
even nonsensical.

There are many other examples. Combination of 田 (field) and 力
(power) gives "male," 男 , no doubt because of the agrarian base of
Chinese society at the time in which the character originated. However, Lambert points out that if this character was thus composed
in modern industrial times, the combination of 田 (field) and 力
(strength) could well signify a tractor or a herbicide.

Delving into the origin of Chinese characters has its own fascination, but such academic pursuits would appear to have no relevance to
the practical world of business. However, basic language affects the
communication process even in modern times and this influences advertising approaches.

Lambert, who was learning Japanese writing in a logical rather than
an intuitive manner, became curious as to how an average modern

Japanese would react to *tsukuriji* (made-up characters) which were nonexistent and thus could not be instantly deciphered. Just as the combination of 田 (field) and 力 (power) would probably not become "male" in a modern industrial society, would not the interpretation of made-up characters reflect modern attitudes? When his hypothesis was tested, the results were indeed complex, the individual interpretations of the made-up characters clearly reflecting the personality of the respondent. The Japanese respondent is invariably surprised to know that other Japanese interpret the new character differently from himself.

As I was listening to this over a drink at the Tokyo Foreign Correspondents' Club—a favorite haunt of most of the younger generation of foreigners in business in those days—it dawned on me why Fred Perry was so interested in introducing me to his friend, George Lambert. While neither Lambert nor I was quite clear how it could be done, we both wondered whether his theory could not be applied as a unique Japanese tool of attitude segmentation.

Reacting to Nonexistent Characters

Lambert himself had a clinical psychology orientation and visualized his techniques as an Oriental Rorschach Test; he had no conception of applying it to large numbers of respondents. Indeed the clinical relevance was immediately apparent; for example, when the character 甥 (a juxtaposition of two males) is shown, some respondents interpret it as "competition," and others as "friendship." Most respondents were surprised to hear the others' interpretation. Lambert had taken this idea in the course of his Ph.D. dissertation at the Sorbonne to Professor Stoetzel, who took an interest in it and suggested that he pursue the matter further. Of course, the expected application was in the area of clinical psychology rather than in marketing. Lambert, in those days, carried a pocket full of *tsukuriji*, showing them to Japanese at all available occasions and continuously doodling to try to create new ones. (The components of the character have to be perfectly balanced for the respondent to perceive any meaning and the stock of suggestive *tsukuriji* was much lower than we originally anticipated.)

To avoid overburdening this discussion, I will here give two experiments only, which reflect cultural values. To the character components already given, 女 (female), 男 (male), and 子 (child), we will add a subcomponent of a character 宀. This in itself has no meaning, but as the following character 家 (house, or family) shows, can signify a "roof." So let us place these individual characters under the roof thus:

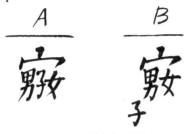

If we pose the question, "Which child appears to be the happier," most Japanese respondents give A, with only about 10 percent choosing B. However, even with the same pair of *tsukurijis*, when the question was changed to "which child is likely to be the more successful," one in three college graduate males this time chose B. We could rationalize that the child in B is a more independent being, not stifled between the parents, but few Japanese would be capable of offering an explanation for their choice in this way. In fact, the choice was instinctive with average lapse time from question to answer taking only four seconds.

We now add 心 (heart) as a component:

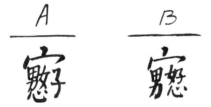

Unlike the first pair, in the answers to the question, "Which is the better wife?" we get polarization. While almost all the young college graduate females chose A, the proportion was only 40 percent among college graduate males. Furthermore, the older the person, the more likely he or she was to choose B. Perhaps B signified the male being allowed greater independence and freedom of action, with the female playing the role of a good mother at home. Or perhaps it signified the traditional role of the male going to work to bring back the paycheck while the female concentrates on bringing up the child.

Kabuki, Not Shakespeare

In any event, insistence on having things explained in this fashion is typically Western; it seemed to be reflected in the logical approach in Western advertising, compared to the more intuitive approach in Japanese advertising. It also explains the superior Japanese perception of "symbolic" communication.

Japan has further cultural overlays. Jack Seward, in his early book *Japanese in Action*, half-jokingly blames the class system of samurai, farmer, artisan, and merchant, for vagueness in Japanese dialogue. Actually, effectively there were the samurais (the ruling class)—and all others, with the former vested with great authority over the rest. The expression *kirisute gomen* literally translates as impunity from killing by sword and abandoning the victim. The samurai class did not necessarily abuse this power, as society has a way of imposing restraint to preserve its fabric, and it was certainly not true that they could kill with impunity. In fact, just as in feudal Sicily, a civil protection group grew up in the late Edo period constituting the roots of the modern *yakuza*, which paralleled the Mafia. Like the British aristocracy, or to a greater degree, the samurai had their codes of honor and obligations to the lower, ruled classes. Nevertheless, Seward argues that one had to be very cautious in the presence of such absolute authority and be very careful that one did not offend through careless utterances. Such verbal ambiguities still linger, perfectly understandable to the Japanese through body language or other nonverbal means, but not comprehensible to the foreigner.

The Japanese use the expression *hara gei* (stomach art), which in turn actually refers to nonverbal means of exploring the other's feelings. They have elevated nonverbal communications to the state of art.

Since the word *art* has been used we can now look for further examples in this field. Haiku—the short Japanese evocative poetic form—and Kabuki both no longer require explaining to most Western readers. One of the masterworks of haiku is Basho's "*furuikeya kawazu tobikomu mizuno oto*," which is, when nonpoetically translated, "An old pond; the sound of a frog jumping in." While a haiku aficionado may take exception, I contend that what is not said, that is, the atmosphere the words evoke, is more important than the actual words used. Haiku are composed of three combinations of vowel sounds, containing five syllables, then seven, and finally five again, and must work within these strict verbal constraints.

If one thinks immediately of Shakespeare as traditional English language theater, in Japan it is Kabuki. I again contend that the reliance on words, qualitatively speaking, differs fundamentally between the two. Can we really appreciate or enjoy Shakespeare without listening carefully to what is being said? This is not the case with Kabuki. It is true that the real aficionado understands every phrase but the average Kabuki-goer is perfectly happy to bask in the visual spectacle and to enjoy the *manner* in which the dialogue is delivered, even if he understands only half of it. In that sense, I have always felt that Kabuki is closer to opera; do we really need to follow the intricate plot of *Il Trovatore* to enjoy it? A Japanese person can't go to a Shakespearean production in London unless he is proficient in the language, without falling asleep during the performance. Many foreigners seem to attend Kabuki productions without knowledge of the language and still enjoy them. However, they cannot go to a modern Japanese play without also falling asleep like their Japanese counterparts at a Shakespearean play.

In the field of art, abstraction has come more easily to the Japanese than to the Europeans. Since one was not compelled to explain things verbally, pure forms such as ikebana developed. Few can read the actual writings in calligraphy but can admire the form. The early European impressionists were stunned by Japanese woodblock prints, a popular art not recognized in their own country at the time, for the degree of nonrepresentational expression. The ability to abstract in art developed earlier in Japan than in Europe.

The Japanese Schizophrenia, or Some Say Their Brains Develop Differently!

We have so far covered so-called nonverbal or symbolic communication fairly thoroughly. Like many others, I do not believe that there is a universally acceptable advertising. We can't dispute that while there are differing arguments, the Japanese language itself and the forms in which it is used differ substantially from most of the European languages. Years ago, when I was still fighting this issue against the big guns, I came across a short piece in the Japanese newspaper, *Asahi*, around 1976, that helped to prove my point.

The piece introduced Dr. Shigeru Yamadori of the psychiatric and neurology department of Kobe University, who had completed a thesis on "the separate memorization of *kanji* in the brain." To the average reader, we must explain that unlike the Chinese, probably the last remaining major ideographic writing, the Japanese incorporates a phonetic system as well. This is a typical demonstration of Japanese adaptability. Writing was originally imported from China, but the Chinese language is totally different from the Japanese, not only in the way words are pronounced, but also in grammatical structure; in fact, for the latter, Chinese is closer to the English than to the Japanese. The Japanese struggled and made do with the Chinese characters but eventually evolved a phonetic compromise. Typically, without abandoning the imported Chinese characters, the Japanese ran the two systems in parallel, evolving the unique form of communication that is currently used. Some now agree that the forced adaptation of unsuitable Chinese characters to their language was a linguistic disaster from which the Japanese are still suffering. Actually, it is the opposite. The Japanese language is more flexible than the Chinese.

Dr. Yamadori believed that the ideographic *kanji* and the phonetic *kana* were stored in different parts of the brain. This was long before the now popular left versus right brain discussions had developed. And the article simply said that, when this thesis was presented at an academic gathering in England, it caused a stir. A culture, such as the European, which had only one system of written communication, could not accept such a phenomenon. I recognized the relevance to my own work and took cognizance of Dr. Yamadori's essay, "Reading of *kanji* under aphasia [loss of the ability to use words]."

A patient who was being treated under Dr. Yamadori after a stroke, incredibly as it seemed then, recovered his ability to read the ideographic *kanji* but not the phonetic *kana*. That meant that he could not read Japanese newspapers. Yamadori continued his testing for three years and came to the conclusion that the brain stored the ideographic *kanji* in the right hemisphere, unlike the phonetic *kana*, which was stored in the left.

In an interview at that time, Dr. Yamadori stated: "I think Japanese that has both the phonetic and ideographic writings has some practical advantages. I am an outsider to the debate conducted by the parliamentary committee on the Japanese language, but I feel greater heed should be taken of the *kanji*, which appeals just to the visual senses." I leapt up from my chair with delight when I read this statement, and that was more than ten years ago. Although Dr. Yamadori does not know it, this piece of information immediately became part of my standard repertoire. It gave me further ammunition to convince the Western advertiser that there was indeed a difference in the way an advertising message could be conveyed and perceived.

The superimposing of writings in a Japanese commercial is a lot more evident than in the West; it obviously serves as visual message reinforcement, compared to the aural enforcement required of scenes in the Western commercial. Various messages, such as next week's program, wriggle across the screen in Japan, which would be considered a gross irritant and intrusion in the West. On the other hand, the Japanese would consider some of the verbal barrage over Western T. V. an intrusion.

The Japanese Further Complicate the Left Brain, Right Brain Argument

Discussions on the left brain versus the right brain entered the popular lexicon, and the winning of the Nobel Prize by Roger Sperry of Caltech has given the debate considerable respectability. Dr. Sidney Weinstein, president of Neuro Communications Research Laboratories in Danbury, Connecticut, and Dr. H. Krugman, formerly of General Electric and now in private practice, have been early advocates of the use of this knowledge for the testing of commercials, and it would be even more interesting if we can somehow settle this matter scientifically on the Japanese versus Western advertising issue.

Like many Japanese, I was fascinated with the theory advanced by Professor Tadanobu Tsunoda that the Japanese brain functions differently than that of most Westerners. His book *The Japanese Brain* details the scientific methods he employed to arrive at this conclusion. He makes the astounding claim that natural sounds are dealt with in the brain in a different manner from the Westerner and that this affects the Japanese psychological makeup. According to Tsunoda, the Japanese left brain not only deals with language and calculations but also deals with human voices, animal cries, and insect sounds. Of course, this is not genetic but a consequence of environment, as he says he conducted the same tests on second- and third-generation Japanese-Americans and found their brain functions to be basically Western; on the other hand, he found a Japanese girl who was adopted into an American family at a young age and lost her Japanese language ability completely, but when tested, produced a Japanese pattern of reception in the brain. From this and other data he draws the conclusion that the vowel-dominant Japanese language is the significant variable, making the Japanese left brain not just a disposer of logic but also that of many natural sounds; it takes in and considers all environmental circumstances. This is obviously an oversimplification of his theory, but such a complex subject is not capable of summary in a paragraph or two.

There are other vowel-dominant languages, and it would be interesting to see whether his theories and consequent attitudes about them could also be validated in these cultures. Tsunoda's claim has been attacked cogently by Roy Andrew Miller, an authority in another sphere—linguistics. The blurb to his book *Japan's Modern Myth* says:

The Japanese have come up with numerous theories to explain themselves, from the "spirit of the Japanese language," an idea popular during the militaristic 1940s, to Dr. Tsunoda's recent "scientific" theory of the uniqueness of the Japanese brain. And in this volume, the author [Miller] debunks them all.

Many observers of Japan and students of the language have a common complaint: the more you understand the facts, the more you grasp the meaning of the words, the less you feel you are understanding the context—why they act the way they do and say the things they say. This dilemma is solved only by pursuing the Japanese view of themselves, especially as it relates to the language.

My own work in this area is of course considerably more modest in dimension. However, as we have seen here, there is enough evidence to suggest that culturally induced factors do affect advertising, and an important part of this seems to be the language. The mistakes Western advertisers in Japan have made in the past cannot be dismissed as another one of those nontariff barriers set up by the devious Japanese. Western advertisers were a bit arrogant in thinking that internationally successful campaigns can also be applied in Japan without modification. Some deserved to fail. Others were victims of the underdeveloped state of advertising research that failed to clearly explain the reason for the differences. Of course, it is difficult enough to measure the effects of a specific advertisement in one's own culture. Still, one can somehow develop empirical guidelines. Although it may be frustrating, Western advertisers have to accept the fact that these guidelines do not necessarily apply in Japan. They have to be prepared to start over—but if they are good advertisers, they will find the new paths of exploration fascinating.

8

You Can't Westernize the Bath

"Do Westerners Use Soap in the Bath?!"

Sitting Cross-Legged on the Sofa in a Yukata *(Traditional Informal Gown) With a Beer*

The way the Japanese live has been undergoing considerable transformation. The traditional tatami flooring is an example. As explained earlier, the tatami was fine in the days when labor costs were low and the apprenticeship system worked. Now that it is more expensive to install and maintain a tatami room it is easier to have Western-type flooring with carpet. Many Japanese still try to have at least one tatami room, but the economic forces are such that there are children growing up in Tokyo who see tatami floors only when they visit other homes or places. Consequently, the demand for Western beds and furniture has increased considerably.

The Japanese themselves think their life-style is becoming Westernized, and it is not surprising that the foreigner gets led up the garden path. What has actually happened is that certain items that are more convenient and more suitable to modern-day living have been readily taken into the Japanese home. As these emanated from the West, their use gives a superficial semblance of a Westernized life-style.

However, things that matter, those based on traditional values, remain invulnerable to the Western onslaught. A Japanese has a Western-type flooring, but would not contemplate walking onto it while wearing shoes. The habit is unclean on two counts: it can dirty the floor, and it keeps the feet in a stuffy and enclosed state from which they are demanding immediate release. Those readers who have traveled to Japan and who have stayed at a Western-style hotel may have noticed the slippers provided in the room. When I travel outside Japan I miss them and the *yukata* (a form of casual kimono) into which you change but in which you can also sleep—no need to pack your pajamas. So right at the doorstep the life-style is not as Western as it may have at first seemed.

The next thing is to take a bath—a very significant part of the day. As stated earlier—very few Western businessmen are invited to a Japanese home. However, a friend who now lives in New York told me that while he was on a three-month assignment in Japan, a Japanese colleague did indeed invite him to his home. The Japanese colleague thinks of himself as Westernized. Working for a foreign-capital firm, he is surrounded by Westerners and does remarkably well in holding his own. He lives a fair way out of town and when they arrived—after about an hour and a half's traveling—the American was asked if he would like to have a bath. He accepted the offer and found the experience pleasant and warming in more ways than one.

After the bath the most relaxing thing is to shed one's Western clothes and get into a *yukata*. The bath is taken very hot—uncomfortably so for Westerners who are not used to it—so the skin is red and the body warm. What is more suitable then than a cool beer—originally a Western product? Dinner follows, and the kitchen is full of modern gadgets—no, not Western gadgets! There may even be an oven. However, what comes out of the oven tends to be quite different from what you'd expect. What comes out of the kitchen is either still traditional Japanese or most likely a unique blend of Japanese and Western foods. Most evening meals are eaten with chopsticks even if you sit on a chair and eat from a Western-style table.

When it is time for bed, if you are lucky enough to get a Japanese tatami bedroom, you will probably sleep on a mattress rolled out onto the floor, though that mattress may no longer be the traditional type stuffed with cotton, which is hard; it may be made of foam rubber. So, aside from making love, if eating and sleeping are the most fundamental of human needs, they are being satisfied in very Japanese ways. Where fundamental values are affected true Westernization does not occur and why should it? Perhaps sleeping is less fundamental than eating or bathing because of the switch of many to Western beds. But

the Western bed in a Japanese room doesn't quite seem the same to me.
As for love making, that may make an interesting study although here
I am prepared to concede that it may transcend East-West differences.
Ah, yes, but there's still the bath.

"Are You Really Telling Me That the Westerner Uses Soap in the Bath?"

Some Japanese are still incredulous at Western bathing habits. The
feeling is, of course, mutual. One of the first to arrive in Japan after her
long seclusion from the outside world were the Dutch. In the diaries
of two Dutch naval officers are references to Japanese bathing habits.
In one the Japanese were observed emerging from the bath looking like
boiled octopuses. Western Puritanism frowned on the sight of men,
women, and children piling into a large tub together and in the altogether. One observer was surprised that nothing untoward happened and remarked that perhaps the Japanese lacked the awareness of
sex. A modern writer may have suspected the Japanese of being asex-
ual! Apart from the sexual hang-ups that the Dutch of the day had,
the mixed bathing offended their sense of hygiene.

If I were to pick the most unique aspect of Japanese culture, it
would be the bath. The first time I became aware of this was, as usual,
when I was doing product research, this time for soap. Since the client
was a multinational company headquartered elsewhere and entering
the Japanese market for the first time in this category, the research
involved describing step-by-step what the Japanese do when they enter the bathroom. I do not intend to give the reader quite the same
detail; suffice to say that this space, which in Japan and the West
happens to be called the bathroom, has as much in common as a
temple has to a church.

The most noticeable difference is that the Japanese wash themselves
thoroughly before they enter the tub. The tub is called *yubune*. The
bune part in the Chinese ideograph is the same as a boat, the *yubune* is a
boat that carries hot water. Your mind drifts while you're in the tub,
which is solely for soaking, just as it would if you were being rocked in
a boat on calm seas. The act of getting oneself clean and the act of
soaking in the tub are distinct and serve entirely different purposes.
One is a rational, practical act while the other is an emotional experi-

ence. The purity of the latter must not be contaminated by bodily dirt and the product that is associated with that dirt—soap. This perception is fundamentally important to the marketing of soap.

The concept that suds that contain dirt are contaminated and must be thoroughly removed extends into the kitchen. A Japanese woman who had lived in England with a British family laughingly told me that one thing she couldn't get used to was the British way of taking care of soiled dishes. "The British," she said, "put the detergent in the sink, get the water to suds up, and then place the dishes in it." Actually, that was not the part that worried her, because it is the same here. What concerned her was that a cloth would be used to wipe off the dishes that were covered with suds. True, the grease was removed with a paper towel or tissue before placing in the sink, which limited the amount of grease in the water, but even so the dishes were still essentially contaminated with soap even if they sparkled after wiping. What the Japanese do is to run clean water over the dishes after they've been washed in soap or detergent and leave them to dry naturally. No suds are allowed to remain on the surface to be wiped off. The parallel with the human body is obvious. The Japanese do not allow any suggestion of soap to remain on the body before they wipe themselves down. In the traditional inn, the foreigner is forever dismayed and puzzled with the lack of a bath towel, finding only a small hand towel. The Japanese rub themselves dry with this small cloth, which has very little power of absorption; the idea is to let your clean body dry as naturally as possible by exposure to air. Since the bath water is piping hot, your body is also steaming red so the experience is not nearly as great a hardship as you would expect, even in winter.

There have been some attempts at introducing Western bath additives to Japan but, not surprisingly, the market is very limited. This bathing characteristic also affects scent levels in the soap and after-bath products. The ideal state when you leave the bath is for your skin to be squeaky clean; having something remain would spoil that state. I have already mentioned the paucity of scent- and odor-related words in the Japanese vocabulary and that it indicated a relatively low positioning of scent in the traditional Japanese culture. The Westerner applies perfume or cologne to express individuality. To the Japanese this seems at times to be rather unsubtle, even vulgar. Only the bar hostess advertises herself in that way.

When the Bath Is Not a Bath

Speaking of words, there are many, many bath-related words that have no equivalent in English. So it is the converse of perfume and indicates how important the bath is to the Japanese. I wonder if there is another culture in which so many books and essays have been produced about the bath. One of the key scenes in Soseki Natsume's *Kusa Makura* ("Pillows of Grass")—and Soseki is generally said to be the father of modern Japanese literature—is one in which the hero has arrived at a country inn and decides to have a nice soak. But let Soseki describe it and its consequences.

It's cold. With the hand towel dangling, I go down to the *yutsubo* [a literal translation would be "hot water jar"].

I shed my clothes in the three mat [room] and as I slowy descend four steps I emerged into a bathroom of about 8 mats. [One tatami mat is approximately 180 cm by 90 cm in size.] It appeared that a *yubune* about the size of a tofu shop is dug down to approximately four feet in depth in the middle with the bottom laid with granite. Although we may call it a tub, it also is laid with stone. As long as it is called a mineral spring, I suppose it contains many ingredients but, being semitransparent, quite agreeable to enter. I even hold [the water] in my mouth from time to time, but it has no special taste or odor. I believe it is good for ailments, but as I have not bothered to ask, I do not know for which sickness it works. The practical values have never entered my mind. [The author now goes into meditating on a classical Chinese poem about the hot spring.]

I supported my head, which was stretched back, on the edge of the hot water tub and let my lightened body in the transparent warm water drift with as little resistance as possible. Lightly, lightly, the soul floats like jellyfish. The world would be easy if you could get yourself in this state, opening the locks of rationality and removing the bars of tenacious attachment to things. You become assimilated with the warm water while in it. You now feel that nothing in the world matters.

This is probably enough to evoke for the Western reader the atmosphere of a contemplative Japanese bath. Things pick up in the ensuing scene for the nineteenth-century reader when a nubile girl accidentally steps into the bathroom, unaware of the author, well concealed in the steam that emanates from the bath and fills the whole room. The author watches her and goes into further flights of fancy, until the girl realizes his presence and flies out of the room. By the way, she was the daughter of the innkeeper. All this was, of course, extremely innocuous from modern day standards but my youthful imagination was titillated by this brief encounter in the bathroom and I read the passage over and over. At the time, Japan was a country of heavy-handed censorship that extended to literature. Words were deleted from passages that had even touched upon the sexual act. (These days, the hang-up is with pubic hair that is air-brushed out in copies of *Playboy* and *Penthouse*.) We used to have great fun guessing the words and filling in the offending passages. I was quite disappointed when after the war, I compared the actual passage with my own; the original seemed quite pallid and insipid when contrasted with what my vivid adolescent imagination had generated.

Soseki's encounter with the nubile form and the ambience needed to make it happen would have occurred only in a Japanese bathroom. Clearly the bathroom is a special place and bathing is a special occasion, even if performed every day. At least, it is different from the Western bathroom so the soap and other bathroom products assume different characteristics from those in the West.

The word for water in Japanese is *mizu*, but the hot or warm water that fills the bathtub is *yu*: In other words, it is not just water; cold water and warm or hot water are not of the same substance as *mizu*. The imagery the word *yu* evokes in a Japanese person would require greater verbal skills than I can generate. A recent book by Kazue Morizaki, entitled *Yukagen Ikaga* (if translated literally it can only be rendered in a very pedestrian manner as "How is the water temperature?"), is an ode to the Japanese bath. This is how the author, a woman, opens it.

It is not that I am exceptionally fond of bathing, but when the children became independent and left home, even a custom as ordinary as bathing seemed to become a vivid experience. And I savor slowly the delights of *yu* [the warm bath water]. All the things that trouble me in the mind will slowly fade away from my gradually warming body and soul and is it because I return to my nonavaricious youth, a gentle feeling spreads within me. In this way, I delight in a complete change in mood and recently when the tension of the day accumulates, no matter what time of day, I will make up the *yu*. The twists and turns of my thoughts vanish completely.

In *yu*, various patterns of life float up and, as it is a moment when un-adorned naked beings shed their soil and grime, it may seem trifling but it really seemed like a belief in tomorrow and the long held custom has a touch of sadness. . . .

To the Japanese, *yu* evokes feelings for a moment of contemplation; it is resuscitation and sensual pleasure. *Yu*, "warm water," is not just water, and any product that enters in the *yudono* (the place of *yu*) must have the right fit. There is a school of thought that half-seriously explains the very small number of psychiatrists in Japan as the result of the Japanese bath. How the worship of *yu* has come about leads to interesting speculation. Japan has been blessed with an abundance of water, and the saying "spending like *yu* and water" is the equivalent of "spending as if money is going out of style." The Japanese equivalent of striking oil is to strike a hot spring that overnight turns the neigh-borhood into a spa to which hordes would flock. There are only a few prefectures in Japan that do not boast a hot spring.

To round off this saga of the *yu*, a book by Chika Otake that de-scribes the shame of being a prisoner of the Soviets after World War II includes a very poignant scene. In the camp each Japanese prisoner was allocated only enough hot water to clean and wipe himself down. Nostalgia for them was to gather around and talk about the wonderful bath they used to have back home—like the World War II American soldier in New Guinea who dreamed of a white Christmas. Unable to bear it any longer they decided to pool their water to fill a tub. Drawing lots, one after another they soaked in the tub until a dis-gusted Soviet guard stopped them from what he saw as a barbaric and unclean act.

Two Words That Drove a Western Marketer Crazy

The Japanese love sensual words, and there are many that are used in conjunction with the bath. The research that I conducted for my multinational client nearly drove me out of my mind. The scenes of the Japanese at bath unfolded somewhat along the preceding lines although not quite as lyrical; if such purple prose had crept into my market research report I most certainly would have been fired.

There are two words that occur frequently in Japanese daily conver-sation to express sensual satisfaction—*sawayaka* and *sappari*; but in the

There are just as many stores in Japan as in the United States, but within an area smaller than California.

Western fast foods are very popular in Japanese cities.

Far more popular in Japan than Western video arcades are the ever-present *pachinko* parlors.

Typical Japanese housing: the traditional Japanese house (right); the new upper-middle-class apartment building (below, left); and the evolving "rabbit hutch," which reflects the crucial space shortage in Japanese cities (below, right).

Whether at a public bathhouse or a country inn, the Japanese bath is a tranquil and contemplative experience.

In the 1960s, traditional furnishing mix with modern appliances, as th low table called the *kotatsu* shares space with the television and sewi machine (left), but by the 1970s, Western-style consumer goods predominate.

Teenage women may dress in 1950s-style clothing and even drink soda pop—but only until they marry and prepare for childbirth.

These Japanese teenagers are enjoying the short period between their school days and their adult life as a *shakaijin*—a member of society.

Jeans are the young Japanese man's uniform, but as soon as he starts his first job, they are no longer appropriate attire.

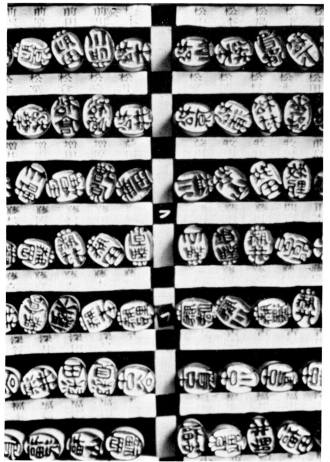

These traditional business seals are the personal signatures on any official papers.

The company badge is the conc. symbol of the Japanese entry int the world of the *shakaijin*.

Japanese-English dictionary the only word that fits them both is "refreshed." So it was important for me to explain to my client that while "refreshing" and "feel refreshed" kept cropping up in consumer responses, depending on the context they had different meanings. When you washed off the day's grime from your body the resultant sensation was more likely to be *sappari*. After the bath, when you went into the living room and opened the window and felt the breeze, it is more likely to be *sawayaka*. One of the great post–World War II advertising phrases was *sukkatto sawayaka* for Coca-Cola. Separately each word describes the sensation of refreshment but the former conveys the feeling when you open the bottle and the carbonation escapes. Combined they make a great advertising phrase, but it is impossible to render the feeling into English—the best I can do is to translate it as "the refreshment that refreshes."

The great frustration of the Westerner is to know that, like a deaf man, there is a world of sound of which he is not aware. As a product and advertising concept was being developed for the soap, the two words began to obsess my client. My worst moment came when I was asked to submit a written explanation on how the two words differed. I did my best but only managed to confuse everyone. I remember those phone calls in the morning, obviously being made during a meeting, "George, which is it: *sappari* or *sawayaka* when it is such and such? The trouble was that often the two words were substitutable, but in the context of the copy, one just seemed to go better than the other.

These linguistic problems have serious consequences in quite a few cases. What inevitably happens in most instances is that the Japanese creative personnel will just give up the struggle to logically explain his copy and start producing advertising that translates well. Worse still, if he takes the line of least resistance he will just take what his client gives him in English and put it into Japanese. The client will get it back in Japanese and will be satisfied that the proper concept is being conveyed, though totally unaware that as advertising execution it is simply awful.

It is strange how translations give a false sense of security if they come out the right way; it is the meaning in the original language that is relevant. On the other hand, when the translations do not agree— and actually, they seldom do—all hell is let loose by the irate Western advertising director who thinks his instructions have been sabotaged. In my early days I used to get myself into so much hot water and into so many futile arguments by carelessly providing my own translation that didn't quite agree with the advertising agency's translator, that I will now generally insist that the client provides his own translation; unless it is totally wrong I will not dispute it. (Anyway, I prefer to read the Japanese.)

Yes, I Use the Shower When I Bathe

But a Western manufacturer who had very successfully marketed bathroom products, bath bubbles, splash-ons, etc., was not dismayed that the Japanese bath was different. He stayed at some of the Japanese hotels that were full of Japanese and had perfect Western-type bathrooms. His Japanese contacts told him that the Japanese bath was becoming Westernized. (The tubs were made of plastic and no longer of wood.) Granted that selling bath bubbles may still be difficult, his question on whether the Japanese bathroom also had a shower elicited an innocent "yes." In fact, when the precaution was taken to have a question in an omnibus survey on this matter, the majority of respondents said they had a shower in their bathroom.

It was then assumed that bath balms that were used under the shower would not be objectionable because they didn't contaminate the water. But it was not that simple. The implement that was called a shower was the same implement as the one in the West—or, at least, usually. On most occasions they are not used in the same way. In many cases the shower is not a fixed attachment, as in the Western bathroom, but simply a flexible device that can be attached to the hot water tap. Any foreigner who has visited a Japanese public bath house or a sauna will have observed these devices. They are used to wash off the soap before getting into the bath tub! We have found a significant proportion of Japanese saying that they also had a soak in the tub *after* using the shower. Unfortunately in this context using and having a shower is not the same thing.

But the most important use for the so-called shower was for shampooing the hair. This is done outside the tub; afterward, one still soaks in a tub of clean hot water. After all, the device is infinitely superior to the traditional basin for washing the hair. As the shower is a different device, even products for the shower have a much more limited market than in the West.

9

Beer, Whiskey, Sake in That Order

How Whiskey and Water Challenged the Establishment

Beer and Whiskey's Challenge to Sake

Whether one drinks it or not, alcohol is an important manifestation of a culture. In many, it is *the* social lubricant while in Islamic countries and in areas that strictly follow Puritan ethics it may be the root of all evil. In those cultures where drinking is acceptable behavior, the most popular alcoholic drink is generally from the local agricultural produce. We find wine in the South of France, made from grapes grown there, rum in Jamaica and Cuba made from sugar cane, tequila in Mexico made from cactus, and, of course, sake in Japan made from rice. In many ways the change in imbibing habits signifies a change in cultural values or a transition from one society to another. Up to the sixties Australia was an extremely male-dominated society and men tested themselves by drinking beer in large quantities. It is consistent with this cultural base that the current Australian prime minister, Bob Hawke, had held since his Oxford days the *Guinness Book of Records* record for imbibing the greatest amount of beer in the shortest time—an image that did not hurt him politically, although he has given up the habit (he also gave up the record).

Australia today is quite a different country; for one thing, while until the end of World War II it was 90 percent Anglo-Saxon, now one in three children born are of immigrant parents, with the greatest infusion being from the Mediterranean region. Wine has thus had an exponential growth in Australia, and the switch from beer to wine, to many, means a change in one's fundamental life-style. In the United States, too, the bourbons and the whiskeys associated with a male-dominated life-style faced the challenge of the Smirnoffs and the Bacardis, and the latters' ascendancy symbolizes a transition from tough pioneer values to more urban values.

In both the United States and Australia, two very similar societies, the new drinks meant admission of women to the circle of drinkers. Once a macho product, alcoholic drinks have become unisexual, and this is clearly reflected in the modern advertising of these products. Once this starts, the two trends feed upon each other producing an evolutionary effect. Alcohol must surely be the champion of product categories in its ability to rapidly change social styles (the automobile may share this position). So if we take the alcoholic drinks consumed in either culture over the years, it could be a barometer of that culture's shift in social values. In this sense the Japanese scene is different from the American and the Australian. The incumbent, sake, was challenged quite early by Western imports, at least among the elite who were the trendsetters. The Meiji pioneers of Westernization were fully aware of wine but it did not take. The intricacies of wine growing—the climate and soil—were not suitable for growing enough grapes for the industry. Beer technology was easier to import; it is a relatively simple matter to import hops. However, this does not explain why whiskey was, beside beer, the Western alcoholic drink that stuck.

My theory on how whiskey took hold starts with my childhood memories of Japan in the thirties and my own environment—the people who visited our home and their worship of the pipe (one of them even sported a homburg and spats) and, of course, Scotch whiskey. It seemed that the Japanese intellectuals identified more with Europe than with the United States—in particular, with the businessmen and the political theorists. After all, the British Empire was the most impressive demonstration of elitist power. The crown prince, now the emperor, visited the U.K. and was the guest of King George V at Buckingham Palace; his brother studied briefly at Oxford. The red brick buildings, almost a replica of London, dominated the government offices of Kasumigaseki and the business offices of Marunouchi until they were largely destroyed by the bombing raids. Only a few remain. Tokyo station is one of them, but alas it is scheduled for demolition, to be inevitably replaced by a more functional modern structure. While many Japanologists lament the Japanese destruction of their cultural heritage—for example, the famous Frank Lloyd Wright–designed Old Imperial Hotel—they forget that unlike the equivalent structures in Europe, these were only temporary phenomena and when the value guideline shifted to the victorious U.S., it was only natural that they would be quickly replaced by the façades of New York.

The Japanese love the word *akogare*, which loosely translates as "yearning." They will fix on something that would be seemingly unattainable; its unattainability imparts a certain romantic glow. Even just being on the fringe of the object of *akogare* is enough. Before World War II, the *akogare* was for London, afterward it became New York. But it was not just the buildings of London that were the object of the establishment's *akogare*, but its life-style. Scotch whiskey fitted very easily into this frame of reference. The yearning for the foreign and "We the Japanese" syndrome combined to help the Suntory brand of whiskey. But then why not sherry or port? Continuing to be entirely conjectural, putting aside its appropriateness with the Japanese cuisine, etc., the fact that whiskey was essentially based on good water and that it could be made locally using imported malt and acquired technology must have contributed greatly. Suntory's own published history testifies to this. For one, Suntory established its distillery in Kyoto and quickly drew attention to the fact that it used the same renowned pure water for its whiskey as did the premier-grade sakes. Suntory still makes a great thing out of the Japanese water culture and had its own pavilion at Expo '70 on this theme.

Suntory was not challenging established values; instead it based its new product introduction entry in a way entirely consistent with their culture. Then, of course, there was the imagery of the drink that came from elitist England that satisfied the *akogare*. Well then, why not port? Suntory did introduce a concoction that is still on the market called Akadama Port Wine, which was positioned as a woman's drink. It carved out a prewar niche in the market and the brand still exists. But unlike the whiskey, the quality of the product is such that it could surely only appeal to the unsophisticated palate and its potential is thus limited.

Suntory's development followed that of many Japanese industries. It was heavily protected from the imported Scotch whiskeys from which it drew its original technology. But after that, their strategy was brilliant. One of the essential myths that they and some other food manufacturers have been able to create is that "the Japanese palate is different from anybody else's." Suntory must have been worried about the days when eventually the protective wall would be lifted and the *agokareno* Scotches would come pouring in, threatening the base of the gigantic business they had built up. Using editorial-type advertising, articles, symposiums, etc., over an extended period of time, a conviction was created that only a Japanese manufacturer could produce something that is truly suitable to the subtle Japanese palate. Scientifically this ignores the fact that tested "blind," Suntory would be indistinguishable from many a Scotch.

The *coup de grace* is that now Suntory or Nikka (its somewhat smaller competitor) with water has joined sake and beer as the drink to be consumed with sushi; you will seldom if ever see Scotch being consumed at a traditional sushi bar. I have had many a Japanese friend say to me quite seriously that Suntory was the only whiskey that went with sushi or tempura. Interestingly, they don't apply the reverse logic that Scotch goes better with foods of Anglo-Saxon origin. The claim would strike most as being ridiculous but not when it concerns Japanese food, which is presumably of a more highly delicate nature. This is where my Western side comes out: alcohol *per se* stimulates the taste buds and White Horse is more than acceptable to me with my sushi.

Unlike the U.S. or Australia, Japan did not have immigrant influences to affect drinking habits. However, after World War II, beer very quickly overcame sake as the number one drink in volume. More recently sake has suffered the ignominy of a continuing declining share due to whiskey. Still, that doesn't quite make Japan Westernized in its drinking habits because these three beverages account for a whopping 90 percent of alcohol consumption. All the others—wine, brandy, vodka, rum, etc.—have to fight it out for the remaining tiny segment. I have already given my cultural reasons for this and why it was not an accident when others had also attempted to introduce alcoholic drinks. The growth of whiskey was accelerated by Suntory's brilliant marketing strategy that simply picked up the right cultural cues.

Beer, the Universal Drink; Mizuwari (Whiskey and Water), a Japanese Drink

The key to this phenomenon of there being, volume-wise, only three major drink categories is still in the much-touted cultural homogeneity of the Japanese. With an almost monotonous and predictable pattern of drinking, it is not difficult to cater a Japanese party, as just the three drinks will do. Drinking is a social act, but it's also an expression of individual personality and recognition of this in the West leads to advertising that appeals to different attitudinal segments. In Japan, the weight is toward the "social" not the "private," at least in volume consumption. Here I do not mean home versus out of home drinking, but rather that the act itself is more social than the expression of individuality as discussed in Chapter 4. In a vertical society, overfragmentation leads to confusion, bewilderment, and rejection. It therefore has been much more difficult to diversify drinking habits, and so we had the gradual progression from sake and its variants, such as *shochu*, to beer, and finally to whiskey. The time is ripe for another entry or perhaps a group of entries.

All evidence so far is that the initiative is still in Japanese hands despite the multitude of Western brands theoretically available. Suntory is promoting "brandy American," which is nothing more than the idea of consuming brandy with water—an extension of the phenomenally successful *mizuwari* (whiskey and water). But the most recent phenomenon is the rise in popularity of *shochu*, a distilled drink made from potatoes, popular in the southern island of Kyushu, that resembles vodka in its clarity but has hitherto had a low-class image.

According to a government white paper prepared in 1982, *shochu* and wine each had a 20 percent increase in volume consumption. Like the traditional sake, neither is served mixed. Because of its low price, its value share is smaller, but on volume *shochu* is almost 80 percent whiskey and brandy combined. Though it resembles vodka, it is not drunk mixed, but straight or with water. Basically, *shochu* fits very well into the traditional drinking pattern; this and its low price are probably the real reasons for its popularity.

There are only a few places in the world where I find the beer undrinkable. Indeed, beer is the universal alcoholic beverage, just as cola is the universal soft drink. My theory for this is that beer is the one drink that fits the values of an industrial society. Industrialization has always been imposed on other traditional forms of social structures; in its wake, some of the more leisurely customs are swept aside.

The advent of the carbonated soft drink seems to fit the desire for stimulation and refreshment as well as for a thirst quencher with a difference. Beer may be an extension of this principle: it starts as a thirst quencher while at the same time satisfying the adult desire for alcohol. Because of the stimulation of alcohol you can drink more of it than you can of a soft drink, which also makes it suitable as a social drink. It simply does not fit any preindustrial-revolution perception of an alcoholic beverage. Perhaps we should not classify beer in the same category as wine, whiskey, etc. Maybe it is unique and happens to be a drink that contains alcohol. This certainly is the case in Japan because the way sake was consumed required a fairly leisurely setting; it was not suitable as a thirst quencher after a hard day's work or after sports. The sake makers, very much aware of this fact, have tried to stem the tide by promoting it as a cold, rather than a heated drink, including "on the rocks" to combat the whiskey boom. Still, the modernization of sake in this way has proved to be quite difficult. Sake is up against traditional perceptions whereas beer simply slipped into an open gap. Nowadays most banquets have shifted from the slower paced, more expensive tatami-floored establishments to the so-called Japanese beer gardens perched on top of modern buildings.

Another way of looking at the Japanese acceptance of beer into the daily menu was suggested by Professor Shozaburo Kimura, an authority on medieval history at Tokyo University. At a recent symposium in Tokyo, he said that meal cultures tended to divide into drink-oriented and food-oriented. The Greeks did not develop a fine cuisine because they produced mainly grapes and olives, with very little meat and only poor quality vegetables. Culturally they tended to concentrate on drinking. In contrast, the Romans were food-oriented, enjoying every meal to its fullest and considering wine only an accom-

paniment. In modern day Japan, though food is plentiful, Professor
Kimura feels that the culture tends, as it always has, more toward
drink. It was once considered very low class to start a proper meal
with rice while still drinking sake. Even now, the Japanese worker
makes the rounds of the bars before retiring with *chazuke* (tea on boiled
rice) dutifully served up by his wife, who has stayed up for his late
return.

Then again we must return to the phenomenal success of whiskey—
in the beginning primarily a drink for the elite rather than the masses.
The fact that the drinking of alcohol is a social act first, then a private
one, is important for a mass-marketed brand.

There is one thing that sake, beer, and whiskey share when you
observe a group of Japanese enjoying a social drink. All three beverages are consumed straight out of the bottle, which is offered to you
by your drinking companions. You, in turn, do the same to him. The
Japanese have the words *sashitsu sasaretsu*, which describe the exchang-
ing of sake cups, and the custom has been continued on to beer and
whiskey. How is this possible with whiskey? Isn't it brought to you by
the waiter? To overcome this problem most Japanese salaried workers
purchase what is known as a "key bottle" from the bar. The bottle has
the customer's name written on it and will be kept scrupulously until
his next visit to that establishment. It saves the customer money and
helps the establishment keep him as a regular customer. It also ensures
that there has been no radical break in the way alcoholic drinks are
consumed. Obviously, this is impossible with the cocktail and hence
the low consumption volume of vodka, gin, and rum.

To reinforce this point, we must not forget the importance of
women in the Japanese drinking environment. Alcohol itself has never
been a taboo for women, although as in most societies there was a time
and a place for them. In the Edo period, preceding the modernization
of Japan, men frequented the pleasure quarters and called the well
known but much misunderstood geisha to their banquets. The women
would sit beside the men and replenish their sake cups, personally.
The geisha system is now an anachronism, and with the economic
advancement of women, the arduous apprenticeship system is no
longer viable. Well-trained geishas are in such short supply that the
average foreign visitor is not likely to have the experience of being
served by them unless in a phony, stage-managed situation that is put

on for a tour group. Sake was the only drink served on those occasions and its small heated bottle and the tiny cup into which it was poured was wonderfully suited to establishing an illusion of intimacy between the male and female.

Anybody who visits Japan cannot but fail to be impressed by the profusion of small eating and drinking establishments. Japan spends 1.5 percent of its Gross National Product on declared entertainment, which is more than what they spend for defense. A sore point for Americans, but as Gregory Clark, the noted Japanologist, has pointed out, they surely have their priorities right for a happy society. The bars now have hostesses who superficially retain the geishas' serving tradition—not, of course, the accoutrements or musical or dancing skills. The hostess sits beside the customer and makes sure his cup is filled, but this time it is with either beer or whiskey. A cocktail would put her out of this job, but since having a hostess pour the drink is more important than the drink itself, the attraction of the bottle on the table is not likely to vanish in the near future.

The Japanese almost always drink their whiskey with water. The Japanese word, *mizuwari* actually means diluted with water and could, theoretically, apply to any base drink. However, it has now become a term for whiskey and water only. Since it is necessary on a social occasion to continue drinking for a while, this is probably the only suitable way to drink whiskey and still preserve your liver. Drinks such as brandy that have not developed an image of being consumed in this way are having a hard time breaking into this environment, at least in the more popular establishments.

Drinking Alcohol the Natural Way

But why water and not soda? Here we are looking at a cultural phenomenon that values purity, or it may be better to say that they abhor impurity. The Japanese value water for its purity and its influence pervades the various Japanese art forms. You are never far from water's influence in this country of islands with their bonsai-like pines and land-locked prefectures in which there are the clear springs (cold as well as hot), streams, and valleys.

Water is natural and does not disturb the essence of whatever it is added to—in this instance whiskey. When it comes to soda or any other manufactured item it is a different matter. By mixing one of them with whiskey you are diluting its essential characteristic. Living in a more or less racially homogeneous society, the Japanese have trouble with the concept of a mixed drink and invariably consider that whichever was the superior of the two items then becomes downgraded. (Extended to race, this has a very unpleasant side.)

We have been using the word *sake* to denote a specific alcoholic beverage. However, when the Japanese opened their doors to the West, this word was generic for all alcoholic drinks. The drinker in Japan is a *sake nomi, nomi* meaning "to drink." (Combined with other words the Chinese character for sake is pronounced "shu." Until recently wine was *budoshu*—now just *wainu*—*budo* meaning grape, so wine was "grape sake.") I have dealt *ad nauseam* with the subject of words that exist in one culture and not another and the significance of this fact in revealing relative values. If sake is generic for all alcoholic drinks, it stands to reason that there are no words like aperitif or liqueur in the Japanese language. And this has obvious ramifications for the company trying to market products in this category.

A beginning, a middle, and an end permeates many Western art forms—perhaps starting with the Greek tragedies, then the sonata form in music, and in the culinary world the concept of a meal starting with hors d'oeuvres, soup, and so on to the dessert. The meal, no matter how elaborate, must finish, and in Japan this is usually signified by the arrival of the rice, at which time you stop drinking. However, although there will be a progression of items up until that point, it has little relationship to the Western concept of a course. While each item is balanced against the other, it is based on a concept of overall harmony; thus in a family meal, all the items, except perhaps the last bowl of soup to go with the rice, can be brought out at once. Just as sake was drunk throughout the meal till the appearance of the rice, the alcoholic beverage selected, whether it be beer or whiskey is likely to be drunk throughout.

An English marketer of Scotch remarked to me in surprise that he observed the Japanese men drinking whiskey throughout the meal. This somewhat offended his perception of the role of whiskey and he wondered how drinking hard liquor in this way did not produce a nation of alcoholics. This, of course, is where the *mizuwari* (whiskey with water) comes in because the alcoholic content can be modified to one's liking.

So far we have identified three elements that make the development of the mixed drink into a popular beverage difficult. First, the idea that mixing dilutes the quality of the superior item—that the cocktail developed in a very mixed society, the United States, seems no accident. Second, blending into the social group is more important than assertion or the display of one's individuality, and the cocktail requires individual attention. Third, the drink selected usually lasts the whole occasion, from before the meal, during it, and on until you feel like stopping.

Still, drinking is no longer the domain of the male; women have changed the pattern in many societies. There is really no social convention in Japan that frowns upon women drinking, and as in many other countries, the courting ritual often takes the form of the girl and boy sharing a drink. However, the cocktail in Japan is regarded more as a female's drink, and in fact suitable for those who really don't like alcohol. When we probed into this aspect in research we conducted among young, office girls who were presumed to be not as bound by social convention as their elder sisters, we found that they were reluctant to deviate from the drinking pattern of their boyfriends. Lest it be said that this is a reflection of the subservient status of the Japanese female, I must contend that this is only seeing the surface; it is of little relevance if you are trying to market gin or vodka. I was struck by the fact that the young women's comments implied a desire to share with their male companions, and this is the very essence of sake drinking that I described earlier and that has developed over the century. The Japanese woman drinks whiskey and water and beer quite often, drinks that are regarded in the West as essentially masculine. Yet even among females, whiskey was more easily acceptable than vodka or gin. Why McDonald's and not Smirnoff? Japan has had a long tradition of their own kinds of fast foods and as the *akogare* (yearning) for the U.S. developed, there was already a cultural base for McDonald's entrance. Mixed drinks, on the other hand, have had to develop in a culture where a similar tradition was hitherto nonexistent.

10

The Inventors of the Non-Religious Pilgrimage

Doing the Japanese Thing When Traveling Overseas

The Greatest Pleasure in Life and You Can Have Your Religion at the Same Time

The Japanese, like the British of yore, are inveterate travelers except that, unlike the British, their travels had been confined to their small islands. They like to see themselves as an island nation like Great Britain, and while there are some similarities, intercourse with the neighboring continent is not one of them. And the quest for an empire occurred rather clumsily and only in the last half century, with a pattern that had nothing to do with the establishment of the great British Empire. Although the literature of Japan shows the people's love of travel, this tended to be restricted quite severely under the feudal government of Tokugawa, and visas were required to cross the many borders of the clans. The checking station at Hakone was particularly notorious for its strictness and the near impossibility of breaking through. Despite all this the word *tabi* (travel) has strong emotional connotations and is said, in an old Japanese proverb, to be the greatest pleasure of life.

According to history, prior to the seventeenth century the Japanese traveled mainly for business, with some special "occupational" travels. Leisure travel by the average person is not evident in the records. However in the seventeenth century a strong centralized government emerged and in the process of consolidating the Japanese political order, travel became more popular. The beginnings of the pleasure trip (*tabi*) by the average person could be perceived.

One of the most representative was called *oise mairi* and its objective was ostensibly religious in that the destination was Ise shrine, the foundation of Shintoism. People of those early times tried to experience a great journey once in their lifetime, and it was usually a worshipping trip to the Ise shrine. Ise is symbolic of the Japanese tradition of ancestor worship and enshrines the emperor's ancestors, the ancestors of the Japanese race. It was the lifelong wish of the citizens of that time to embark on an extended trip on foot to where this shrine stood—midway between the current Tokyo and Osaka.

This Ise trip has similarities to a Moslem's pilgrimage to Mecca in that religion appears to be the prime motive. However, in the case of the Japanese there are very few religious taboos. All that was needed was to reach the Ise shrine and worship. On the way there were absolutely no conditions or precepts that one had to observe other than those normally imposed by society. Hence the resemblance between the *oise mairi* and the pilgrimage to Mecca is only superficial and in the case of the former fundamentally closer to the modern-day pleasure trip. The citizens of the day called upon the noted spots and ruins in the course of their travels, tasted the specialties of the various districts, and traveled in a completely tourist mood. In other words, their lifetime leisure work was that which satisfied two things: the sight-seeing urge and religious fervor.

These travels were seldom embarked upon alone, but rather in groups consisting, in many cases, of neighbors or work mates. (This followed the policy of citizen control by the government of the time.) For this I would like to note a book that has been keenly read by the Japanese since its publication two hundred years ago known as *Yaji and Kita's travel notes (Yajikita Dochuki)* or *Hiking down the Tokaido (Tokaido Hiza Kurige)*—Tokaido being the route that connected the administrative capital of Edo (now Tokyo) with the symbolic capital of Kyoto, where the Emperor resided. (Lovers of woodblock prints will be familiar with the exquisite series produced by Hiroshige of the fifty-three stops of the Tokaido.) The story concerns two men (friends) who save for a trip to Ise and finally set out from Edo and recounts how they traveled while having fun. It is one of the great humorous works in Japanese literature and has been a best-seller for two centuries. Even now it is continuously adapted for movies and T.V., and there is hardly a Japanese who does not know of it.

One notices on reading it, however, that not a scrap of religious feeling intrudes. The theme is purely the pleasures of travel and dwells on the unexpected happenings that befall the two, the embarrassments in strange places and how they laugh and are laughed at. Even today the book is hardly dated, is full of gags and humorous situations, and makes enjoyable reading. No book makes clearer the Japanese sense of anticipation toward *oise mairi*.

What is interesting in this instance is that the ostensible principle and the real motivation for travel by the Japanese are quite different. While the motivation is to have fun, this is not openly admitted; the Japanese attitude toward travel at the time was to bring out "religion," which was really the subsidiary motive. (The custom of *oise mairi* still remains with some of the older folk in the rural districts.)

Similar examples could be seen during the same period for the other religion—Buddhism. Zenkoji, a famous temple, was pivotal to a certain sect, but there was a commonly held belief that by worshipping at the temple once, one was assured a path to the Elysian field. Travel under these circumstances would appear to have a strong religious base but in fact, in this case, the age composition was heavily weighted toward the old, and it had strong overtones of a recreation trip for the senior citizens. From the seventeenth to the nineteenth centuries, old people belonging to this sect organized groups and embarked on trips to Zenkoji en masse, again without being bound by any commandments or taboos on the way, and when they reached the temple they prayed for their passage to the blissful land after their deaths. On the way back they would visit the hot spring resorts in the neighborhood—the districts around the temple simply abound with these—and spend delightful days at leisure.

Zenkoji, unlike the *oise mairi*, failed to give birth to literature such as the *Travel Notes*. But it has left a very famous saying: "To worship at Zenkoji, led by a cow." Just when the saying originated is not clear and very few modern Japanese know the supposed story behind it. An old lady was said to have been hanging out her wash, when a passing cow took one of the items and trotted off. The old woman pursued the cow and found herself in the Zenkoji temple—so she started to pray. But today, the Japanese use the saying to invoke a leisurely trip, in which one takes in the sights and pleasures on the way. It obliquely suggests that what happens on the way is more important than reaching the destination. As with haiku, the literal Westerner may find it hard to conjure up such an image from the terse saying. But the proverb could almost stand as a television commercial slogan for a Zenkoji trip, expressing a mood of relaxation and enjoyment.

The Japanese Travel: Looking at One's Reflections

These centuries of domestic travel have developed in the Japanese a very narcissistic tendency of examining everything in each locality in minute detail. Travel has always been a big industry, and the centuries of isolation have produced attitudes that have become basic even in today's overseas travel. In our research, repeated remarks by returned travelers were, "It was great because I was able to reevaluate myself as a Japanese." This self-consciousness is cultivated early with *shugaku ryokos*, three- to four-day school trips to places like Kyoto, the ancient capital, if you happen to live in the Eastern region. Temples, shrines, and historical relics are visited on these trips, with the tour guide continuously extolling the marvels of the past and imparting the feeling of historical continuity.

The key to Japanese travel is that it has to have a motive. In the past, it was religion, but what was gained was the enjoyment of being away from home. Bound to their clans and their rice paddies, travel was a lifetime adventure to be saved for over an extended period; it therefore had to have a serious motive. Though this is no longer the case, the older Japanese still insist on a defined objective, as if they feel guilt in traveling simply for pleasure. Once on the way, with the Japanese genius of not holding onto absolutes, pleasure naturally takes over. Once the motive has been provided they can indulge. There is even a Japanese saying to cover it: "Any shame committed on travel, can be written off."

In the days of the feudal Tokugawa, a single traveler could be an object of suspicion, but a delegation of villagers on their pilgrimage was not a matter of concern. The Japanese may have been the first to invent the group tour as a way of traveling for pleasure. Although the industrial revolution has ushered in a period of intensive drive toward work and little spare time, it has not been long enough to completely

erase values and attitudes of generations. In the area of domestic travel
this traditional form most certainly continues; in addition to school
excursions there are now annual company trips—and unlike business
conventions in the West, wives are not invited.

The domestic travel market is, by definition, the domain of the
Japanese and is of little interest to the foreign marketer—the airlines,
the travel agents, hotels, etc.—or so it may seem. Actually it helps the
foreign travel marketer to know the traditional attitudes. Japan just has
not had the tradition of overseas travel for the average person, though
selected persons were, of course, sent overseas, even during the so-
called closed period. When the country opened its doors, first under
the duress of Commodore Perry's guns but later with great gusto,
overseas travel developed in stages. The first stage was the aristocratic
traveler, much as in eighteenth- and nineteenth-century England, and
these intellectuals had a profound influence on Japan. In politics, John
Stuart Mill's *On Liberty* and other nineteenth-century works were immediately translated and hotly debated; even a parliamentary system,
superficially modeled on the British, was introduced. In literature,
translations of Shakespeare were already available in the late 1800s,
and Soseki, the father of the modern Japanese novel, spent two years at
Cambridge and contributed marvelous vignettes of turn of the century
London. In an even more remarkable experiment, Western music was
brought to Japan from the United States and immediately ordered into
the standard curriculum of the schools—Japan now has a vibrant community of musicians in the Western discipline and some first-rate
orchestras. Painters with such names as Fujita and Umebara were now
seen in the cafés of Montmartre. There is even a record of a young
Japanese of the merchant class who, having worked for the French
legation, somehow wangled a trip abroad to learn French cooking, but
unfortunately died in the streets of Paris as an innocent bystander of
the Commune uprising. Those were heady times for the privileged
few who could get abroad, and the excitement still lingered when I
was a small boy in the outskirts of Tokyo.

Alas, the dark clouds of war and the militarist adventurism of the
thirties snuffed out this enormous intellectual curiosity, but the duration, looking back now, was mercifully short. The postwar period in
Japan lasted until 1963 as far as overseas travel was concerned. Travel
was still restricted by the government because of the scars of war and

the acute awareness on the part of the leaders—but not necessarily the man on the street—of strong anti-Japanese feelings in many parts of the world. (Of course, there was also a lack of foreign currency, and this was another important reason.) Memories of Pearl Harbor, the Bataan death march, the Burma-Siam Railways, Changi, were far too vivid for the Japanese to travel with peace of mind. I know; I was in Sydney those days and it would not have been safe for a Japanese to step into a pub on a Saturday afternoon.

Even if cut off from the world because of defeat and past behavior, life must go on, and unlike the late 1800s and the early 1900s, those who were now permitted to travel were businessmen engaged in export sales, journalists, and students—the latter with a similar mission as during the Meiji period, but this time the mecca was the United States, not Europe.

In the late fifties and early sixties, once Japan was readmitted into the international community, some pleasure travelers began to emerge; but like the travelers of the seventeenth and eighteenth centuries, they too were required to provide a serious reason for the trip. So groups were leaving the Japanese shores with such objectives as research, surveys, inspections, and attending academic conventions. In the early days when the villagers who were selected to go "abroad" (to other parts of Japan) returned, they were greeted by the whole village and were expected to regale them with stories of their experiences. They were expected to bring back something of the outside and thus enrich the community. The Japanese traveler prior to 1964 still carried the same feeling of obligation; there was a sense of mission that they too, having been privileged to go abroad, should contribute something of benefit to their country as a result.

Travelers With a Mission

Just a few exerpts would show that the selected travelers of the late fifties and early sixties were not the same in their perception of travel as their later compatriots. *The World Through These Eyes*, a preliberalization book, published in 1958, written by Tadao Yoshida, the president of the world's largest manufacturer of fasteners, Y.K.K., is a record of Yoshida's business travels. Business talks and inspections of factories in various places occupy most of the book, and read now, it seems more like a succession of business memoranda and lacks interest to the general reader. However, because of the very special privilege awarded him to travel abroad, this book sold well and became a topic of conversation by people who envied the author's luck. He states in a postscript:

So long as one operates a business, one must not be ignorant of the moves in the world economy. Surely, there is no true development of business unless I research with my own eyes in my own way rather than rely on what is reported through the eyes and pens of others. This was my motive for travel. . . . Utilizing this precious experience to the full, I hope to contribute in the future to my utmost powers by working for my company and my country. . . ."

The book typifies the attitude of that time that business was a perfectly clear motive and the sense of obligation that accompanied it was dedicated to the country and to the enterprise.

A Traveller's Journal by Soich Oya, published in 1959, is in another genre, being the reportage of the various countries of the world by a noted Japanese journalist. There is no fixed theme and the reporting is fairly simple, introducing sundry aspects of various countries. The author compiled his overseas reports into a runaway best-seller, but his following words are of interest to us as indicative of his attitude toward travel.

The desire to escape from my current daily routine was heightened to the state of a biological urge and there are times when I can't keep still. At such times, I would literally pawn my wife [to raise the money] to set forth on travel. . . . Surely, the greatest pleasures of travel is to dream about the unknown world?"

In the days when overseas travel was still not freely available, the author cleverly used his profession to satisfy the desire for world travel. The fact that his overseas reportings became the best-seller of the time was probably because he spoke to the many Japanese who were not permitted to travel and satisfied some of their curiosity.

I'll Look at Anything by Makoto Oda was published in 1961. As one of the only reasons for overseas travel available to the author, he went as "a student abroad" to Harvard and stayed for several years. On his way back, this unknown youth (twenty-eight at the time) traveled through the Near and Middle East and Southeast Asia on a shoe-string. He collected his notes over approximately six months. When the book was first published, it became an immediate runaway best-seller and was still being widely read ten years after its first ap-pearance. It is famous as a travel book of the Japan modernized by the Meiji restoration, and the book has sold more copies than any other of its kind. In substance, this is not a simple travel book like the others; it is a record of the reactions of a young Japanese man to foreign cultures and, specifically, to the gap between the United States, worshipped at the time as the pinnacle of world power, and the underdeveloped countries. Furthermore, it records the rebirth of nationalism in a Japa-nese youth who was seeing his homeland from many points of the earth.

This book captivated many Japanese youths and created a minor boom for shoestring travel. Through his book, Makoto Oda became, in one leap, the opinion leader of the Japanese younger generation. To this day he is still in the limelight though now he is a middle-aged radical. At the time he described his feelings as follows:

I thought, now let's just go to America. The reasons were very simple. It was one of the two great powers on which our survival or demise depended, and for better or worse she represented the ultimate to which our civilization had reached or brought to a stall; if that society was shaking, just to what extent; if it was solid, how secure was the homestead; these were the things I wanted to see firmly with my own eyes. . . . I think the fact that I was fond of modern American literature, undiscriminatingly, was one of the factors that drove me to America. . . . The things I especially craved to see in America were the skyscrapers in New York, the Mississippi River, and the plains of Texas."

This one overseas travel book changed his destiny, making him the center of an anti-establishment movement and an internationally known personality in the peace movement. It was said that for at least a few years his living expenses were provided for by the income from this one book. Overseas travel could, in Japan, in those recent days, suddenly produce a hero. And the beginning was his yearning for American literature, skyscrapers, the Mississippi River, and the plains of Texas.

The last of the preliberalization books was *Dew Drops of Travel* by Kakuzo Matsutani, published in 1962. In it are travel sketches from the president of a wholesale company that handled the products of a French chemical firm. Before leaving for a round-the-world trip his words were:

I was born near the 99 *ri* [mile] beach. Morning and nights, without being overly conscious of it, I spent my days gazing at the distant horizon. And I pictured in my mind, the America and the Europe which lay beyond that horizon. These countries which were pictured in my mind, in my own way, swelled as the years went by. In order to nurture the America and Europe in my dreams, I just stared at the distant horizon. . . . These were incomparable moments of pleasure for my awakening and retiring moments. I continued to hold and nurture my faint dreams of boyhood. I am now at the airport to visit America and Europe—pictured in my dreams and nurtured. My heart beats fast and refuses to be calmed, because of my emotions.

The sixty-year-old Matsutani was aquiver with emotion because he was embarking in reality to the land of his dreams. The honest joys are well described. This book was published in a rather unusual form. Strictly speaking, it was not published for sale, but as a private edition printed for Mr. Matsutani for distribution among close acquaintants and friends. Thus it has none of the pretensions and embellishments of the usual travel book. The narrative form is simple and relaxed—a colloquial mood as if speaking to his wife and children. While there are many reasons for the Japanese to travel, such cases as Mr. Matsutani's—the fulfillment of a boyhood dream—seem to be quite common even for the middle-aged generation.

In the early sixties, I was able to observe a Japanese travel group first hand. My boss at the time was one of the first Australians to take an active interest in creating an industrial productivity movement in Australia. The Australian Productivity Center was created, but those engaged in the movement were purely volunteers, unlike its Japanese counterpart, which was funded by the government and boasted and still boasts of a large full-time staff housed in its own building. It was through my then boss' efforts that a Japanese visited Australia to explain how the Japanese productivity movement was set up—this was long before the Japanese had become famous with their quality circles. Susumu Morota was a veteran who was fluent in English and mixed easily with Westerners. Australia and its relaxed environment was a new experience for him and he became quite an enthusiast for the country. When he returned to Japan he talked to all his friends about the charms of Australia and thus the first delegation of top-level Japanese businessmen to visit Australia was formed, headed by the late Mr. Tashiro, the chairman of Toray.

The mission was hosted by the Australian Institute of Management and the Chamber of Manufacturers, and an itinerary was duly drawn up. The delegation included, apart from Mr. Tashiro of Toray, senior executives from such companies as Fuji Film, Toppan (the largest printer in the East), Ajinomoto (the largest food manufacturer), as well as others of that ilk; in scale of operation there were few manufacturers in Australia that could match them. I was part of the team who looked after them, and I realized very quickly, since I understood their conversations in Japanese, that the real purpose for their visit to Australia was to satisfy their curiosity by "seeing" this continent. It was unlikely that the factory inspection tours and the various meetings contributed much to their stock of knowledge, but since this was the supposed purpose of the trip, they went through the motion dutifully. I know Syndey Harbor, Taronge Park Zoo, and the Blue Mountains were the key experiences that they sought.

Sombreros, Greyhound Bus, and *Women Alone in Alaska*

Once travel became liberalized the pool of overseas travelers naturally widened, and we began to see a new breed. Those awaiting the day of the lifting of the overseas travel ban—men and women, the eager young, the wealthy middle aged—all embarked on their trip. *Leaving the Sombrero to the Winds* by Minoru Nagao and published in 1966 was from one such person; the book contains the travel notes of an illustrator in his thirties.

The author was in charge of illustrating a serial novel in one of the weeklies. It was at a farewell party at the conclusion of this long serial that the feeling to escape overwhelmed him:

You are more often left with a lonely blankness than a feeling of relief when work for a very long serialization ends. This is followed by a sense of uneasiness of losing one piece of work until the next one comes along.

It was then that a certain novelist started to say that "I intend to travel to South America within the year" and my vacant, blank feeling was blown away. Rather than taking the completion of a stage in my work with uneasiness, I switched over at the opportunity.

The clear differences in motivation from the preceding travelers would not escape the reader.

Round America by Bus by Ichiro Ishi was published in 1966 and relates the wanderings of Mr. and Mrs. Ishi in America. Like *Leaving the Sombrero to the Winds*, it contains only notes of escape from one's own life-style, which were expressed as:

We thought we would go to America for the summer holidays. From the spring of the year before last, overseas travel had been so-called liberalized. Although one was restricted to $500 a year for taking out, anybody could freely leave the country and it seemed that travel fervor was suddenly being whipped up and I heard that planes to Hawaii were booked to capacity. I couldn't deny that I too was touched somewhat by this travel fever and mentioned touring America using the summer holidays (of two months). Astonishingly, my wife was all for it and made faces to indicate that she would be losing out if she didn't go herself.

The departure for America by this high school teacher and his wife was truly lighthearted.

Women Alone in Alaska by Sakae Kishi was published in 1969. The author, a spinster of thirty, is a mountaineer. Why did she head for Alaska?

I think I was about five years old when I first knew that there was such a place as Alaska in the world. At the time . . . there was a large picture book called *The Story of Dogs* that contained one on Alaskan sleigh dogs.

She said that her recollections when she was five stayed with her even in adulthood so she chose Alaska for her first overseas trip. Her purpose was simply to climb a mountain there in the 3,000 meter class. Her departure for Alaska was fairly impulsive as were Mr. and Mrs. Ishi's trip to America and Mr. Nagao's to Mexico.

The motives of the Japanese overseas traveler were changing toward a more impulsive nature after the liberalization of 1964. In each case, although the direct causes were different, the impulses were all set forth by image factors of the country (fairly strongly held since, in many cases, they involved childhood memories), picture books, fairy tales, literature, music. The so-called impulses were, therefore, firmly emotionally based. These travelers were the opening of the dam, and it took only a few more years for the situation to settle down to produce the current hordes of package tourists who simply extended their domestic travel attitudes to overseas trips.

European Travels by an Office Girl by Haruko Hattori was published in 1969. The book, which has the subtitle "Secret Hints for the Young Girl Traveling in Europe," is a guidebook that sets out to show how safe, cheap, and interesting it is for a young girl to travel alone. It is an individually written tour guide. In the book the author attempts to describe her motives:

I want to go to Europe. . . . Surely everybody has hopes like that. . . . However, some people lack the money, some the time, and some the courage to decide. I was, in the past, one of those without money, time, or courage. I didn't have a family who would just fork out the money for travel and I used to think that I would be fired if I was absent for a month and to start with, I had a timid nature. I even believed that overseas travel was the privilege of the wealthy.

But one day I decided "I will go to Europe" and that was the beginning of everything.

It was not possible to find, in any of her sentences, what motivated her to go to Europe. Perhaps she too acted on impulse. In any event, the Japanese woman has been proving to be a more independent consumer than the male, and this time it was in the travel category.

Charlie Walk—the Relaxed Mechanic From Melbourne Who Got the Raspberry in Japan

In the mid-sixties, before the avalanche of package tourists started to exit Japan, the attention of the airlines was on the business traveler. (Even now, advertising concentrates on the business traveler—the tour group end of the business is heavily dependent on the travel trade.) It was then that some of the airlines had started to examine their television advertising to the Japanese business traveler, and airlines are notorious in thinking that the same approach could be used throughout the world. Create a commercial in New York, dub it, and use it anywhere seemed to be the philosophy, which made sense only in that it saved production costs.

I remember only one of the commercials from a series that was created for a European airline; it caused quite a few comments in the

Western advertising community. The commercials were tested among Japanese businessmen and most left them nonplussed. The one I distinctly remember opened with a peaceful scene of an ordinary-looking fellow relaxing while dangling a fishing line. The voice-over announcement explained that this was Charlie Walk, a mechanic from Melbourne, Australia, who worked for the particular European airline. The story that unfolded was that this airline was so concerned about maintaining its planes that their mechanics need only work two days out of three, so they could relax every third day and return to work refreshed. This was how much this airline was prepared to go to maintain its service reputation.

This approach caused a stir because there is an unwritten law among airlines that safety must not be a feature in their advertising. The law is sensible in that with the latent fears some people have of flying, mentioning safety only draws their attention to the other possibility. Besides, on a common sense basis, it would be dangerous for an airline to feature safety because one crash could wipe out their claim—at least for a short time. The heavy emphasis on maintenance did skirt the forbidden area rather perilously.

However, the other airlines need not have worried about this approach as far as Japan was concerned. When the commercial was shown to them, the Japanese businessmen were stunned. They felt that any airline that took such a casual approach to maintenance was acting irresponsibly! After all, how can you expect a person to retain his sharp edge if he only worked two out of three days? Like the sportsman, the truly efficient worker was the one who put in long hours. But more fundamentally, pitted against the Japanese work ethic, the commercial stirred up unconscious resentment in the hardworking Japanese executives. The commercial was not shown in Japan.

Little Boy Lost—the Trials and Tribulations of the Early Japanese Business Traveler

The Japanese who crossed the ocean before 1964 were the samurais who were selected for their language ability and mettle. The other exceptions wrote books, some of which have been quoted. They were not representative of the average businessman and were in the minority. Americans, with the strength of the dollar and the English language—almost the international language—behind them, could respond to a foreign airline's appeal of exoticism; this was not so for the majority of Japanese businessmen. As the demand for these warriors grew, a shortage soon developed. The succeeding waves were those who first had to spend time at a training center at the foot of Mt. Fuji learning how to use knives and forks, step back for ladies, eat soup the way a Westerner would, and tip the bellboy properly. But the assignment to go overseas was exciting enough until the send-off at Haneda Airport when the realization suddenly dawns that one was now on one's own in unfriendly foreign seas. Like magic, all the English conversation lessons were forgotten and helplessness set in.

The local branch of an international advertising agency decided to conduct its own motivational research among Japanese business travelers. The Western account supervisor had majored in psychology and had an excellent research background. What came out of the study delighted his Freudian heart. The research revealed that the Japanese businessman embarking on his overseas assignment was ridden with anxieties, paramount being the language problem. It also showed that once he arrived at his destination he always had somebody from the branch or a local representative to meet him, to smooth the shock of entry to a foreign environment and assure him that his troubles will be over. While airborne and in transit he had no desire to be left to his own devices. No wonder he preferred Japan Air Lines; they extended his home environment until he reached his destination.

Faced with this data, our American advertising man sat down to develop an advertising concept and showed his Japanese colleagues how it's really done. First, it was obvious that the businessman was a helpless little boy being pushed out into the big world. Next, he pointed out that the research revealed that the businessman's greatest fear upon entering the aircraft cabin was its foreignness, and particularly the female. The blonde, friendly stewardess approaching him as he slunk in his chair was a veritable Brünhilde of towering dimensions. What to do if she speaks to you? Worse still, if you can't understand her or if she can't understand you! Such humiliation would be unbearable. The instinct was to beat an exit to the toilet or pretend to be asleep.

Put these together and you had an advertising concept that went like this. A little boy is taken to Haneda Airport and handed over to an, oh, so sweet, ground hostess. He is embarking on an overseas trip to meet his folks. On the plane he is looked after by a pretty blonde stewardess. Who would not want to be mothered by such a woman? Our Freudian friend also pointed out that it was well known that Japanese men like to be mothered. After this delightful experience on the plane the boy is duly handed over at a European airport to a smiling Asian couple. Now, the latter obviously represented, in the subconscious of the businessman, the local staff who will look after him from that point. So the scenario was set and the commercial was shot.

I regret to say that the reception given to the commercial was no better than that given to our Melbourne mechanic, Charlie Walk. Probes revealed a very simple fact: like Charlie Walk and his fishing, nobody identified with the situation. The little boy of Oriental heritage was never specifically identified as being Japanese, and probes revealed that many viewers thought that he was a Chinese residing in some part of Southeast Asia. It turned out to be inconceivable for any Japanese family to dispatch a boy of that age to an overseas destination unaccompanied, especially in the care of foreigners. Therefore the commercial depicted an overseas Chinese boy, probably in Hong Kong, traveling in a foreign airline, being greeted by an overseas Chinese family at a European airport. "What's that got to do with me?" asked the Japanese business traveler. So much for the advertising concept.

Overseas Travel Is Not a Leisure Activity

Package tours are always hectic affairs of the if-it's-Wednesday-this-must-be-Belgium–type. If this concept is at all conceivable, it is even more so if you join a Japanese group, which I have done on two occasions. The first was a trip to Europe when we found ourselves in the middle of the Tokyo summer with unexpected free time. At that late time of year it was easier, and not much more expensive, to join an organized overseas package tour as all the Japanese summer resort hotels were either completely booked or charged exorbitant rates for the odd days available. The hotel bills alone would have paid for a trip to Hong Kong and back. The package we joined—to several European countries—was appropriately called Look Tour and is, in fact, the largest of its kind. The group was an incredible mixture ranging from the operators of small businesses in a provincial city, traveling without their wives, to a widow in her sixties whose late husband's unfulfilled ambition was to see London—the lady, without a word of English, set forth in London and promptly got lost without remembering the name of the hotel—a medical student, an office girl from a provincial capital, and so on. Presiding over the group was an intensely worried young man who later confided to us that at the age of thirty-one he had developed ulcers and was hoping for an easier job. A tour group leader's, and in fact the agent's, social responsibilities are substantial and are distinct from any legal requirements. If an airplane crashes the tour agent gets involved and has to go through a considerable amount of work in helping family members of the victims—normally the sole responsibility of the airlines in other parts of the world.

The group leader was, at first, far from happy to see himself landed with a foreign family; he had enough worries. But by the time the group happily disbanded, I believe we were his favorites—we were the only ones that were not totally dependent on him. The fact that such a hodgepodge could form a group and happily go their way may seem a contradiction to what I have earlier said about the tightly knit and self-contained "primary group." Their group shared one thing in common—except for us, everybody was Japanese. Once outside their own country they banded together to forge a tight primary group and the airline and hotel staffs became the secondary group with whom they came into contact. The rest, in the tertiary group, did not exist for all intents and purposes as social contacts.

Actually, this temporary forging of travelers into a group also has historical precedence in Japan. The *hatagos*, the inns in the old days, brought together a hodgepodge of travelers, sometimes in groups but most often individually. Once under the roof of the *hatago*, the idea was that you entered a temporary family. The sliding paper doors did not have locks and that night's guests shared a common fate. The temporary nature of the group is implicity acknowledged. I have observed groups that formed very quickly only to disband equally quickly when the common fate dissolved. Our Look group also disbanded, and although name cards were exchanged, further contacts were unlikely. The one exception was the medical student and the office girl who, completely unnoticed by the group, must have formed a personal attachment, for about a year or so later we ran into them at the ballet.

None of the group members, except ourselves, had been overseas before. To sit with them was to realize how momentous the event was to people who have never been in direct contact with another culture. Americans, with the multiplicity of ethnic groups within their own culture, and Europeans, who share numerous borders with one another, cannot possibly conceive the likes of such a group. The tour was definitely not for rest, relaxation, or fun. It was to satisfy a tremendous curiosity about the unreality of the outside world. It was a revelation to me as the continuous "oohs," and "ahs" were uttered at things and events that Westerners would not normally notice. As the bus crossed the border between Switzerland and France on the way to Mont Blanc there was tremendous excitement and the cameras were out—of course, there are no borders in Japan. In Spain it became evident that we were not going to keep up with the group. What with jet lag and the time differences, our eyelids were heavy by the time the flamenco dancers came out (after midnight), so we cut out and went back to our hotel. There was an optional tour to Toledo that next morning, starting at 6:00 A.M., but we slept in. We were the only ones that exercised our option. A few years later we again found ourselves with a few days to spare, so we joined a group going to Bali, but we had learned our lesson. We stayed on the beach most of the day and joined the group in the evening for the dance feasts. There are no beaches like them in Japan, but that did not constitute an experience to the rest of the group members, who managed to squeeze in an hour or two before and after the guided tours. The idea that a vacation could be spent overseas lying on the sand for a few weeks or staying in one spot relaxing is still inconceivable for most Japanese. The rich, of course, do have their villas in Japanese summer resorts, but the target-oriented Japanese feel guilty if all they do on an overseas trip is to relax.

In early 1983 there was an international market research conference in San Francisco, and the Japan Market Research Association duly got up a group. My colleague, who also happens to be an Australian, was nominated to represent us. After a direct flight from Tokyo to San

Francisco he was looking forward to going to his hotel and cleaning up. Yet after a ten-hour flight the group boarded a chartered bus at the airport to go on a guided tour of the city. After all, there was still a full afternoon ahead.

11

How It's Being Said Is More Important Than What Is Being Said

The Relationship Between Japanese Labor Negotiations and Consumer Behavior

Sandwiched Between My American Boss and My Japanese Staff

Japan is a country that has few wildcat strikes; management is usually forewarned, at least by a few weeks or at most by several months of a pending strike. Even its probable duration is announced, though most strikes end sooner than expected. Labor negotiations are always conducted in the spring, and the ritual is called the Spring Offensive. For the Western manager all this seems silly at first and unnecessarily time-consuming because the outcome is predictable to both management and labor. However, once you get used to the system, there are some significant advantages. I must confess, though, I will never quite reach the state of enjoying the ritual. The negotiating table is an important area of communication and enables management to learn what the staff thinks about them. In the strictly structured day-to-day environment, the only other way to get a candid picture is to go out drinking with the boys and piece together the inebriated comments that have a degree of seriousness that cannot be ignored. At the negotiating table employee views are presented as a group, where there is considerable security and no individual offense in telling the boss that he is really mismanaging the company. Management can then present a counterargument or defend its policy.

To the Western reader this must seem more like a shareholders' meeting than a labor-management confrontation. Shareholders' meetings in Japan last, on the average, about ten minutes and there is rarely any open discussion. There are enough books written about this aspect of Japan so I need not go any further than to say it is okay to treat shareholders in a cavalier manner, but woe to management who does not show its sincerity to the staff by spending interminable hours listening to their suggestions and complaints. Everytime I go to the United States I come back madly jealous of the men who carry the title chairman and the respect their words carry and the terror they strike in the hearts of lesser mortals. Maybe its just me—I have the title, but you might as well say it's a different job.

Another advantage the Spring Offensive system offers is that since everybody is doing it at the same time, a total community consensus is obtained. There are deviations from the national average but that is based on known performance of the respective industries. So if your competitor gives a 6 percent raise to his employees, the chances are that you will do roughly the same. Cost-wise, the competitive balance is preserved and so none of this business of a militant union sending you to the wall or an obstinate management creating a prolonged dispute.

So it came as a shock to everyone in Japan when this very orderly labor force seemed to go temporarily insane. It was the year of the oil shock. Great anxiety gripped the nation and the housewife was buying enough detergent and toilet tissue to last for twelve months. There was inflation of 25 percent and wage demands of 35 percent. Foreign companies were particularly badly hit because they were rightly suspected of considering such demands not accompanied by a corresponding rise in profits to be irrational and unreasonable. Unions sprang up in many companies and many Western managers reacted with hostility to the situation, turning some of them militant, for which they still suffer. It all seems so unnecessary now.

Although we are a small company—about seventy full-time employees at the time—we were not exempt from the turmoil. A small group of workers walked into my office one day during the oil shock when our business seemed to be in temporary suspension—what's the use of measuring the detergent market when everybody is frantically buying up anything in sight—and announced they were representing the Employees' Mutual Consultation Committee. I was stunned. Call it what you may, this was a euphemism for a pending union.

Their purpose was to negotiate and ensure that they were not left behind in wage settlements. Clearly I had a serious problem on my hands for which I had not been trained. It wasn't really that long since the company had turned the corner in writing off accumulated losses—as is true everywhere, it took a few years for us to become established and start making profits, and the head office was not prepared to let us slide back into a loss situation.

The argument that everybody else in Japan does it never got very far with my chairman in the States. He does, to this day, maintain that in the crunch, the Japanese businessman is no different from the American. The branch manager represents the head office to the staff, so he will be fired if he doesn't discharge his duties. The employees know this so there is a certain amount of trade-off—sometimes they will compromise and settle for the devil they know rather than have him replaced by someone tougher. However, this play must be made with great subtlety because neither side—head office or local staff—can tolerate a branch manager who is too skewed one way.

I am convinced that a Western branch manager has more problems in Japan because of the reversed pecking order in the importance rating when making corporate decisions—in the West: stockholders, management, and employees; in Japan: employees, management, and stockholders. So in tough business situations in Japan, profits are sacrificed first, next senior management takes salary cuts, and finally bonuses and overtime cuts for the average employee. The possibility of lay-offs is never mentioned although they do occur—euphemistically called voluntary retirement. Japan is a country of euphemisms.

Pierre Marquis, my chairman, was an entrepreneur and an excellent delegator. However, he is not a patient man—like many American entrepreneurs—and it was my duty to keep him away from long-winded Japanese negotiations. Unlike me, he did not have the Japanese instinct to avoid confrontation. But as the sign on Harry Truman's desk said, "The buck stops here," and a good boss is the person you pass the buck to—which was exactly what I did. Since assuming the top spot in Japan, I am sorely aware that there is no exit for me now except out the window.

Via an overseas phone call, I explained about the demands that were being made and added that this was going on all over Japan and most management seemed to be giving in—this last statement was like waving a red flag in front of a bull. Pierre pointed out that ours was a small firm, that we only recently started to make money, and that we could not be compared with the Mitsubishi's and the IBMs in what we do and what we are expected to do. I wonder how many Western branch managers are capable of standing up to a logical onslaught of this kind from their boss. As I've said earlier, it is sometimes a disadvantage to be a Westerner fluent in Japanese; I would also add that it is a disadvantage in many cases for a Western branch manager in Japan to put forth the Japanese viewpoint too strongly. The comment "He's been in Japan too long" has been the kiss of death to many a Japan expert—the implication being that he has lost his objectivity and therefore can be a hindrance rather than an asset to an international firm.

If you want to keep your job there is less danger in stressing the illogicality of the Japanese than in trying to explain the differences to your boss—"I've heard it all before" is the best you can expect. Needless to say, this eventually leads to isolation of the branch manager from his local staff, a general mistrust in management, and another disillusioned or bitter Western senior executive who is equally distrustful of the Japanese. But this is not a Japanese conspiracy. A Japanese company that handles the situation in a Western manner will—and some do—find itself with serious labor problems too.

The Western head office has another serious disadvantage and that is communication. The absence of the ultimate decision-making personnel from the daily scene prevents the sort of daily contact management in which the Japanese excel and which informs and involves the employees in the decision process. Such a system means more local control than many Western companies are prepared to give their branches.

The Japanese Art of Negotiation

The brief excursion into management philosophizing was meant to be a preamble to what happened rather than a serious discourse. After all, there has been a spate of books on this subject, for example, Richard Tanner Pascale and Anthony G. Athos' *The Art of Japanese Management* as well as many fragmentary observations by Peter Drucker. So we return to the oil shock, high wage demands, and a poor business outlook—the latter turning out to be resoundingly wrong.

I did exactly what most branch managers would have done. I decided to let my chairman find out for himself, which he was dying to do and which he would have done anyway. If he blew it, he at least couldn't pass the buck.

So Pierre came roaring in and found the strange ambivalence of the Japanese. Still the same courteous people when meeting individually in the usual workplace, they turn into a solid mass of disagreers when together as a group. However, he had two things going for him: he was a doer and the man who had built the company. The Japanese have a genuine respect for the founder and are not by instinct knockers. To the Japanese, founders have passion and conviction, qualities that are often lacking in professional managers, and contrary to the stereotype of the bureaucratic Japanese business managers, many of Japan's companies are led by founder/innovators with strong personalities—Matsushita, Honda, Morita of Sony, to name a few. Since such men of action are rather more conspicuous in this society, they are looked upon as models of leadership; the Matsushitas and Hondas of today are the Nobunagas and Hideyoshis, the historical warlord heroes, of yore. They can break tradition and be applauded for their courage in doing so.

Apart from these personal assets, Pierre also had a weapon—he did not speak a word of Japanese. This meant that everything he said had to be interpreted and anything that didn't come through could be blamed on bad interpreting or on different customs and manners. He did not have to follow formal Japanese protocol—a very important advantage he had over me. When said in Japanese, some things could cause a war, but they are listened to with bemusement and put down to the Westerner's eccentricity when propounded in English. By the way, interpreters usually modify wordings to fit the Japanese form and sometimes pointedly refuse to say anything that would be, to the Japanese ears, offensive. When Pierre came to town, I was the interpreter. Despite my competence in both languages, I don't like interpreting because it is a strain to continuously shift conceptual gears; I now usually refuse the role.

I had made up my mind to go along with Pierre; not only was it my duty to do so, but there is nothing more cowardly than trying to be a friend to both sides. Mediation is one thing, toadying is another. I decided that if Pierre went too far, I could always candidly debate the situation with him later; I kept my fingers crossed that this would not be necessary. Aside from some filtering when interpreting, I could not stop Pierre from saying what he wanted. But then, he was a good businessman and not likely to push the button.

In due course a meeting was arranged with the nonexecutive employees. Generally, unless you are a Matsushita, it is not a good idea, in the Japanese context, for the big boss to show up in front of the nonexecutive staff in a situation of negotiation because his is the last word and does not allow for compromise. On the other hand, it is more than appropriate that he seek an area of communication where company policy could be explained. There should never be a shoot-out at the O.K. Corral unless you are prepared for permanent damage. Diplomats rather than cowboys are necessary, but maybe this viewpoint reveals my Japanese bias. No doubt Pierre was prepared to pull his gun if necessary. In essence, the representative American attitude under these circumstances is that if you give way even an inch, you will have to continue to give way in the future. The Japanese attitude is that you give away an affordable amount on condition that if things get worse some of it may be taken back—it puts the other under certain obligations and leaves room for further negotiations.

The retreat by Japanese management that year—with scarcely a fight, just enormous wage increases—bewildered many Western managers. At an international conference held not too long after this turmoil, Mr. Morita, the chairman of Sony, was asked why Japanese management conceded to the enormous wage demands and how did they expect to absorb such large labor cost increases. Morita's answer was that the cost was probably not as high as industrial turmoil, and since profits over the years were high, it was exactly the right time for many corporations to carry the one-time burden. This is exactly what happened: Japanese management bought industrial peace and the price was not very high, just a one-time increase, and labor cost increases have been kept less than in most advanced industrial societies ever since. This philosophy of sacrificing immediate returns for possible future gains is conspicuously absent in U.S. management circles, and I had not the ability to communicate this to Pierre, nor would he have been inclined to listen.

With such differences in attitudes and temperament, Pierre and I certainly made a strange combination. When we entered the conference room, the American entrepreneur was prepared to pull his gun, and the local manager wanted to follow his instincts, developed over ten years in Japan, to compromise. However, our objective was the same: to pull everyone together and get on with business. What we lacked, in those days, in sophistication, we made up for with earnest striving for accomplishment. So the meeting started with Pierre explaining, with his usual passion, the corporate standpoint. That the company could only do so much under circumstances of such business uncertainty. However, the whole thing was a little bit of an anticlimax as the passion was all on one side and we faced a wall of impassivity. Pierre was therefore forced to keep talking and inevitably to repeat himself—something an interpreter becomes acutely aware of. As the interpreter, I was having considerable trouble getting his directly phrased English into appropriate Japanese. (Incidentally, never ask your local top management to act as an interpreter, no matter how good his language ability—it merely downgrades them and makes them look like incompetent "yes men.") I hasten to add that I always volunteered for the role; it would not have occurred to Pierre to ask anybody else.

"If You Don't Like It, You Can Quit" Is Not Japanese Logic

Pierre followed the Western rule of debate, which is the only rule he knows. We tend to forget the Greek origin of this form of resolving differences and don't realize that it was only recently introduced into Japan. The nonverbal form of communication that the Japanese love to call *haragei* (stomach art) means psyching out the other guy with subtle demonstrations of reserve power. The guy who shoots off his mouth too readily is considered rather superficial, particularly when the subject matter is of importance and affects the livelihood of those involved. So when Pierre called for questions, there were none. When he asked if anybody disagreed, there was total silence. Silence of this kind, exerted by a group, can put tremendous pressure on the speaker. His natural instinct is to try to break the impasse and that invariably means that he goes a step further than intended.

Now on the defensive, since nobody has said anything, Pierre said "I suppose you all understand and agree with me?" Silence. Then the breaking of the taboo, "Well, all of you who agree with me raise your hands." Nobody moved. "Does that mean, you all disagree with me?" Silence. The ones who were in the best position were the key Japanese staff. With all that torrent of words it was becoming difficult to unscramble areas of agreement and disagreement, and they couldn't possibly be seen to agree with everything that was being said. This much I explained to Pierre. I had now departed from my role as an interpreter and was committing the unpardonable sin of explaining Japanese form to a foreigner in front of the Japanese staff.

So Pierre changed his tactics and stepped over the final line. "Nobody need be forced to work for a company he doesn't like. But so long as you remain, the company is entitled to expect that you abide by its decisions. Anybody who disagrees should raise his hand." I thought, well this is it. Perhaps it was the moment of peace the condemned feels while waiting for the executioner, or perhaps it is the same feeling as when the soul leaves the body and looks down on the throng with detachment; in any case I suddenly felt a sense of tranquility. Most would understand that much English, so I didn't bother to translate; Pierre must have arrived at the same conclusion because he did not insist. It may have given the impression of my trying to distance myself from my boss but that was not intended. The shock that the situation may have been irretrievably lost probably put me in a state of resignation.

Why such a state of shock? Because to the Japanese an employer is supposed to be the custodian of the employees' entire remaining life. A Japanese president can reprimand and punish his employees, but he is not allowed to turn any out because of disagreement, no more than a father would kick his child out of the home because of disobedience. Similarly, only a minority of employees would think of changing jobs as their first option—though of course this does occur and figures can be cited showing that lifetime employment applies only to the larger companies. But the difference is in priorities. Working in the Western context, I changed jobs several times till I settled into the current one, and each time I changed it was because I wanted to improve my position or pay, but actually both. It certainly was not an action of last resort, as it is in Japan.

The Western president strives to retain the ablest; the Japanese president contrives and maneuvers to get the most out of the average.

You can show this conceptual difference with two baseball teams. The first team has some stars batting close to the .4s but the rest will be lucky to be in the early .2s. The second team doesn't have any stars but just about everybody bats around .25 or slightly over. An experienced team manager may opt for the second team because it produces more closely fought but winning games. Is it because of the employees' sense of values that companies become constituted this way or is it because of corporate policy? It's a chicken or the egg question. Having had to shift my way of thinking in the past eighteen years I am inclined to believe it is the culturally based values of the individual employees that gradually constitute the character of the company and that it is difficult for a manager, no matter how strong-willed, to buck them. For the reverse reasoning, I believe the jury is still out on whether the so-called Japanese management system, which has become a fad in the U.S., will be successful in the long run in cultures that do not share this bottom-up tendency.

If lifetime employment is a professed basic policy of industry, even if not actually a fact, it stands to reason that it is more difficult to relocate in Japan. The Westerner generally changes jobs to try something new or go up the ladder, but in Japan relocation may not be accompanied by an absolute gain. For example, you move to a smaller company who needs your experience and credentials acquired by the training in a larger company; you receive a higher remuneration but the trade-off is that you lose the higher social status of working for the larger corporation. These are not steps taken lightly. "If you don't like it you can go elsewhere" is barely a reasonable option. Considering the depressed state of today's economy, it is that way in the United States and Australia now too, but the difference is that it is a temporary phenomenon imposed by economic circumstances; in Japan it's a long-term state based on deeply rooted social values.

Fortunately, Pierre's statement was so far out of the Japanese staff's conceptual framework that they were astonished rather than angry. Since the seed was sown, it meant that I had to try just that much harder in the following years to demonstrate the company's sincerity—a favorite Japanese word—but in the long run that was not a bad thing. I almost forgot to mention that nobody quit on the spot though we did lose a few sometime later.

The Process Is More Important Than the Decision

This book is not about industrial relations in Japan or about the art of Japanese management, about which plenty has been written of late. The extended preamble was to show how the attitudes reflected in labor-management negotiations affect consumer behavior. The confidence the consumer places on brands has its foundation in the importance of corporate identity and springs from the sort of cultural attitudes I have described. The Japanese consumer is not satisfied with the short-term promise of a product but on whether the corporation has the ability to fulfill such a public pledge. In a "blind" test many products are not discernably different from their main competitors, but the perception of the corporation to deliver may give a particular brand an edge in the marketplace and we must take that into account. So the Japanese companies place enormous importance to after-service—if the village carpenter doesn't do a decent job with that cupboard he was asked to put in for Mrs. A, the rest of the village will soon learn about it. Public apologies proliferate and corporations would rather settle quickly and publicly humiliate themselves than fight consumer claims. Such gestures of sincerity are interpreted as meaning that the act of negligence is not likely to be repeated.

Pressures are exerted but they are social rather than legal. A corporation goes to great lengths to avoid going to court. Japan, with half the population of the United States, has only as many lawyers as the state of Illinois. Whether the consumer is better protected through legal or social means can make an interesting topic for debate, there are many pros and cons. But one thing is obvious, the Japanese approach is far more emotional than the American, and this extends to product selection with greater emphasis on the nebulous qualities of brand image. A recent scandal involving the largest department store in Japan, Mitsukoshi, revealed that the store was charging enormous prices for fake Persian antiques. It was not, however, the exorbitant prices that upset everybody but the betrayal of social trust by not correctly vetting the authenticity of the merchandise. As far as I know, no private legal actions have been instituted by individual consumers, but Mitsukoshi has suffered enormously through a drastic drop in sales as a result of a collective, though not overtly stated, boycott.

Returning then to our internal crisis, what would have been a logical challenge in the U.S. was verboten in Japan. There were, however, two things that saved the day. One was our chairman's obvious straightforwardness and faith in what he said. He was not indulging in political maneuvering to reach a compromise later, but acting with the utter conviction that he was right. The Japanese, the eternal compromisers, have difficulty handling this sort of attitude. The second element was even more important and that was the final value judgment by the Japanese employees to go for harmony rather than confrontation. As I have pointed out, if lifetime employment is postulated as an ideal, then the company cannot indulge in layoffs, let alone in firings. The converse is that if the company went under, the employees are in serious trouble for if everyone practiced lifetime employment there would be no other jobs available. The majority of Japanese unions are company based rather than industrial, and this prevents them from pushing the company to the extent that it may lose its competitive edge. In the case of a foreign company, there is, in addition, the fear that it may close shop and retreat. There have been several such cases that, considering the size of their operations, received more publicity in this respect than was warranted. But, it was still news to the media and implicit in their coverage was the reminder that this option was not open to Japanese companies.

As long as branch employees have this fear of the company simply pulling out and going back to where it came from—and if they are reminded that they work for unseen shareholders, a concept that is almost impossible for them to grasp—they will not show the renowned Japanese devotion to their company. Foreign companies then finish up in the worst of two worlds and are left wondering about the myth of the efficient Japanese work force. After we changed into an employee-owned company, incorporated in Japan, I noticed a remarkable change in morale even though the basic management personnel remain the same, at least in the Japanese component. Since the Japanese temperament favors gradual and steady transition rather than dramatic moves, there are fewer corporate coups to replace the president. When it does occur—as it did with the Mitsukoshi department store and not because of any dictatorial behavior by Mr. Okada, the president—it's because the president has allowed the corporation to lose face and social prestige, an unforgivable sin that would have led to a demand for hara-kiri in the olden days.

The incident that was called "the Marquis hurricane" created a great deal of internal discussion. In the West it would be a debate requiring a solution one way or the other. In Japan a resolution is not necessarily demanded and if there is a difference of opinion the discussion will be resumed another day. Sometimes these discussions will go on for so long without a resolution that eventually everybody gets tired of the issue and the whole thing simply fizzles out to wait the natural consequences or the next eruption. In a village, one serious error in judgment may disrupt the whole community, so rather than risk this it is considered preferable to let the situation drift. Since my U.S. boss could not stay forever, he dropped the bomb and departed, leaving the resolution in my hands—or perhaps I should say the nonresolution. From the staff's point of view it was, of course, senseless to indulge in a confrontation with a hardheaded U.S. businessman, and it was a lot wiser to take the whole matter up again with the hapless branch manager.

Since that traumatic experience, I have learned how the process of arriving at a decision is more important than the decision itself. I have also learned that the boss is not supposed to communicate orders downward in a one-sided way but to pose the problem, ask for opinions, select options, and in turn communicate the options downward. It takes a long time to arrive at a decision, but at least everybody has been informed and you receive a lot less flak afterward. The employees' association in our case, the unions in others, serve as an important sounding board for management, although many Western managers would consider the opinions offered by them as being presumptions and usurping of his function.

The Japanese corporation is not a place for the impatient. Not long after the Marquis hurricane, I made a decision that I wanted executed rather quickly and issued a memo to this effect. It came under considerable criticism and I had to call a meeting with the association. The representative of the staff, later to advance to management position himself, advised me of the general unhappiness with my decision. I went to great lengths to explain the logical base of the decision and wanted to know why they objected. "Ah," said the rep, "it is not the decision we object to, Fields san, but the way you made it." Incidentally, union heads invariably go on to management positions in a Japanese corporation, who regard the union as a testing ground for handling people and displaying leadership qualities. Senior management do not find it strange to have somebody sitting across the table arguing against them and a little later be sitting with them, on the same side of the table. It is not strange for the Japanese to regard role divisions as the result of circumstances beyond the individual's strict control. If the circumstances change, then there is nothing strange in having the roles change. Fixed positions are dangerous in corporations as well as in diplomacy, and absolute principles are more likely to cause wars than encourage peace. These days my expatriate staff tends to criticize my slowness and procrastination. In the early days, my Japanese staff used to criticize me in making decisions too quickly and capriciously. If I had a head office no doubt the comment would be that George has been in Japan too long.

In the strictly structured Japanese society it is difficult to get candid individual criticism. The association came right out and hit me with comments that immediately made me defensive. But the group anonymity enabled me to hear criticisms that would not reach the ears of the chief executives in a Western corporation. While at times I resented their comments, at least it afforded me an opportunity to take stock. Everytime I go to the States I am impressed with the tremendous power the chief executives yield, and I'm filled with envy. Respected for their authority, they are used to issuing directives. Their critics are the stockholders against whom they are sometimes put on the defensive; a critical staff member will more than likely leave, voluntarily or otherwise. In any country, including Japan, nobody gains by antagonizing the boss. Without the option to leave, the critical platform provided to the group acts as a safety valve for the functioning of the organization, a process individual Western staff members find frustrating and stifling.

When the Package Is More Important Than the Contents— Japanese-Style Marketing

The process described above, when translated into the area of marketing, leads the Westerner to comment "form before substance." To him it is the ultimate decision that is of importance and not the process that leads to it. It is like saying that the way in which a commercial is made is more important than what is said about the product. Western deductive reasoning requires major and minor premises to draw a conclusion. Then you start all over again. For the Japanese, results are only a moment in a flow of time and need not necessarily be conclusive. The phenomenon is induced and is transitory.

Chie Nakane, a Japanese female sociologist, was quoted in a *Newsweek* interview as saying that "the Japanese have no principles." The Western interpretation of her statement was not what she had intended to convey. It was another way of saying that the Japanese think in relative rather than in absolute terms and nothing is therefore considered as definite. The principle can be bent or changed if circumstances change. The Japanese have showed themselves as being extremely adept at completely turning around at certain moments in history. The Westerner may see this as duplicity and a lack of principle, but those do not exist here.

Thus the Royalist samurais, who were wielding their swords at the hairy barbarian invaders, decided that this was not the wisest course and, forming the Meiji government, strove to open the doors to Western technology. The surviving kamikaze pilots and those who were sharpening bamboo spears for the final resistance in World War II greeted MacArthur as the greatest savior of modern times and embraced democracy. This lack of absolutist positions creates the greatest problems in business when contracts are involved. The Westerner will stick to the letter of the law, and if there's any deviation he'll go to court; the Japanese will rewrite the contract to suit the changing circumstances.

So to repeat, what is said cannot be divorced from how it is said and the latter is, in turn, dependent on the circumstance that surrounds the act. Twice a year Japan goes on a binge of gift giving—to be precise, during December and the mid-summer months. To illustrate how important this gift giving is to marketing, more than half the Japanese homes never buy toilet soap—they are given enough on these two occasions to last the whole year. This custom of giving gifts demands that certain forms be observed; you just don't give any old thing, you match the recipient's status, and the dues given are what he deserves. Giving too many gifts, although not as troublesome as under-gifting, can cause embarrassment and be counterproductive.

When a Westerner buys a gift he will usually wrap it himself before giving it. This cannot happen in Japan; the gift must retain the original department store wrapper to be of any value. The newer department store chains run commercials featuring their wrapping papers. The same box of Lux toilet soap would be almost unacceptable if it came in a supermarket wrapper instead of the paper the Takashimaya department store uses. The Japanese logic is simple: if you cannot go to the courtesy and trouble of selecting the product from a decent store, you cannot be placing too much importance on the act. This is just like my decision that was delivered without the due process and therefore did not carry any weight with the staff. We knew the Mitsukoshi department store was in real trouble after the scandal when its crucial gift sales plummeted—the consumer, temporarily at least, did not want to identify with its wrapping paper.

The house brand concept—in which the cost to the consumer is reduced by minimum packaging—was introduced to Japan at the onset of slower growth. This concept, which caught fire in some parts of Europe, failed in Japan and the reasons are now obvious. The powerful Diaei supermarket chain—led by Mr. Nakauchi, a dynamic upstart, considered a maverick by the establishment—started with only a few stores several decades ago and has grown to be the largest retail chain in Japan, overtaking the prestigious department stores. But even Nakauchi could not make his house brands stick. Contrary to what has been happening in most advanced markets, in Japan the house brands have threatened the major brands only in those limited categories where corporate identification is not important.

In my Western marketing training I was taught that, in advertising, the concept took precedence over execution. In other words, if you had a good concept and poor execution all was not lost because you could always improve the latter. On the other hand the reverse was not possible—no matter how good the execution, it cannot save a bad concept. I would argue that in Japan poor execution can kill a good concept no matter how powerful the latter may be. The importance of form, as represented in packaging, and the importance of how you give the message, as represented in the execution of a T.V. commercial, cannot be overemphasized. How to say what you mean is difficult even for the Japanese among themselves. The following letter is from a twenty-three-year-old female store attendant to the *Asahi* newspaper.

As I am engaged in work that brings me in contact with people, I am always on tenterhooks on the words I choose. It happened when I was being trained on the job to acquire skills. On the last day, as an aside I said, "I was unable to do anything special. . . ." I meant to convey the feeling that I was not able to render great assistance, but the store person apparently did not take it that way. He seemed to have interpreted it as a protest for my not being taught enough. Thinking back on the manager's expression at the time, I regret that I had not said, "it was great that I could learn many things," but it is too late for me to offer any excuses now. On-the-job training, unlike part-time work, probably carries little expectation from the store of any real contribution. So the trainee needs only to put her best foot forward, but I had arrogantly considered that I had helped out. I did not properly understand my role. I imagine there are many who have entered society and have had trouble coming out of habits of expression of student days. It is difficult to use expressions that are suited to the moment or take action that is suited to the situation, but I suppose you are called a social being only when you can do those things. I feel I must strive to that end so that I can become a full-fledged store attendant soon.

This pressure for the proper form obviously places great strain on the individual toward conformity, and one Japanophile confided to me that he loved Japan because he could remain a foreigner and that he could not, himself, live under the same social pressures as did the Japanese. It is unlikely that an American would agonize over the manner of expression as did the young Japanese store attendant. That the Westerner lacks this meticulous attention to the proper expression is, to the Japanese, reflected in his advertising. In personal dealings the difference in social customs will be taken into account to smooth the relationship, but no such concessions will be made for advertising that enters the living room. The Japanese expression for entering a home without removing one's shoes—*"dosoku no mama agaru"*—is actually a phrase that is used to describe brutish and contemptible social behavior and unfortunately some Western concepts, not couched in the proper expressions, have a similar effect. The failure of the advertising and the lack of progress of the product in the marketplace has little to do with the advertising concept, which may have been just fine. The Japanese feel that if you don't go to the trouble of presenting your ideas properly, how can they be any good?

The Dangers of Living in a Nonlitigious Society

The Japanese aversion to direct confrontation as a form of conduct does not mean that the foreign marketer has less to worry about in consumer litigations, although superficially this may seem the case. In early 1982, a Japan Air Lines plane crashed into the bay adjacent to Haneda, the domestic airport, resulting in injuries and deaths. It was a freak accident in that the pilot was later adjudged to be schizophrenic, but considerable criticism was leveled at JAL management for not detecting this dangerous ailment in an employee who literally held the fate of many lives in his hands. In fact, some evidence has emerged to indicate that the airline was aware before the accident that the pilot may have been mentally disturbed. If this had happened to any of the Western airlines, we could expect an avalanche of lawsuits, but at the time of writing, more than a year later, only one woman—the widow of a business executive—has announced her intention to sue.

What happened was that immediately after the crash the president of the company visited every family that had a member involved in the crash, and humbled himself. Some say this gesture of sincerity and humility prevented a rash of lawsuits. It certainly conformed to the accepted social attitude that the head of the organization should take full responsibility for anything that happens. JAL, however, did pay compensation thereby matching gesture with deed. Another disaster that occurred coincidentally about the same time—a hotel fire with a number of fatalities—did not follow this pattern. The president in this case refused to acknowledge liability and a number of lawsuits resulted. He has, as a result, been totally ostracized and the mass media has had a field day dragging before the country every aspect of his past, present, public, and private life with what seems to be little regard for any verification of truth or falsity. It's as if the media found it necessary to explain why anybody would behave in such a socially unacceptable manner. As he is beyond the pale of society, he was considered un-Japanese and is currently everybody's favorite villain.

Two ritualistic resignations remain in my mind since returning to Japan; both were pointless in Western logic but unqueried in the Japanese context. In one, a junior police officer turned out to be a dangerous sexual pervert and raped a college girl who was living alone in an apartment. He had taken advantage of his position for he had called on her in uniform several times, not an unusual act *per se* since a policeman in Japan is responsible for those in his block and makes periodic checks. He knows who lives where, as does everybody in the neighborhood, and that without a doubt is the reason for the high crime-detection rate in Japan. The betrayal of trust by a man in uniform was, of course, appalling and the consequence shocking. Some other college girls who lived alone had encountered his visits and sensed something odd and this led to his quick arrest. As the final denouement, the police commissioner took responsibility and resigned. I don't know exactly how many policemen there are in Japan, but in Western logic, the commissioner could hardly be responsible for the conduct of each and every one of his force, particularly for one on the beat. He, of course, does not resign when one is caught driving while drunk. But the crime was such that it was appropriate for him to commit ritual hara-kiri for the "lack of discipline on the forces."

The other incident was when a self-defense force—a euphemism for the Japanese army—fighter plane collided with a civilian passenger aircraft that then crashed. The minister for defense resigned because of the ineptitude of the pilot. It is in this environment that the marketer has to operate, so when anything goes wrong he must do his utmost to ensure that the right postures are displayed and his sincerity not questioned. To the Westerner, Japanese management displays extraordinary concern toward even one complaint and will do anything to keep the complaint from surfacing. I have experienced a situation where a claimant, whom I considered to be a concealed blackmailer, got his way on a charge he couldn't substantiate.

While all this is going on at the corporate or public level, what is happening among private individuals? To be able to sue on a matter of private dispute is one of the most fundamental of human rights in a free society. In early 1983 a very significant event occurred in this respect in the prefecture of Mie. A mother was taking her infant son shopping and passed a neighbor who volunteered to take care of him for the short time. The neighbor said she was asked to take care of the child and could hardly refuse in her exercise of usual civility. Unfortunately, the infant, who was seen to be playing with other children, wandered off, fell into a pond, and drowned. The parents of the dead child sued the neighbor for negligence and won a compensatory award of approximately $25,000.

The parents' action aroused considerable passion throughout Japan. The parents who suffered the loss of the child and who sued were heaped abuse day and night, by phone and by letter, for their un-forgivable action of taking a well-meaning neighbor to court. In a free system the principle is to respect divergent opinions and actions; the courts are supposed to act as the arbiter. In this instance the unfortu-nate parents withdrew their suit, despite the fact that they had actu-ally won in court, because of the pressure of the village community. Life had become unbearable for them and the language used toward them was unbelievably harsh—devil, animal, traders of children's souls for money, etc. The defendants, who were prepared to fight the case in a higher court, were also harassed. The man in the street thought that a tragedy such as a child's death could not be resolved by money and should not be subject to litigation. Furthermore, it was maintained that disputes of this kind, between neighbors, destroy the basis of community living.

The incident prompted the Ministry of Justice to issue an extraordi-nary statement concerning the right of individuals to sue and deplor-ing the duress that was exercised by the community on this right. The event also prompted intellectuals to again raise the question, "Does Japanese culture prevent lawsuits?" As reported in the *Asian Wall Street Journal*, John Owen Haley, a Japanese-speaking University of Wash-ington law professor, considers this to be a "pernicious myth." To quote the *AWSJ*: "What inhibits the Japanese from bringing more suits, Mr. Haley argues, isn't some unique nonlitigious strain in Japa-nese character, it's the Japanese legal system, which was deliberately designed in the feudal era"—another example of the influence of basic cultural factors on the market—"and then redesigned in the 1920s and 1930s"—or was it? Was it not just another example that what goes against basic values has only a temporary effect?—"to limit oppor-tunities to sue and to encourage people to resolve their differences informally." Haley argues that the Japanese "bring so few lawsuits in part because the government and the bar so sharply restrict the num-ber of lawyers, making suing difficult." I said before that Japan, with approximately half the population of the United States, has fewer lawyers than the state of Illinois, but the *AWSJ* has it that the numbers are "fewer than there are in the U.S. city of Philadelphia."

Setting up a marketing organization in Japan has another wrinkle:

when something goes wrong in the market one cannot rely on the usual coterie of lawyers but must use some other apparatus. Haley's position notwithstanding, there are at least three possible viewpoints concerning the Japanese preference or, if not that, prevalence of group harmony over individual litigation. The first postulates the lack in Japanese society of a "modern" sense of justice. The modern legal system was rather hurriedly introduced by the Meiji government without full understanding of the philosophies on which it was based; somewhat similar to our examples of products being introduced hurriedly without taking into account cultural factors. Thus a Roman system that did not share Confucian values was imposed on a basic culture.

The second theory is the easiest and most often used: Western societies are combative and competitive while the Japanese society values empathy and harmony among its individual members. It is argued that it is not a question of who is right or wrong but that of societal values. This argument wholly ignores the numerous blood lettings in Japanese history and the very savage clan and family feuds that dot even the so-called peaceful Tokugawa era.

The third contends that the Japanese are incurably sentimental and do not go by logic alone—sort of an Oriental Latino. None of these views really address the fact that there were disputations galore in Japanese history—Haley only pointed out the twenties and thirties, which could have been a temporary aberration. The argument will only be resolved and we will really see whether the proponents of group harmony are correct when there is a reform of the legal system and corporations and individuals do not have to resort to extrajudicial solutions. Haley cites statistics suggesting that the typical Japanese judge "handles anywhere from two to five times as many cases as his American counterpart." Thus any Japanese who contemplates suing must face the prospect of waiting as long as ten years for a final solution. Currently as many as 30,000 law school graduates vie for the three-year, government-run apprentice program that accepts only about 500 a year. Still, to the marketer all this is academic. He must accept and contend with what exists. It is an internal matter in which no foreign government can interfere.

12
Arranged Marriages Versus Love Marriages

Aspirations of Joint Ventures

Miai ("Here's Looking at You Kid," With a View to Marriage)—Between Samurai and Merchant Families

A joint venture is like a marriage and involves a clash of corporate personalities. Some Japanese claim that marriages arranged by the old custom, by progressing cautiously and obtaining the consensus of both the bride and bridegroom's families, have a lower divorce rate than marriages based on love because there is less emotion and a more cool-headed examination of family backgrounds. While the term arranged marriage has a bad connotation in the West, half or more of the marriages in Japan were, until recently, contracted in the old way. However, like the image of the geisha girl, the Western perception of the arranged marriage, at least as it applies to Japan, is not entirely accurate. The Japanese words for arranged marriage are *miai kekkon*, the word *kekkon* meaning marriage. However, the word *miai* that precedes it does not mean "arranged." The literal translation would be "look and match." In other words, it starts with the process of introducing the boy and girl with the respective families present. This look-see can occur in a hotel dining room, a restaurant, or at the Kabuki theater. It seems to be a very embarrassing affair for both the young man and woman. What is probably less known in the West is that the young couple then have the option of proceeding to the next stage of courtship or calling the whole thing off. Admittedly, since they have consented to the introduction, the groundwork is laid for an eventual marriage, but a surprising number of people opt for a second or third try at *miai*, which means that both or one of the young parties must have said "no." While this whole procedure is certainly unromantic, the tradition of romanticism does not really have a long history even in the West. One need not go any further back than Jane Austen to observe the habit of families getting together to introduce eligible bachelors to nubile maids.

Aristocratic marriages in the nineteenth century were probably more "arranged" than are *miai* marriages in modern-day Japan. The principles were no different for the Western aristocrats than they were for the Japanese samurais. Some "establishment" marriages even in the United States seem to have the element of a *miai*—the elaborately organized balls and parties, etc. However, in a new nomadic society such as the United States it stands to reason that only a minority would practice the custom. In Japan love marriages therefore grow on different social soil and cannot be equated to the American.

International joint ventures are like intercultural marriages, and unless each partner fully realizes the differences in the other's values the failure rate is likely to be higher than that of the purely local get-together. Love alone may not be enough to sustain them through the tensions created by clashes in values, and besides, love is notoriously ephemeral. If the illusions created by passion are strong, the more the disappointment when love fades. It seems that too many joint ventures have been formed because each party was enamored by some specific quality of the other. Peter Drucker points out that, of the Japanese companies, Sumitomo had a good record of joint ventures while Toshiba had a poor one. I would suggest that it is no coincidence that Sumitomo is a company with its roots in Osaka, which was a merchant city for three centuries with no incumbent samurai class. Osaka merchants, separated from the rigidity of samurai values, merrily indulged in commerce during the Tokugawa shogunate period. Even today, the favorite Osaka-ite's greeting is "Are you making any money" or "How's business," a form that is eschewed by the more circumspect Tokyo-ite. On the other hand, Toshiba—Tokyo Shibaura Electric—is a true-blue Tokyo company and may have all the rigidity of a samurai. It is not surprising that Sumitomo's values may be closer to those of a Western corporation than are Toshiba's. Sumitomo is a blanket name for many companies—trading, metal, chemicals, etc.—that band together as a group and share the common financial resources of the Sumitomo Bank. Incidentally, of the many Japanese banks, Sumitomo has been the most profitable for quite a few years running.

As a provider and analyzer of information concerning the Japanese market, I often have the opportunity of observing a *miai* between Western and Japanese firms. One such marriage, because it occurred relatively early in my Japanese career, has stuck in my mind.

Must the Data Be Purely Japanese?—Seeds of Conflict

In order to investigate the feasibility of entering the Japanese market and forming a joint venture, one of *Fortune's* top one hundred companies in the U.S. dispatched an executive to commission research in Japan. The research was to be funded by both the U.S.-based company and the prospective Japanese partner, the latter seemingly anxious to have access to the former's technology.

Proposals were requested from several research companies, and as this promised to be an important project we put in a fair bit of effort to submit the winning bid. Our key pitch to the American company was not only that we had the technical competency, but that we were truly bicultural and thus could serve as a bridge in communicating the information accurately to both parties. This is still our tenet. We emphasized that while a research company may be fully competent in its execution of field work, in a project of this kind the proper definition of the problems and the understanding of these, language competency especially of the bilingual kind, plus technical qualification were necessary—a difficult combination that we strove to acquire. In our ability to communicate with the American executives we certainly had the advantage over our purely Japanese competitors, and so as far as the Americans were concerned the field was narrowed to us and another Western firm.

However, it was the first time I served two masters. For this type of custom-designed research almost all our clients up to then had been Western; our Japanese clients used us for a specific advertising research technique that we had successfully imported. The consultancy profession has been very slow to develop in Japan and most companies processed nonsyndicated-type research in-house, or simply farmed out the field work portion only. The low or nonexistent status of the consultant stems from the distrust and contempt held for the outsider, a feeling nurtured over the centuries in the *han* or clan system of feudal lords. The *gaijin* (the foreigner) is the ultimate outsider. I am continuously reminded that the Japanese corporation embodies all the values of the feudal clan; absolute loyalty is demanded to the clan, which acts as a tightly knit group, although internecine squabbles are common. Doing everything in-house is fine for a major corporation, although inherently wasteful and subjective. But the smaller companies do not have the infrastructure and are precluded from having access to this type of know-how, further reinforcing the larger companies' already formidable strength. The in-house paranoia is so deeply rooted that even outside auditors are a fairly recent occurrence. A consultant, to be truly effective, must be admitted as part of the team, and this is still rare in Japan.

The Japanese corporation that was the prospective partner saw no need for employing a research agency and was insulted that the Americans were not prepared to accept their internally collected data, which was not what the Americans had demanded. Basically their attitude was that "We are a major corporation. Why should we go to a small specialist office? Moreover, we are the customer but they seem to expect to be treated as equals or more."

So this was the opening scenario. The Americans settled on us as the most appropriate gatherers and interpreters of information and the Japanese reluctantly went along because the Americans wanted it that way. The fact that we were a branch of an American company also made us closer, in the eyes of the Japanese to the American camp and it was only till we neared the end of the project that we were able to win their trust by demonstrating that the data were after all data, and while interpretation could vary, the data themselves were tamperproof. Our open debates with the American client at meetings, without a doubt, struck the Japanese side as unusual but helped them understand our objectivity. Neutrality in international affairs is near impossible, and it was inevitable that we were suspected of taking sides even though we openly disagreed with our American client. In any event, it was difficult to conceal the easy rapport we were able to establish with our American client. In the first place he was a single individual while the Japanese side involved vast numbers. In the second place we spoke the same professional language.

Japanese market research, even now, tends to be heavily weighted toward after-the-fact data, such as market share figures and audience ratings. The industry tends to be weak on the systematic testing of concepts before the product is introduced, and they have the tendency to feel that they should follow instinct. The argument often advanced is that the Japanese society is more homogeneous than most other advanced societies and that therefore it is easier for the Japanese to know what other Japanese feel than it is for an American to do for other Americans. An "average American" was a nebulous concept while, it is argued, Japan is a land of the "average." Unfortunately this argument precludes any foreigner from entering into crucial decisions in a joint venture and was, of course, not acceptable. The American client had had his fingers burned with another joint venture in Japan when his Japanese partners proved to be fallible in knowing how the average Japanese consumer felt.

There is another reason the Japanese felt they did not need prior information. The Japanese have been going through an explosion in consumer demand—a demand fed by its economic miracle but also by a consumer economy that, unlike the United States, had only recently reached maturity. The Japanese were real supply-siders in that they firmly believed that a superior product created its own demand. Typical is the case of the origin of Sony.

The Japanese were completely shut off from information from the rest of the world during World War II as they had been during the three hundred years of the Tokugawa shogunate. The now-legendary founders of Sony were excellent technologists with a profound love of electronic equipment and were one of the first to assemble shortwave radio sets after the war. They inserted a small classified ad for their radio in the newspaper and were amazed to find a line forming in front of their small factory by Japanese who were starved for sounds from the outside world. The rest is history. Western willingness to sell technology minimized subsequent development risks. Quite recently the research director of a major Japanese consumer firm told me, "In Japan, we don't test market. We stick the new product on the market and if it doesn't sell, we withdraw it. We put the cost down as that for education." And I was trying to sell him a pretest market simulation model!

The need for research is in proportion to the risk involved, and the

Japanese market has only recently become mature for consumer products. In theory, less maturity should mean a lower failure rate for new products, though no statistics are available to verify this proposition. At the time of the feasibility study, the two managements therefore approached the problem from totally different backgrounds and viewpoints.

The Teams Line Up

Although economic environments may change fairly quickly, management philosophies do not. I have had this fact displayed right before my eyes, and to the Western businessman who has been dispatched to Japan for negotiations, the scene I describe will be totally familiar. The first thing that strikes you when you enter the conference room is the imbalance in numbers. The Americans had a vice president who was responsible for policy; a research specialist; and a local bilingual executive. Each had a specific role that was clear at the outset. On the other hand the Japanese side could only be described as an amorphous mass—I didn't say mess—distinguishable only in its pecking order, which was indicated by their seating. Those who could not sit around the large conference table sat on small auxiliary chairs along the wall. These were the apprentice learners—at the start of their long road of lifetime training—who were not expected to contribute in any way to the proceedings; they were to simply observe the mysterious way things are done.

We also had a project team of four—those who would supervise the various phases of the project excluding the heads of such departments as field work, data processing, and discussion moderating. Even if this were a big project it was not the only one we were handling at the time, so a small company like ours had to go on the principle of business as usual and could not hope to match our Japanese client in numbers. We sat between the two parties because we belonged to neither side, which put us at the head of the table. Despite their large numbers, the Japanese all sat on their side; so the visual imbalance in the room was startling. For an instant, looking at the grim image of the Americans, I wondered whether they felt like pioneers who were suddenly confronted by Red Indians who outnumbered them by a wide margin. Because of their organizational infrastructures no Western corporations can hope or wish to mount project teams similar in size to those of the Japanese. This American corporation had three on its team, but I have actually witnessed a solitary Westerner facing a similar number of Japanese during negotiations.

The unschooled Westerner generally assumes that the man sitting at the head of the table is the one to whom he should make his pitch. In most cases he would be wrong, though one can never be sure, and it's usually after a lapse of considerable time, just as he is thinking he is making great strides because of the amicable nods from the guy at the head of the table, that he realizes the person he should be making the pitch to is one of those who has been busy taking notes and asking questions to ostensibly clarify those notes. Unfortunately in these situations practically everybody is taking meticulous notes, so it is impossible to tell who the key personnel are. I hasten to add that these observations do not apply to the Japanese trading companies—the Mitsubishis, Mitsuis, Sumitomos, Marubenis—who will fairly quickly identify to whom the initial action is entrusted. In Japan, however, they are the exceptions rather than the rule.

Before the discussions begin there is the customary exchange of cards, which lulls the novice Westerner into a false sense of security, particularly if he recognizes some of the titles as meaningful in his own context. They are simply rough translations of the Japanese titles, some of which have no Western equivalent; in these cases, the Japanese have blithely fitted a Western title as an approximation. The art of deciphering the significance of name card titles requires years of prac-tice and should not be indulged in by amateurs. Sometimes transla-tions that are meant to help the foreigner instead further add to the confusion. Recently a former business colleague, who was running a successful business that included the utilization of Japanese electronic equipment, visited Japan and made a courtesy call to his supplier. His was a medium-sized company in the U.S. while his supplier was one of the electronic giants. Since he had visited Japan on numerous pre-vious occasions he knew the differences between Japanese and U.S. business titles, but alas he could not read the Japanese side of the name card. He was therefore flattered and pleased to tell me that he was received by the vice president of the organization. Vice president in a Japanese corporation perhaps should be more properly called deputy president and there is usually only one. In any case his status is second only to that of the president. In Japan the chairmanship is generally only a honorary designation for a retired president; so in the Japanese context the president is a closer equivalent to the U.S. chairman or chief executive officer, and to be second to him is indeed an important position.

I must confess I too was slightly surprised, but on seeing the Japanese on the flipside I realized what had happened. The status of his Japanese host was *kacho*, which roughly translates as division or section head—still a very important position in a major corporation as he is the man who institutes the action. His Japanese card indicated that he was in the overseas business section and what had clearly happened was that most of his visitors from U.S. corporations, roughly of his own status, carried the title of vice president—not executive or senior V.P. He was obviously entitled to assign to himself the same designation.

Back to the card-exchange ceremony. Our first-time visitor was panic-stricken as he must have thought that he had to exchange cards with all twenty or so attendees. Actually, this is where the apprentices drop out; they do not join the parade but quietly sit where they are. Even so, a dozen or so Japanese cards were passed over. If one is looking for a general rule as to the key persons at these initial stages, they are not those with obvious authority and carry titles of *bucho* (division head or above). The *bucho* will assign the roles to the team members after the initial phase and will probably, for all intents and purposes, fade out for a while. He will serve as a reviewer of what the team comes up with. In almost all "How to Do Business in Japan" literature, the *kacho* is regarded as the key person. In a large corporation he is probably in his late thirties to mid-forties; if the employee hasn't made it to *bucho* by this time he will still carry the title but will more likely be relegated to a minor administrative function or staff role as his experience would be considered of use, but he will no longer be considered action-oriented. The mid-thirties is therefore a critical phase in the Japanese corporate career development, and your *kacho* is likely to be a tiger if he is in this age group. At this meeting, however, there was more than one *kacho*, so just who was going to be the guy that would be the team leader was not revealed till later.

When the ceremony is finally over and everybody has regained their seats—the Westerner sometimes doing his bit to confuse by sitting in the wrong place—you line up the name cards in front of you according to the seating on the opposite side of the table (a clever trick that helps you identify the person, his name and rank, in a shorter time). This can be a difficult task if there are more than five cards to handle.

The Hare and the Tortoise in Decision Making

Much has been made of the superiority of the Japanese decision-making process because of their outstanding achievements in recent years. Even though I have actually been involved in it, it is still difficult for me to concede that superiority on a practical basis. I am virtually Japanese in my management attitudes, but I still find the process agonizing. It seems that interminable time is wasted in trying to convince that one obtuse guy when, in a committee situation, a majority vote would seem to clear the stage for the next necessary action. Since the Americans had come all that way to accomplish specific objectives, any sidetracking of the real issue was not only a waste of time but had serious personal consequences as they had already booked their return flight. They had one simple task to perform—to commission the research—and then they were leaving.

The Japanese are sticklers on keeping to a fixed schedule but only after the total schedule has been drawn up. It would be wrong to say that they have no fixed timing at the early stage, but it is best described as stretchable. They tend to allocate more time upfront, then, once the target is set, go hell for leather. I have noticed that the American time allocation is almost the opposite. American businessmen insist on making decisions within a very specified time—decision making is after all what managers are for. Once the decisions are made, all sorts of things can change and so the latter half is stretchable. However, it does seem to me that the American businessman often does not allow himself enough time just so he can show his mettle later. When the priorities are so different we are bound to have trouble right from the start.

Peter Drucker, whom I prefer to call a management philosopher rather than a management scientist—a reason why he is so popular here—put it rather well while ruminating at an informal seminar for Western managers held in Tokyo recently. Drucker said the difference in the allocation of time between decision and execution reminded him of the difference between *sumie* (an Eastern brush painting done in black ink monochrome) and oil painting. Drucker, (Clarke Professor of Social Science at Claremont graduate school in California) teaches Oriental art, a hobby that has no doubt helped him in his very perceptive observations of Japanese management methods.

In *sumie* the artist prepares the ink and paper and then contemplates for a long time before the brush strokes are applied. He does this because in this particular art form no corrections are possible once the brush hits the paper. In swift moves the artist's conceptualization materializes, finishing either as a commendable work or a failure. No wonder then that the artist must take plenty of time before the execution of the strokes. On the other hand, in oil painting the artist can amend as he goes along. Because of this the Western oil painter spends incomparably longer in executing his work than the *sumie* artist.

Drucker wondered whether the total time to completion is so different between the two artists—just that they allocated the time between decision and execution differently. A perfect parallel to our story of the American executives in a hurry to get the ball rolling and the Japanese insisting on getting everything straight in their minds before we could even start the research.

Drucker's thoughts set me to thinking about other parallels in Western-Japanese attitudes toward time allocation. Two sports came immediately to mind—one is wrestling, the other baseball. To the uninitiated, Japanese sumo wrestling is a pointless spectacle. I happen to love it and there are many Westerners in Japan who have become hooked on it. But if you have never seen sumo it may only seem to be two usually obese and hence unathletic-looking characters repeatedly squatting and staring at each other before finally charging. The one advantage about sumo is that anybody can understand the rules within minutes. The wrestlers tackle each other in a ring that seems very small because of their size; if either wrestler steps out or any part of his body other than the soles of his feet touches the ground he is the loser. Now the staring and crouching takes about three minutes but the average action time is less than twenty seconds. So you spend more time watching, or not watching, the combatants psyching each other out than the actual action. Contrast this with Western wrestling that goes straight into action and takes considerably longer to arrive at the final denouement. A somewhat similar comparison can be made in Japanese-style fencing in which there is considerable staring before the attack.

But what about baseball? Yes, the same rules are adopted but, as Robert Whiting amusingly demonstrates in his book *The Chrysanthemum and the Bat*, like many things imported to Japan it has undergone transformations to fit the culture. Baseball as played in Japan is a very, very Japanese game. It is a national sport commanding an enormous following—even more than sumo. Reggie Smith is now a million-dollar player for the Yomiuri Giants, but as Whiting's book points out, the *gaijin* player is still an outsider. He is the exception to the group and cannot expect the customary protection. It is a difficult and lonely life, very much the same as the Western manager arriving from Detroit, Peoria, or wherever.

But how can baseball be a Japanese game? Well, like sumo wrestling there is the long-winded staring match between the pitcher and the batter. Japanese baseball lovers who go to the States are forever impressed by the short intervals in which the ball is pitched. Actually, in Japanese baseball there is supposed to be a time limit for pitching the ball as in the U.S. games, but the observation of the rule is more notable for being the exception. So there is the interminable negotiation between the pitcher and the batter, and the average baseball game in Japan, for the same nine innings, lasts from a quarter to one-third longer than the U.S. game. Still, the fans love it because it embodies the true Japanese spirit of combat and provides the requisite tragic hero—the pitcher whose pitch gets hit over the scoreboard.

Play the Japanese Business Game in the Spirit of Go, Not Chess

We finally got through the preliminary sparring, à la sumo or Japanese baseball, and the American research specialist left for home and family. Now it was our turn to get down to business. This was when I learned an important lesson in dealing with a joint commission: allow yourself twice the time that is needed when there is only one client involved. I was naive in assuming that English would be the primary language on the premise that more understood it than Japanese. We are perfectly capable of handling both languages but a report is best not written by a committee and thus an American colleague and I decided to write the reports in English based on the Japanese data. Although we are bilingual, writing in two languages simultaneously is not possible.

It was perfectly reasonable for the Japanese to feel at a disadvantage if they had to cope with data in another language. So why not simply have the English report translated? Well, market research reports, unless they are the most basic kind, do not render well in direct translation. A good report translated directly from English into Japanese reads terribly, and vice versa. (This book was first written in Japanese, but it is not a direct translation. As I am the author, I am not a judge on whether it reads well in English, but I can assure the English reader that it had to be rewritten.) So this research project demanded a bilingual basis, but based on the schedule in the proposal there was only time for the submission of the report in one language—something that turned into a nightmare.

To compound the difficulty, we had to contend with all those numbers on the Japanese team. In a Western context it is inconceivable for the client to mount a team that is larger than the agency's, but this is what happened. There were queries galore from the diligent pursuers of our data and every typo was delightedly pointed out. I have made sure I won't have to go through the same experience again by extending the deadlines for any project that requires bilingual reporting. Anyway, we churned out all the data and it now came time to get the results down in detail. The U.S. research specialist returned at this point. He had a hard science background, was a stickler for detail, and was a numbers man. And he had every intention of constructing a mathematical model for forecasting the expected size of the market for the new product. Numerical inputs were all important. He was, for an American, unusually meticulous on details, and he and the Japanese "committee" made life sheer hell for us for a while.

In the final count, we estimated the market to be quite small, at least for the immediate future, and an adequate return for the fairly large investment in facilities seemed unlikely. This created an agony of decision making on the American side, but the Japanese, quite surprisingly, seemed unconcerned. To them, numbers were numbers, interesting but quite irrelevant. After all, how can human behavior be reduced to numbers. Here the differing institutional framework and resultant management attitudes become crucial. From the Western viewpoint, the longer one has to wait for an adequate return on investment, the greater the risk for the management who made the initial decision. After all, the shareholders may not be prepared to wait. The

Japanese corporation was not concerned about the shareholders. Under the lifetime employment system, they were worried about where the company would be in a number of years; the fact that the immediate market was limited was not a great matter. The Japanese are fascinated by a new technology—"Has it ever failed?"; as a matter of fact yes, but not so much in Japan since in those days only proven technology had been imported. The United States and others, who were the innovators, experienced plenty of failures and could not afford a cavalier attitude. I believe the Japanese are for the first time beginning to realize that newness alone does not ensure the success of the technology.

In any event, the American side, who had been so impatient to get the project rolling, suddenly became cautious and agonized over the data while the Japanese wanted to get cracking. The positions were now reversed. Because responsibility was shared by a group, decisions were easier to make when there was a possibility of failure. The Americans were afforded no such luxury. It was only because of the technology the Americans possessed that the Japanese were prepared to consider *miai* marriage; the quality that interested them, the new technology, was still there. The Japanese must have been bewildered by the American insistence on going by numbers. Research, to them, was only a detour to a foregone conclusion.

There was some time lapse after the rough passage that left us older and wiser for the experience. It was clear from the research that the product had concept problems, and the way it was presented the Japanese consumer perceived little need for it. So in came another American researcher of a completely different mold. A greater contrast from the previous researcher could not be imagined. This man was a conceptualizer and was not a bit concerned with all the detail we were compelled to produce and slaved over during many sleepless nights. He dismissed the volumes of data as obscuring the forest for the trees. The Japanese too had doubts about the relevance of the reams of data to the ultimate decision, but had been persuaded that this was the way of scientific marketing. But, lo, a change in management mid-stream and a change in style to boot. Sanity was preserved on their side only by muttering about eccentric foreign ways. To the Japanese, who work in teams, such a quick turn around on their own volition would have been impossible. There was still a way to go before the marriage could be consumated.

At this stage there was every indication that the Japanese intended for the marriage to take place. A team, not quite as large as the one fielded on homegrounds, had already visited the United States. The Americans who thought they had hosted the last of such visits were amazed to find there were several more waves to come. Having gotten through the *miai* it was now time for all the relatives to have a look at the prospective bride. (Remember, since the marriage is to take place in Japan, it would be an American bride and a Japanese bridegroom.) It was definitely to be a *miai* marriage but the Americans were still not certain whether they were in love enough to get married.

As the new man was a conceptualizer, he correctly perceived that the original forecast was not very meaningful because it was based on an ill-formulated concept, so breathing space was obtained to explore the concept further. To the Americans this was a last-ditch salvage operation, but the Japanese were seeing it as just another detour imposed upon them by scientific marketers. This meant a different type of research, qualitative rather than quantitative, and only after the viability of the concept was established was there to be the final assessment of its potential in the market. The new man also brought a different style of approaching the Japanese team even though his was a staff function and he did not have any negotiating responsibility. Incredible enough, his difference in approach came from his enthusiasm for the Japanese game of *go*, which he had learned in the States—he had never visited Japan before. I still remember his early contention that the business game as played in Japan is closer to *go* than it is to *chess*—the Japanese have a more complicated version of the latter. It certainly made sense to me and I have since plagiarized this thought on a number of occasions.

I am neither a chess nor a *go* player but understand the difference, in terms of gamesmanship, to be as follows. Chess is essentially a game based on the law of probability, as are many Western games. There are moves and countermoves, and each time a move is made the player has to calculate the effects of the countermoves open to the opponent and plan accordingly. Of course, the permutations are so great that there is no way one can anticipate all the possible moves except for the first few after some well-known opening gambits. The various chessmen are not functionally equal, complicating the calculations. In Japanese chess, when a pawn reaches the other side of the board it turns into a queen and can mount devastating attacks by reversing its direction. Furthermore, by an interesting twist, captured chess pieces can be reused as one's own pieces and placed on any part of the board. A pawn cannot be too casually sacrificed as a result. The Japanese word *mochigoma*, which means captured chessmen, has also been used about people one has on one's side.

Go, on the surface, is less complicated. Each player is provided with an enormous number of black pieces or white ones—the first indication that the game is not to be over quickly. Checkmating in the first ten moves is impossible in *go*. The first stone is placed on a large checkered board, and this is where the Japanese saying "*isseki o tozuru*" (throwing down a stone) comes from, implying the starting of something for which the consequence cannot be foreseen. Gradually, a pattern emerges as the stones are placed one at a time, and the game ends when one side is completely surrounded by the other—quite a long drawn-out process. *Go* masters are just as venerated as chess masters and the main newspapers run a weekly *go* column as well as a chess column. Now, the essential difference, as I see it, between chess and *go* is that the latter is not based on a move by move calculation of probability, but by observation of a developing pattern. Perhaps it is more right brain than left brain? As my very perceptive American friend said, to be good at *go* you have to be able to see the whole board. A more long-ranged perspective is required because the game is not decided on short-term moves and countermoves. A game that could surely not be further removed from *go* is poker; chess is at least a board game. Most of the business negotiations I see between Americans and Japanese seem to proceed along the lines of the former playing chess and the latter playing *go*. But sometimes the American is playing poker! I would say, mixing my metaphors, that if the ball park is Japan, you must at least know the rules that are being applied. The strike zone in Japanese baseball is different to the American—a fact that has given more than one visiting player problems.

Despite all the research and the numerous meetings, and despite the various games played in its course, this international marriage was never consummated. This all happened a number of years ago and the decision was the right one for the American management because we just could not find a concept that would strike a chord with the Japanese consumer. On the other hand, some Japanese firms did enter the market with this product and had very poor initial results. But as predicted, the market for the product is slowly but surely increasing. Although because of our test results the joint venture was aborted, I cherish the experience because it gave me a firsthand observation of different management philosophies long before all the books on Japanese management.

13

To Be or Not to Be a Youth

How to Enjoy Being in Limbo in a Structured Society

An Adult But Not Necessarily a Member of Society . . . Yet

My daughter, who has just graduated from college in the United States, received a postcard from the local ward office last year, while she was home in Japan on term vacation. It was an invitation for her to attend an "Adult's Day" ceremony on January 15. She was now to be officially received as an adult in society. Fortunately, she was not offended and found the thought charming and cute. On this day, all over Japan, the Japanese girls dress up in pretty kimonos and blossom forth. It is a nice day for a tourist to be in a hotel lobby, for many private parties are held and one gets the impression that this attractive attire that is naturally suited to the national character is what the girls normally wear. But the next day it will be different, and one would have to venture to an overpriced Ginza bar to see a live specimen in kimono.

Despite this formality, which is really a good excuse for a public holiday, reaching twenty does not automatically admit a person into society. The Japanese have a word, *shakaijin*, which is given in the dictionary as "a public person" or "a member of society," and to become a *shakaijin*—which means "going out into the world"—actually has little to do with age. In the period that preceded Commodore Perry, a boy went through an initiation ceremony in which his head was shaved and he was made a full-fledged samurai. In those days, this initiation—*genpuku*, as it was called—only applied to the elite samurai class. Now, everybody is entitled to a *genpuku*.

Becoming a *shakaijin* is another thing altogether. While the word is in daily use in Japan, there is no equivalent for it in the West. A *shakaijin*—literally, *shakai* is society, and *jin*, a person—is one who assumes social responsibilities. The corollary is that if you are not a *shakaijin*, you are absolved of many responsibilities. In modern Japan, when does one become a *shakaijin*? Simple. For the men it is when they get a job, and for the women, when they get married. (Though things are changing, work is still seen as a transitory period for a woman.) There is a twilight period between rigid school days and becoming a *shakaijin*, the latter bound by innumerable social conventions, mostly short, and for some, shorter than for others.

Making Use of One's Free Time—There May Not Be Any for Quite a While

This twilight time zone creates a special situation for the marketer. There is a frenzy of consumer activity that comes to a halt when one becomes a *shakaijin*. Jeans are the uniform for non-*shakaijin*, but once men start wearing a suit to the office, most also stop wearing jeans. Young women drink copious amounts of colas—until they enter the family as a potential mother.

Young Japanese with free time before they become *shakaijin* create their own subculture. An American visitor in my office the other day expounded to me that the Japanese were not as different as they were said to be. They share most of the common joys of life—and he could see that particularly among the young. Why, he even saw Japanese girls wearing bobby sox in the trendy streets of Harajuku. I wish I could have shown those very girls at home or at school; he would not have recognized them.

Throughout history, so-called adults have looked askance at the behavior of youth, often out of envy. Considering the traumatic changes in youthful behavior, Japanese society has behaved with remarkable tolerance. This has helped marketers to introduce new products and services and created the phenomena which visitors mistake for Westernization. (As I said before, you may like sushi but that doesn't make you Japanized.) The fact that these new products are aimed at non-*shakaijin*—those not bound by conventional rules of society—helped enormously.

But why the tolerance that many other societies do not show? Perhaps, unlike Christian or Islamic societies, the Japanese do not have absolute principles. However, even more than that, the shame—not guilt, by the way—of losing the war weighs heavily on members of the preceding generation. They were the ones who opened the gates to the invaders, leading to the possibility of destruction of social modes. They "invited" the Western occupation forces, so how could they complain about what the visitors did? In fact, in pragmatic Japanese fashion, since the Americans were victors, they must have had superior forces behind them, and it is a lot less painful to ascribe these forces to material rather than spiritual elements. Adapt the material aspects as quickly as possible, bringing the culture to par in this respect, and then the superior social modes of Japan will prevail. There was considerable risk in this approach to the traditionalist, who faced this situation twice, at the Meiji restoration after Commodore Perry and after the World War II occupation. Parents of contemporary youths were those who yearned for the products that the occupation forces enjoyed and that were denied to them.

What has not changed, however, is the basic social fabric, and the key to not letting the youth fads take over society is the *shakaijin* concept. By limiting freedom to such a short period of a person's life, the menace of social transformation is contained. When we compare the non-*shakaijin's* behavior in the marketplace with those who have become *shakaijin*, we realize the dual standards under which the Japanese operate. They exercise tolerance because they assume that youth is only a temporary aberration.

So among other things, what does a non-*shakaijin* office girl do? She goes on a package tour to Europe. When we were examining Japanese overseas travel attitudes, we had to look into a phenomenon that all tour operators knew. The best customers of the European nonbusiness travel market were single girls. When we heard a number of them who had been to Europe chatting away, in a group discussion, it became apparent that they did not expect their very pleasant experience to be repeated. In Western terms, they were having their last fling! Marriage awaited them, the responsibilities of keeping house and bringing up the children, and above all, caring for a husband who, if he was a responsible member of society, would have little free time, let alone consecutive holidays that would allow a break of more than a week, which was necessary for going to Europe.

A Westerner listening to the discussion would expect a note of bitterness to creep into the girls' comments. But they remained extremely happy and serene. That *shakaijins* had to behave in a certain way was comparable to a farmer going out to plow the field when the sun comes up, and there is no cause for rebellion. Accepting this does not mean that there is total rigidity. Many farm youths head for the city and some Japanese youths head overseas. But when it is large scale, the drift to the city or overseas is usually economically enforced rather than voluntary and is another way of accepting the situation; an example of this was the mass migration of the Japanese to Hawaii, California, and Brazil.

James Dean, Forever

The Levi Strauss story in Japan, together with the Cake Mix failure, the success of a laxative called Colac, and the transformation of Avon in Japan—the last is not told in this book—is one that I will cherish; all these cases taught me again, through the grace of clients, some interesting aspects about the Japanese.

In Japan, Levi's had a tough row to hoe. Unlike its place elsewhere, in Japan, Levi's was not, and still is not, generic for jeans. Japan was also one of the few places in the world where Levi's had not developed the market. Quick off the mark, Japanese manufacturers had developed the jeans market, emulating cowboy imagery—very American indeed—with brand names like Big John. There was little to tell from the advertising of these brands that they were not American, and by the time Levi's arrived, the claim of American origin seemed to have been preempted.

Then, there was the formidable Japanese distribution system, even tougher to crack in the clothing trade, in which there were traditional personal ties. After a number of years of struggle, Chris Walker, a young Australian manager, launched into a do-or-die effort to crack the conceptual barrier. He also challenged the distribution and pricing systems. Research was conducted to better understand the jeans-wearing Japanese youths. As I mentioned before, jeans were practically a uniform for the non-*shakaijin*, who stopped wearing them when they became *shakaijin*. While some marketers might think about expanding the pie by extending jeans usage to *shakaijins*, this would involve changing basic social values which would be difficult for any one brand to tackle.

The only course seemed to be to create an image that was irresistible to the non-*shakaijin* youths. Based on research, this was what Levi's proceeded to do, in a brilliantly executed campaign developed entirely in Japan. As I understand it, Japan is one of the few areas in the world in which Levi's deviated from their international approach. (Another successful company, Avon, also deviated from their renowned marketing method only in Japan, again through the intelligent use of research.)

One of the things that Levi's had which few of the major competitors had was that they were the genuine, traditional American jean. Research suggested that the majority of consumers no longer cared for a genuine American jean. However, they yearned for symbolic freedom from social conventions, and American society, in this respect, was seen as a society that provided for it. A fourteen-year-old once told me why she liked jeans: "I get into jeans as soon as I can when I get back from school. It's like getting into my pajamas. I get a complete sense of freedom. You see, I can sit on the tatami floor with my legs crossed. If I did that with my skirts, I would expose my thighs and be scolded by my mother as behaving in an unbecoming way." This desire can, of course, be satisfied by any jean. But the feeling behind it was important for Levi's in developing an image.

Three advertising agencies were briefed to submit concepts that embodied the feeling that "Levi's was the true, original American jean" and that this was relevant to Japanese youths. No mean task. Research after all cannot create advertising, it can only suggest directions. A series of concept tests were conducted, and two concepts, each from a different agency, tied as being viable for the Japanese market, but for different reasons. It was in consideration of these reasons and of the way the agency team worked to develop the concept that swung Chris Walker toward one.

The concept was an unlikely one because it used two deceased American movie stars—James Dean and Marilyn Monroe. Nevertheless, since the person watching the commercial was identifying with symbols rather than real, living persons, the fact that they had to be spoken of in the past tense was not relevant even for a modern product like jeans.

However, Marilyn wearing the jeans she wore in Arthur Miller's *Misfits* was dropped because she was too voluptuous for the female Japanese teenager to identify with. But Levi's took off with Dean.

Understanding the fascination modern-day Japanese youth has with this idol of the fifties offers us some clues to their feelings about society, which are distinctly ambivalent. Before examining the reasons Dean has achieved the status of an idealized projection of youth in Japanese society, it must be said that a product's success is not ensured just because a popular star endorses the product. What Dean conveyed for Levi's is exactly what the original brief to the agency set out—traditional Americanness and more. Although my American readers may dispute this or think of others who may be more representative of American tradition, the fact remains that there were aspects which I shall explain that no other could match in Japan. Levi's followed up with another American hero—John Wayne—but it was the young Wayne, as he appeared in John Ford's classic, *Stagecoach*, that Levi's used.

But back to Dean. Although *Rebel Without a Cause* and *Giant* were also popular, they are in the shadow of *East of Eden*. Each year, there is a highly rated T.V. program with all the musical stars that features the most popular movie music over the years, based on a popular ballot. For as far back as I can remember, the music from *East of Eden* has been the perennial winner, beating out even *Gone with the Wind* and *Star Wars*, so the appeal of *East of Eden* is universal and not just limited to the youth segment.

Heroes Wear Levi's—and Why It Had to Be James Dean

In *East of Eden*—and in the character of Cal, the recalcitrant son, the image of Dean is created. The two scenes that create the greatest impact come, first when Cal breaks down because his gestures to help his father are scorned and second, when his father, on his deathbed, communicates for the first time (and in a nonverbal manner) that he really loves his son. The latter scene has many parallels in Japanese dramatic art, especially in the *shimpa* stage presentations—a spin-off from the rigid formalism of Kabuki but degenerating into professionally executed, but nevertheless, what can only be described as "soap." I often go to *shimpa* to wallow in its sentimentality while admiring the skills that are displayed in executing melodrama.

The lack of communication between father and son would seem a fairly typical phenomenon in the Japanese home. In a survey conducted in 1970—but I have no reason to think that the finding has changed—less than half of the youths between eighteen and twenty-two interviewed said they had any dialogue with their fathers, while the proportion was about four in five who had dialogue with their mothers.

The archetypal father in a Japanese drama is admired for his silent qualities. A popular advertising phrase is, "A man drinks his Sapporo beer silently." The Japanese male is not supposed to communicate his feelings well—at least if he wants to be admired. However, to any son who wants to identify with the father, there is a subtle line between silent love and benign neglect; probably spanking at least shows involvement. Cal's efforts, in *East of Eden*, to be noticed and loved by his strict father who obviously favored the less troublesome elder brother, must have struck a chord in many a Japanese teenager's heart—and that helped to make James Dean a legend.

The other aspect—Dean's untimely and dramatic death—would be a common factor to lend to his legend, both in Japan and in the U.S. However, superimposed on this is the great appeal of the tragic heroes in Japanese drama, developed especially by the great playwrights for the Kabuki and Bunraku (puppet play) theaters. If one was a samurai, there was the glorious but nevertheless tragic exit by hara-kiri. If one was a commoner, this course was precluded—death by hara-kiri was a samurai's prerogative—but nevertheless many joined their lovers in suicide pacts, to escape social conventions. The shadow of death hangs over many of the popular plays.

Unlike the West, Japan has no Christian proscriptions against suicide, so ending one's life is often seen as the only solution to an insoluble personal or a social problem. Ophelia is a much beloved character on the Japanese stage and is played with considerable gusto by young Japanese actresses, but the Japanese audience's interpretation of her exit from life would be different from that of Shakespeare.

This attitude still has unfortunate modern-day manifestations in "family suicides." A father in serious financial trouble not only takes his own life, but also that of his wife and children. In the West, it could only be seen as a child murder, since no individual has the right to take the life of another. However, the way many see it in Japan, an individual without a family support system faces a tough future, and it may even be compassion that forces the unfortunate father to murder his children—he cannot bear to think of the problems they may face, abandoned in society without a family.

So the perception of death is distinctly different, and I have touched upon it only superficially. But returning to the Dean theme, the tragic hero dominates Japanese history, the best known being Yoshitsune, who together with his elder half brother, Yoritomo, unifies Japan to create the relatively short-lived Kamakura government. Yoshitsune was a master tactician on the field, but his very popularity created an Abel and Cain situation, and he later became a hounded refugee, fleeing from his jealous brother in power through various picturesque spots in Japan with a handful of faithful retainers. Yoshitsune provided some of the great moments in Kabuki drama and is the epitome of the Japanese tragic hero, but there are many others, documented in the late Ivan Morris' masterwork, *Nobility of Failure*.

Now, you have the two elements in the Japanese culture that enabled Dean, as a spokesman, to turn around the fortunes of Levi's in Japan. He was a misunderstood son and ended his life tragically—not voluntarily but certainly in a suicidally reckless manner. Incidentally, the catch phrase that was created for Levi's for the campaign by the agency, McCann-Erickson-Hakuhodo, was "Heroes wear Levi's"! It was a triumph for a Western marketer who had the courage to drop his other frame of reference and properly take up that of the consumer in another culture.

Mothers Take Up the Slack with a Vengeance

Where the fathers lack in communication and indulgence, the mothers make up for it with a vengeance. In the confined Japanese home, children are seldom far from their mothers. In an earlier chapter, I discussed the women's role as financial controller, but this male delegation of a key function also extends to the bringing up of the children. A new expression which entered the Japanese vocabulary—*kyoiku mama*—literally translated as "education mother," aptly describes many of the Japanese mothers I know. Particularly with their sons, there is fierce attention, and I cannot help suspecting that the neglect mothers suffer from their hardworking "silent" partners leads to sublimation toward their sons.

Japan can, in this sense, be said to be a matriarchal society. A moving publication after World War II—and a best-seller—was a collection of letters to their mothers by university students who were conscripted to fight at the front. Many, including the kamikaze pilots, knew that their odds for survival were infinitesimal. The letters reveal surprising sensitivity—surprising only to the Westerner who can conceive of them only as savage warriors. The letters express doubt, longing for home, and even some questions about the rightness of war. None of these feelings would have been expressed to their fathers. So the Japanese youth is close to his or her mother. And if the man she married is pampered, she continues to perpetuate the cycle by overindulging her son. Incidentally, it is a fairly commonly held observation by foreign women married to Japanese men that the latter expect them to be a mother even more than a wife.

The way the mother's situation with her children is perceived is as unfortunate as, the slightly derogatory "education mother" tag. She tends to receive all the blame and little of the glory. Even I, brought up in Japan, sometimes wish that she wouldn't overdo things to such an extent. For example, a recent letter in the newspaper deplores the number of youths sitting for their university entrance examination who arrive accompanied by their mother. Our studies show that the youths' freedom in buying products is much more limited than in the West, at least in the home. Open the fridge and pick a soft drink that mother bought for you. Study late at night and mother emerges with a pizza that she had bought during her afternoon shopping trip. Incidentally, the husband is surprisingly docile in this respect too. Of course, he can expect to have his favorite beer in the fridge but when it comes to something like a soft drink, he will accept her choice as being final. After all, the house is her domain.

Coffee Shops and Love Hotels—Essential Ingredients for Social Harmony

Because of the conditions I have described, places outside the home assume enormous importance once one reaches the late teens. This is probably the same in many cultures. But unlike the United States, there is much less home entertainment; home parties are just not possible for most. The service industry that has grown up to cater to this out-of-home need is, of course, not limited just to the youth segment, but youths constitute a great portion of it.

For example most Japanese youths spend their dates at the coffee shops—there are approximately 120,000 in Japan. If coffee shops were to disappear overnight, the void in the life of a Japanese youth would be horrible.

Of course, having tea, coffee, or any other drink is a common social practice in any culture. Some say the French Revolution was hatched in coffeehouses. But for the space-starved Japanese youth, they are necessary places to escape the suffocation of motherly devotion in the home and the group pressures of school. And then there are the outstanding selections of love hotels available. Off the Tomei expressway, a one- to two-hour drive from Tokyo, a foreigner may be excused for thinking that he has accidentally happened on a nocturnal Disneyland. There are Hans Andersen's Castle, the S.S. *Queen Elizabeth*, an ancient Japanese fortress—all enticing facades calling in the young people whose dates in the coffee shops have taken a serious turn. I am told that within these fantasy palaces, Japanese ingenuity runs riot. A young foreign friend told me that he spent so much time exploring the various titilating devices that he ran out of time! Another arrived with his paramour on a Saturday night—the peak, of course—only to be confronted by a computer-operated electric sign that said, "Sorry, rooms full now. Estimated waiting time, 45 minutes."

Incidentally, in most of the drive-ins, one need not have any human contact, except, of course, with one's chosen partner. You drive up, the automatic gate opens, you drive in to a spare garage, the door automatically descends so the evidence of your license plate is quickly concealed, you enter the room, a voice addresses you from an intercom on whether you want any room service food, which then comes up a shaft with an outlet to the room, and finally, when you are signing out, at the exit a disembodied tray comes out, you place your notes, get back the change, and even a receipt if you want to charge it, and off you go. All this may seem sordid, but everything is carried off with an air of innocence, an ability that only the Japanese seem to have mastered in matters of sex.

All in all, the Westerner tends to see only the social pressures and not the superb tension release mechanism that the Japanese society provides, including the *pachinko*—the vertical pinball-machine parlors. Since societal needs are different, the market for escape has developed differently from the West.

Helplessness in a Harmonious Society—Loneliness in a Crowd

I tend to be a little bit suspicious of surveys that purport to give international comparisons of attitudes. Just struggling to make U.S. and British questionnaires fit the Japanese language has taught me the pitfalls; for example, differences may be caused by semantics rather than substance. Nevertheless, I find a Japanese government-commissioned survey of youths in eleven countries, conducted by the Gallup organization in 1972, very illuminating. Although more then ten years have elapsed, much of it probably holds, and when the items are taken individually, most contain no surprises. Looked at overall, a picture does emerge of the Japanese youth, and despite some of my Western friends' observations that they are becoming rapidly Westernized, there is still a chasm between the U.S. counterpart.

- Of the eight items presented on what is "sought in life," "love and good relationship with others" topped in both cultures, but the proportion selecting was two in three for the U.S. versus only one in three for Japan. The difference was—as might be guessed—"to have satisfying work": only 9 percent in the U.S. and 28 percent in Japan. Also 19 percent of Japanese youths did not know what to seek, versus only 7 percent for the U.S.

- You can be lonely in a crowd. Just because you are in a group-oriented culture doesn't mean that you get the necessary individual support. One in four Japanese youths said that they had "no close friends in whom they can confide" versus less than one in ten in the U.S.

- Most would affirm the proposition that "life is to love and to be loved." At least, it is easier to say "yes" than to say "no." Even so, almost one in five denied the proposition in Japan versus only 6 percent in the U.S. Of course, Japan does not operate under the same basis of Romanticism. The English word "love" translates rather stiffly into Japanese.

- In a village culture, extending a helpful hand to a stranger may mean establishing an unwanted personal relationship, with consequent obligations. To the question, "If you saw somebody who seemed to have lost his or her way, would you speak to that person?" slightly under half the American youths answered in the affirmative but the corresponding proportion was only about one in three in Japan.

- The Japanese society is closest to being one that lacks a strong religion—it exists in the ritualistic sense, but moral guidance tends to come from social rather than religious precepts. Still it is a harmonious society, and one is surprised at the pessimistic view of human nature. One in three Japanese youths consider it to be "basically evil," while the Americans were on the optimistic end with only 16 percent holding this view. (Incidentally, most Western cultures share this optimistic view. Man was created in the image of God.)

- Not surprisingly, the great majority of Japanese youths—more than four in five—had no interest in religion, or, to a lesser extent, did not believe in God. The corresponding proportion in the U.S. was only 13 percent.

- Perhaps the most surprising result is that the Japanese youths top the responses for all advanced societies in their dissatisfaction with aspects of daily living—from society in general, home, school, workplace, to socializing. This does not fit with the currently popular perception of the Japanese as an amorphous mass happily dedicated primarily to work but also to family. On the survey responses, the restless American youths come out as contented and happy beings, compared to the Japanese.

- When those who expressed dissatisfaction with their society—about three-fourths of Japanese youths and one-third of the American— were probed about why they did not take any action on the matter, the main response from the Japanese was that "there was nothing an individual could do about it," while the Americans said that "there were other appropriate persons to look after this issue."

- This sense of helplessness as an individual and mistrustfulness of human nature that we have observed results in the paradox of a desire for establishing an intense personal relationship. To the question of "whether it was better to enter into a deep personal relation-

ship with a friend," 69 percent of the Japanese youths answered in
the affirmative versus 45 percent for the American.

As before, to quote Robert Benchley, there are two types of people:
those who classify people into two types and those who don't. So let
us just say that in many aspects the Japanese youths are similar to the
American. They have made the blue jeans a uniform and McDonald's an outstanding business success—but just maybe, for different
reasons?

Bachelor Aristocrats and Those Glorious College Days

But are these youths the same people, who, when entering a corporation, turn themselves into "working bees," as the Japanese themselves like to describe themselves? Yes, and there is a strong link
between their school days and later corporate life. Again, comparisons
with the United States are enlightening. In high school, there is a
startling difference between the two cultures in the number of hours
devoted to study. Another study conducted in 1978, showed that almost one in four Japanese high school students studied more than
three hours a day, but the proportion was only 5 percent—one-fifth
that of Japan—in the U.S. While for the Japanese, high school is
associated with heavy slogging and cramming, for the Americans, it is
a period of preparation for society.

In any event, the hard work habit in the children is imbued from
even earlier days. At the primary and junior high school stages, a large
proportion of children attend tutorial colleges after their regular
schooling. The highly competitive battle to eventually get into the
better colleges starts from kindergarten.

As a consumer, I would imagine the American school kids to be a
lot more varied in their activities than their Japanese counterparts.
Since Japanese kids have so little time to themselves, they concentrate
their spendings solely on recreational items—records, tapes, rock con-
cert tickets. Shopping for clothes, food, and furniture is left to Japanese mothers far more than is the case with American kids. But all this
changes with a vengeance when Japanese kids reach college and satisfy
all their pent-up frustrations about free time.

Again, the same 1978 study comparing student attitudes between

Japan and the U.S. shows that the U.S. high school students engage significantly more in extracurricular activities. While the majority of U.S. students—three in five—said they "tried to attain knowledge and skills that would be useful for a further career," this answer was given by only one in ten of the Japanese students. Basically, for the Japanese students, senior high school is a place that prepares you to sit for the university entrance examination!

There is a carrot at the other end of the stick. Japanese students look forward to an easygoing university life, enjoying the fruits of their previous efforts and freedom for the first time to enjoy nonscholastic activities. The tough competition that prevails in U.S. colleges is lacking in Japanese universities, except for the handful of Japanese students who are destined to be the "elites." Generally, it is assumed that everybody will graduate. College is the time to socialize and have some fun before the shackles of lifetime employment grab you.

Japanese companies like to say that they hire people, not skills. In running a company in Japan for almost twenty years, I can say that I do not expect new recruits from colleges to be immediately useful. They are highly dependent beings. Dependent on their mothers and teachers during their school days and now dependent on their office superiors. Japanese companies expect to train their employees on the job in a long, drawn out, lifetime process. Nobody need be in a hurry, and there wouldn't be much point anyway, because the company is structured so that to jump over those ahead of you is virtually impossible until you get to management status. Thus, although four in five U.S. college students expected to acquire knowledge and skills which will be useful in a job, the corresponding proportion was only one in three among the Japanese. The proportions were reversed when the question was posed to the Japanese and U.S. white-collar workers on acquiring skills "through company-run educational schemes." During the very short period of college days and before one enters a company, the title of *Dokushin Kizoku*, which literally translates as "bachelor aristocrats," is bestowed on the fortunate young people. Most still live with their parents and do not contribute at all to board and housekeeping; whatever they earn with part-time work is theirs to spend. No one begrudges them because of the long years of regimentation that are to follow.

Moving From a "Bachelor Aristocrat" (Dokushin Kizoku) *to a*
"Social Being" (Shakaijin)

As mentioned, men become social beings when they start a job, and
women, when they marry. Our research shows a remarkable transformation in consuming behavior when a "bachelor aristocrat" becomes a
"social being." Women will, for example, stop drinking certain soft
drinks that they believe will be bad for small children. (Perhaps in
psychological preparation, this seems to occur the moment they get
engaged!) Men will start drinking beer and stop drinking soft drinks.
Both sexes will stop wearing jeans.

And like many other things, all this happens like clockwork. Currently, the average marrying age for the male is twenty-seven and for
the female, twenty-four. They will have an average of 2.3 children.
The Prime Minister's Department, which is always interested in
whether the threatened social revolution is going ᵗo occur because of
the obviously peculiar behavior of the modern generation, periodically
conducts a survey into youthful attitudes. The one completed in July
1983 shows that as far as marriage is concerned, the young people have
remained stolidly the same for quite a few years. Of course, the overwhelming majority expect to get married.

To the question, "At what age do you want to marry?" the males'
answers clustered in the twenty-five to twenty-eight years range, while
those for the females, in the twenty-three to twenty-five years range.
As I said before, this has been the tendency for quite a few years and
the American trend toward later marriages has had little impact. A
three-year difference in age, with the female as the younger, is considered to be the ideal: a twenty-seven-year-old male and a twenty-four-
year-old female are the ideal newly marrieds. Here for once, expressed
attitude coincides with behavior.

Only 16 percent of females refused to live with their husbands'
parents; about half said "it depends," and about one-third felt "it
didn't matter." On the other hand, the males polarized between "acceptance" of and "refusal" to living with their wives' parents, the
proportion being about one in five each. Most of the rest and about
half of the total said "it depended." An overwhelming 70 percent of
bachelor males wished to continue living with their parents, and one
in five even after marriage.

A poll is also conducted each year on work expectations, which continually shows that most young graduates expect to stay in the same job for the rest of their lives. The picture that emerges, especially of the young males, is that of a remarkably conservative and even complacent generation. Most are aware that carefree days are over when they get a job but they also have little fear about job security. While free time is cut drastically, there are other pleasures to look forward to: the feeling of accomplishment when achieving a target with like-minded souls, and the group rapport after work, at the beer halls or yakitori restaurants, with one's buddies, when most of the conversation revolves around—yes—complaining about one's superiors. A unique and extraordinary market has grown to cater to these very special needs, but the products and services have, understandably, a heavy Japanese emphasis. This market includes the *pachinko*—or Japanese pinball—parlors, crowded with workers, and prohibited for juveniles; or the *akachochin*—literally meaning "red paper lanterns"— the small stalls serving food and sake, where workers sit knee to knee; or the Mah-Jongg parlor, the best excuse for a man returning home in the early hours of the morning; or the *arusaros*, cabarets where the hostesses who sit with you are ostensibly office girls or college students. All of these are services that are unique in atmosphere and almost impossible to describe in words, but that serve to help the Japanese worker escape temporarily from his rigidly structured daytime existence.

Conclusion: Products That Challenge Basic Values Will Not Sell

A Truism, But Why Then Ignore It?

The Causes of Some Product Failures

This book has dealt with the various cultural elements that make the Japanese market different from the Western. The underlying theme is that while the product is physically the same, it is often not the same in positioning and perception. Entering the Eastern culture, a Western product undergoes a transformation and establishes its *raison d'être* on Japanese values rather than on Western—though many, of course, coincide. This applies also to the transfer of American products to European cultures and vice versa, but when the historical roots of the values are considered, it is only natural that there is a greater probability for transformation to occur in Japan. I have tried to qualify this by saying that the uncompromising position of "Japan is different" in all things overstates the case. In some instances Japan displays greater similarities to the United States than many European cultures do. The notable attitude shared by the two is the love affair with things new and the ability to pull down older, established institutions with few qualms. And this makes for exciting markets in both cases.

It would be overstating the case to say that all Western products that have failed in the Japanese marketplace did so because the marketer went against basic cultural factors. The reasons for a product's failure are usually multifaceted and not accreditable to a single cause; only a few fall neatly into a clearly discernible pattern, such as the cake mix example earlier. Overemphasizing differences can be counterproductive in that it can generate a defeatist attitude. A good marketer is not resentful of the differences but adapts his approaches accordingly.

Application of sophisticated marketing methods presupposes that we understand the consumer, and at least some failures could have been avoided if more efforts had been expended in this direction. We need only to look around to see the evidence of the success of Western brands: Nescafé, Coca-Cola, Band-Aid, Levi's, Avon, Max Factor, Tupperware, McDonald's, Kentucky Fried Chicken, Schick, and so on.

Why have some Western products succeeded and others have not? A recent McKinsey report attempted to arrive at some general rules. The report contained the interesting observation that in many cases the number-two brand in one country does better than the number-one brand in another. Schick and Dunkin' Donuts were among the examples given. Perhaps there is a clue here. Not unlike the old Avis slogan, "We are number two, so we try harder," perhaps these brands were less immodest and did not have the handicap of being the strongest brand elsewhere and therefore feeling the situation was transferable. By not insisting on a positioning based on prior success, the second-ranked brands can be more flexible and able to consider local conditions and values.

When all is said and done, it is probably more useful for the Western marketer not to be bedazzled by superficial similarities—sure Japanese teenagers even wear bobby socks—but to delve for possible differences. In doing so he should be conscious of the fact that what he observes did not spring from a vacuum. They are consequences of a pattern that has been evolving over the years; in some cases they seem to spring up suddenly, but in others it is far more gradual, working to the current stage over a considerable time span. Some seeds have not sprouted. Like plants, some need layers of subsoil while others may take root on just a thin crust. This is conceptualized in the following pyramid.

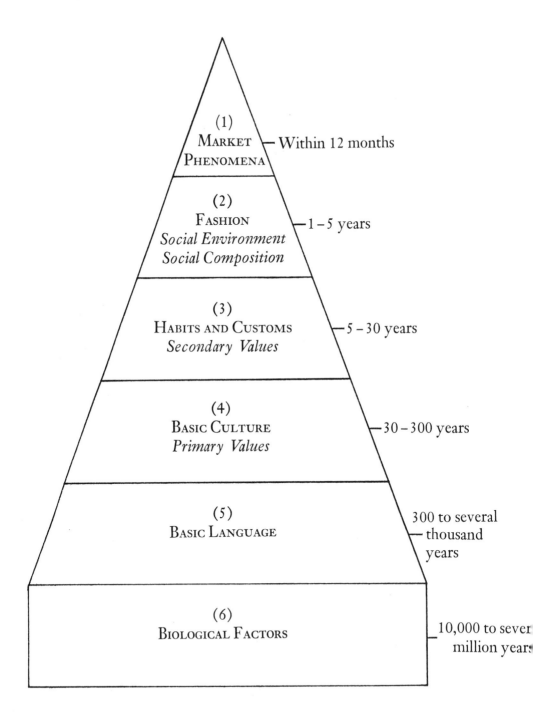

(1)
MARKET
PHENOMENA ⊢ Within 12 months

(2)
FASHION
Social Environment
Social Composition ⊢ 1 – 5 years

(3)
HABITS AND CUSTOMS
Secondary Values ⊢ 5 – 30 years

(4)
BASIC CULTURE
Primary Values ⊢ 30 – 300 years

(5)
BASIC LANGUAGE ⊢ 300 to several thousand years

(6)
BIOLOGICAL FACTORS ⊢ 10,000 to sever million year

The Transitory and the Immutable

Layer (1) in the pyramid is the phenomenon observable before our eyes, the genesis of which occurred sometime earlier. Layer (2) may be simply fashion or a change in the social environment imposed by external events. Examples are the oil shock, which created a change in the attitudes toward cars and other products, or the emergence of video games in Japanese coffee shops, accomplished by the combining of computer graphics with the T.V. screen. In Japan the latter at first threatened the *pachinko* parlors—the vertical pinball machines, originally mechanically operated—but turned out to be opposite. Events that burst upon us may only have a temporary effect unless they are consistent with layer (3). When going against basic customs, consumers will simply revert to their original habits or switch to another course that later emerges because of its being more consistent with the values in (3). This is the difference between short-lived fashions that have come and gone and those that took root.

If things are consistent with layer (3), even if they seem to appear on the scene suddenly, they will stay. Video games in coffee shops failed to take root and the consumer went back to the *pachinko* game. Western fast-food stuck and has become a major industry. In Chapter 1, I explained how Japanese housing and transportation conditions have affected the marketplace. But both are subject to change. Here it is necessary for us to distinguish secondary from primary values. The former can change over a generation as conditions change and housing and transportation are good examples. If primary values are not challenged, then over a generation a product can contribute toward the transformation of consumer habits. Cola drinks and instant coffee are representative examples of this phenomenon.

Normally in business—at least in the consumer field—we expect to see our efforts bear fruit in time spans of, at the longest, five to ten years. We should know not to challenge primary values as indicated in layer (4). These values cannot be changed overnight; some may change after a generation; some may not change for centuries. The lack of success of cake mix and bath additives are examples of this. The Japanese corporations still embody values that were established over the three centuries of Tokugawa rule. We will have to accept these values in their home ground when entering into any joint ventures.

The Japanese distribution system is a natural outcome of its social organization; it has not been set up deliberately to snare the unwary foreigner who is not conversant in the values that make the system work. No single foreign enterprise or government can hope to change the system overnight. The only recourse, when confronted with layer (4), is to evolve ways that go with it, not against it. The adage "when in Rome" applies strongest here, and ignoring it only courts failure. Avon has adapted its methods successfully, carefully taking into account layer (4) values.

Basic language, layer (5), may appear to be irrelevant to marketing and more in the area of semantics or linguistics. If this is the reader's feeling, then my communication abilities are sorely lacking, for in a more-specialized vein than in the rest of the book, I attempted to deal with this matter in Chapters 6 and 7: In these chapters I had the greatest difficulty in addressing the nonspecialist reader, avoiding as much as possible the use of jargon; research into this area is still in its infancy and we can look forward to more debate on the matter.

The proposition that the Japanese language has an effect on the receptive mechanism of the Japanese that differentiates it from many Western cultures has important implications for the marketer. It is a proposition that is challenged and is likely to be challenged further. I have taken sides on this issue based on perhaps simple but nevertheless empirical evidence. Language, despite the infusion of many foreign words, retains its basic structure for a long time, and it is the least challengeable of all the layers in the pyramid. Basic change will not occur in a person's lifetime. Since advertising depends on language, either verbal or nonverbal, it is affected by layer (5).

It is argued that it is the cognizance of the vertical links of the layers formed over time that is necessary in successful intercultural marketing. While simulation models can deal with short-term stabilizations, where major investments are involved it is whether we are here to stay—and not just for this year but for a respectable future time span—that is the key issue. You can be lucky, of course, by not bothering with the cultural issues, but in most cases you will find a local competitor emerging who will take over your role as leader simply because he is better at basing his strategy on local values. Tariff barriers, visible or invisible, are not the only causes for a product's inability to penetrate the market.

Index